Charles T. Griffes

Da Capo Press Music Reprint Series

GENERAL EDITOR

FREDERICK FREEDMAN

VASSAR COLLEGE

Charles T. Griffes

The Life of an American Composer

BY

EDWARD M. MAISEL

New Preface by Donna K. Anderson, *State University of New York, College at Cortland*

DA CAPO PRESS • NEW YORK • 1972

Library of Congress Cataloging in Publication Data

Maisel, Edward M   1917-
    Charles T. Griffes; the life of an American composer.

    (Da Capo Press music reprint series)
    Reprint of the 1943 ed.
    1. Griffes, Charles Tomlinson, 1884-1920.
    ML410.G9134M2   1972   780'.92'4 [B]   69-11668
    ISBN 0-306-71551-1

This Da Capo Press edition of *Charles T. Griffes* is an
unabridged republication of the first edition published
in New York in 1943. It is reprinted by special
arrangement with Alfred A. Knopf, Inc.

Published by Da Capo Press, Inc.
A Subsidiary of Plenum Publishing Corporation
227 West 17th Street, New York, New York 10011

Manufactured in the United States of America

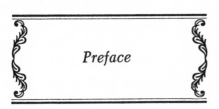

Preface

Charles Tomlinson Griffes, one of the first important American composers of the twentieth century, was born in Elmira, New York on September 17, 1884 and died in New York City on April 8, 1920, at the age of 35. Four cities hold a special significance in his career as composer: Elmira, where he was born and where he had his first "music lessons" from his sister, Katharine, and from Mary Selena Broughton; Berlin, where he studied piano, theory and composition from 1903 to 1907; Tarrytown, New York, where he taught at the Hackley School for Boys from 1907 until his death; and, finally, New York City, where from 1907 to 1920 he spent every spare moment he could find during the school year, and where he usually spent his summers composing.

Several of Griffes' compositions were first performed in New York City, but possibly the single most important first performance of his music was the one given in Boston on November 28, 1919, when Pierre Monteux conducted the Boston Symphony Orchestra in the premiere of Griffes' tone-poem, *The Pleasure-Dome of Kubla Khan.* This performance was one of the most significant events

in the composer's career, and, had he not died five
months later, it might have marked the beginning of universal recognition. One more city should be mentioned in
completing Griffes' story—Bloomfield, New Jersey—
where the composer lies buried at Bloomfield Cemetery
in a grave marked by an unpretentious stone bearing the
inscription: "Charles Tomlinson Griffes 1884-1920."

Griffes died just as his music was beginning to gain
wider acceptance and recognition in the United States,
and especially in the music centers of the East Coast,
where several important presentations of his music had
been staged during his lifetime. *Five Poems of Ancient
China and Japan*, Opus 10, was sung by soprano Eva Gauthier with Griffes at the piano on November 1, 1917 at
Aeolian Hall (no longer extant; once located on 42nd
Street between Fifth and Sixth Avenues) New York
City; the piano *Sonata* was performed by Griffes on February 26, 1918, at the MacDowell Club, New York City;
The Pleasure-Dome of Kubla Khan, as mentioned earlier,
was performed in Boston; *Poem for Flute and Orchestra*
was performed by Georges Barrère and the New York
Symphony Orchestra, Walter Damrosch conducting, on
November 16, 1919 in Aeolian Hall, New York City; *Not-
turno für Orchester* was performed by the Philadelphia
Orchestra, with Leopold Stokowski conducting on December 19, 1919, at the Academy of Music, Philadelphia.
About thirty-five of Griffes' works were published by G.
Schirmer, Inc., during his lifetime, and a handful appeared posthumously. His name, while not a household
word, was, at least in the New York area, comparatively
well known.

Griffes was well liked and respected in music circles,
and his untimely death was felt by his colleagues as a per-

sonal loss as well as a loss to the world of music. Following his death, articles about him appeared in several newspapers and music periodicals, including *The Christian Science Monitor* (May 15, 1920), *The New York Times* (April 18, 1920), *Musical America* (January 15, 1921), *The Chesterian* (March 1923), and G. Schirmer's *Course in Contemporary Biography* (1923). Mezzo-soprano Edna Thomas, pianist Olga Steeb, and violinist Sascha Jacobinoff, while not personal friends of the composer, formed the Griffes Group "to perpetuate his essentially American aims and ideals" (see *Musical America,* April 23, 1921). This group of young musicians made its debut in Aeolian Hall in New York City, December 30, 1920 (reviewed in *Musical America,* January 8, 1921), and during their career as a concert touring company, they always included at least one work by Griffes on each of their programs.

But the lively interest in Griffes and his music gradually subsided and he was eventually consigned to a neat but inadequate place in music history books as an "American Impressionist." Careful study of the published and available unpublished music of Griffes shows clearly that this label is both misleading and inaccurate. Many of his works, such as *The White Peacock,* the *Poem for Flute and Orchestra,* and the *Three Tone-Pictures,* Opus 5, do justify his reputation as an "American Impressionist"; but Griffes spent his entire life in an incessant search for a musical language that could fulfill his artistic personality, and no label can tell the entire story. In his early career he was influenced by German Romanticism, as evidenced by many of his early songs, such as *Auf geheimem Waldespfade* and the unpublished *Symphonische Phantasie* for orchestra; later, he was influenced by French Impressionism. He shared with many the interest in the Orient, so prevalent in all art forms during the early decades of the twentieth century, the flavor of which is reflected so skillfully in *Five Poems of the Ancient Far East,* Opus 10, and in the unpublished songs *Djakoan, Kinanti* and *Hampelas.* At the end of his career he adopted a stark, dissonant idiom peculiarly his own, of which the remarkable piano *Sonata* is an excellent example. But, paradoxically, Griffes was able to remain a distinct musical personality, never content to be merely an imitator, and his music always retained freshness and originality.

Griffes was, in the last analysis, a self-made artist. He was neither decisively shaped nor permanently influenced by any one person or any one prevailing musical style—inspired, yes; guided, of course; but never artistically dominated. His artistic credo was uniquely his own—the product of his curiosity, his vivid imagination, his driving ambition, his desire to assimilate and turn to his own use every possible experience, his modesty and utter lack of pretense, his search for artistic fulfilment, and, finally, his devotion to his art. These traits enabled Griffes to emerge in the scant dozen or so years of his active career as one of America's most significant composers.

Since his death, Griffes' music has gained critical prestige and has won a small but significant position in the orchestral and solo repertoire of the concert stage as well as in the teaching studio. More recently, his compositions have been the center of renewed interest. In 1967 C.F. Peters published *Three Preludes* for piano (which appear to be Griffes' last completed works), and several songs were published in 1970. *Legend,* for piano, is scheduled for publication by Scribner & Sons in 1972.

Studies dealing with the life of Griffes have been, for

the most part, rather superficial and limited in scope. One of the few exceptions is the article, "Charles T. Griffes As I Remember Him," which appeared in *The Musical Quarterly* (July 1943), written by his friend, composer Marion Bauer. Edward M. Maisel's biography of Griffes, first published in 1943 by Alfred A. Knopf and reprinted here, is the only book-length study of the composer's life available today.

Studies of Griffes' music have been based primarily on his published music and thus do not give a complete picture of his development or of the influences that helped shape his career. Four of the most important works dealing with his published compositions are William Treat Upton's "The Songs of Charles T. Griffes," *The Musical Quarterly* (July 1923); Donald Morrison's *Influences of Impressionist Tonality on Selected Works of Delius, Griffes, Falla and Respighi . . .* , unpublished doctoral dissertation, Indiana University (1950); George Arnold Conrey's *The Published Songs of Charles Tomlinson Griffes*, doctoral thesis, Chicago Musical College (1955); and Daniel Boda's *The Music of Charles T. Griffes*, unpublished doctoral dissertation, Florida State University (1962).

In the introduction to his biography (page xiii), Maisel states that "a definitive bibliography of Griffes' compositions will not be possible for some time." Believing the task to be a necessary one, I undertook the compilation of such a bibliography in 1964 and completed it in 1966. It is entitled *The Works of Charles T. Griffes: A Descriptive Catalogue*, and is now available from University Microfilms. This annotated catalogue presents a comprehensive list of all known Griffes works, which I have numbered A1-141. It lists dates of origin; dates of publications; dates,

places, and performers of first performances; and specific
locations of manuscripts. It includes comparisons of all
published editions, descriptions of first drafts and
sketches, and comparisons of different versions of the
same work. Also discussed are Griffes' arrangements or
orchestrations of his own works and those of other composers, as well as arrangements of Griffes' compositions
by other composers.The study includes copious quotations
from the composer's private correspondence and diaries,
as well as numerous excerpts from his music. It also contains commentary on aspects of style, form, evolution, on
unusual circumstances surrounding the creation of certain works, and other pertinent information. I examined
personally every manuscript and document discussed,
and in the process enjoyed the cooperation and assistance
of the Griffes family, which kindly allowed me free access
to the composer's diaries and other important papers.

Scholars interested in undertaking a more thorough
study of the man and his music should be aware of three
important collections of Griffes material. The New York
Public Library's Music Division (at Lincoln Center) has
several complete autograph manuscripts, including the
full orchestral score of *Symphonische Phantasie* (unpublished; listed in my catalogue of Griffes' complete works
as A89); the full orchestral score of the third version of
The Pleasure-Dome of Kubla Khan (A91); the score of
Sho-Jo (unpublished; A92); and, *Scherzo* for piano
(A73). This library also possesses several unidentified
manuscript sketches; three sketchbooks; more than 150
autograph letters (written primarily to the composer's
mother and to his former teacher, Mary Selena Broughton, and particularly revealing in tracing Griffes' activities in Berlin while he was a student); a large iconog-

raphy file; three scrapbooks (maintained by Griffes and members of his family) which are invaluable for determining dates of first performances; several superb pencil sketches, watercolors, and etchings by Griffes; and other memorabilia. The Library of Congress, Music Division houses twenty-five autograph manuscripts, including the full score of the final version of *The Pleasure-Dome of Kubla Khan* (the one used by Pierre Monteux when he conducted the premiere performance at Boston in 1919), of the final version of *The White Peacock* for piano (A77), and of *The Lament of Ian the Proud* for voice and piano (A57). The Hamilton Library collection at Elmira College, Elmira, New York, is not as large as the two previous ones, but it contains what to my knowledge is the only complete manuscript of the piano *Sonata* (A85) (an early version largely in the hand of a copyist), autograph copies of *The White Peacock* (A77), Griffes' woodwind and harp arrangements of his piano solo, *The Lake at Evening* (A108), several autograph letters dating from the Berlin years, and Griffes' collection of wild flowers.

❋ ❋ ❋ ❋ ❋

Almost half a century has passed since the death of Charles Tomlinson Griffes, and a quarter century since publication of Edward M. Maisel's biography of the composer. Maisel's work occupies a fairly significant place in Griffes research. While writing the biography Maisel was acquainted with and enjoyed the cooperation of the Griffes family, including Mrs. Clara Griffes, the composer's mother, now dead. Maisel was given access to the composer's letters and diaries, and was also able to gain much information simply from talking with members of the family, who, from my experience, are delightful, warm, hospitable people, somewhat startled at continuing interest in their brother, Charlie.

No biography can be perfect nor can it please everyone; and Maisel's work is no exception. He approached his subject with great zeal and dedication, and the result is a readable, entertaining biography, packed with a mass of detail. Its primary value is an introduction to Griffes for the "average reader." One can quarrel, however, with its lack of scholarly incisiveness, its unwarranted overemphasis of Griffes' homosexuality, its meandering presentation of incidental and peripheral "data" (see page 136 for example), and, finally the most serious defect, its lack of documentation. Maisel states in the Introduction (pages xv-xvi): "A few notes may be appended here for the benefit of musicologists and students of American culture. Since almost every statement in an original work of this kind refers to some interview, document, or piece of correspondence, it would not be feasible to cite authority without recourse to some formidable footnote apparatus that would alienate the average reader. A fully annotated copy of the book will, however, be deposited with the Music Division of the Library of Congress or with the Harvard College Library." Communication with both institutions, however, failed to turn up this "fully annotated copy." It is hoped that Maisel will some day fulfill his long-standing promise.

Maisel also notes (page xvi) that "exact wording has been retained in all quotations from Griffes, but the spelling has been corrected in some instances, and the punctuation been made to conform to the general text. Obvious slips of the pen have been rectified instead of the customary reproduction with accompanying *sic*. Versed in German, French and Italian, Griffes found it natural oc-

casionally to write in these languages, and an English
translation is given in most cases without any indication
to this effect." While this is obviously a matter of editorial
policy and opinion, it is clear today that verbatim trans-
script of the originals, followed by edited and/or translated versions would have made Griffes' texts more mean-
ingful. This is a matter of particular significance, since
Griffes often wrote those diary entries which were of a
personal nature in German.

Maisel's constant reference to Griffes' homosexuality
would seem to imply that this was one of the major forces
in shaping Griffes' music. He states (page 141): "For
from this time forth [1914] Griffes' music would reflect
in greater and greater degree his relentless struggle to
achieve honesty and balance in his emotional life."
Through my study and performance of the composer's
music I have not found this to be true. I believe that the
change in Griffes' music was not the result of an emotional struggle in his personal life, but rather the logical
musical evolution in his continuing artistic growth. Carl
Engel, reviewing Maisel's biography in *The Musical
Quarterly* xxix/4 (October 1943), 406, wrote: "Only if
there were artistic abnormality, might there be an excuse
for seeking its roots in emotional abnormality." I completely agree.

Mr. Maisel's biography of Griffes is, as I have pointed
out, the only book dealing exclusively with the life of the
composer. As such it fills a certain need in the study of
Griffes as well as in the study of early twentieth-century
American music. But a definitive biography has yet to be
written—one that would take a scholarly approach, be
fully documented, and serve as a basic research tool for
those interested in further study of this important Amer-

ican composer. The growing interest in American music makes it essential that an authoritative study of the man and his music be written. Until such time as a fresh scholarly work appears, however, we must remain indebted to Maisel for his work and to Da Capo Press for this reprint.

Donna K. Anderson

State University of New York
College at Cortland
Cortland, New York

CHARLES T. GRIFFES

Charles T.
GRIFFES

The Life of an American Composer

BY

EDWARD M. MAISEL

NEW YORK: ALFRED · A · KNOPF

1 9 4 3

TO
Elizabeth

"Colpa è di chi m'ha destinato al foco."

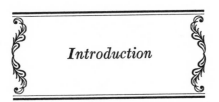

Introduction

THE HISTORY of American music, with certain honorable exceptions, has consisted in the application of inspired adjectives to uninspired music. Diligent inquiry has been as lacking on the one hand as vital creation on the other. In both respects it is hoped that the present contribution may form one of the exceptions.

Few American artists in any field enjoy a greater critical prestige than Charles T. Griffes, and almost no American music is rated higher by the mass of concert-goers than his *Pleasure-Dome of Kubla Khan* and *White Peacock*. A recent survey of contemporary American music dismisses the Old Guard " with the exception of Charles T. Griffes, who was so in advance of his time that he belongs to the present day. . . ." Yet very little if anything is known about the man who stands behind the reputation and who produced these works. Worse than that, a good deal of misinformation has been accepted about him. There is the Griffes legend to contend with. It is no exaggeration to say that almost everything written about the composer since his death has been inaccurate. Every year over the radio the story is trotted forth by some lugubrious announcer, and then the Griffes legend acquires a new detail or two. It may prove instructive to examine some of the more popular stock in trade.

With regard to Griffes's musical development Bauer and Peyser in their *Music Through the Ages* tell of "a turning point in his life. In his pension he heard an unfamiliar type of composition played in a nearby apartment. He was so impressed that he went to the pianist's door and found Rudolph Ganz playing Ravel's *Jeux d'Eau*. A new Griffes thereafter appeared in his two Oscar Wilde's songs, *La Fuite de la Lune* (*The Flight of the Moon*) and *Symphony in Yellow*." Bauer expands the incident somewhat in her *Twentieth Century Music*. "While studying in good conservative fashion in Berlin, he heard someone practicing an unfamiliar composition which so impressed him that he went to the pianist's door to ask its name. It was Ravel's *Jeux d'Eau* and the pianist was Rudolph Ganz. It seems incredible that an incident seemingly of such trifling import could change a man's career." Incredible indeed. Misinformation and misinterpretation could scarcely have combined to greater confusion. Fortunately it is possible to nip this sprout of the Griffes legend in the bud. For Griffes ate scarcely a bun in Germany of which there does not exist some evidence either in the detailed and voluminous correspondence that he poured forth during those years or in the recollections of his pension friends. It is inconceivable that this "turning point in his life" would not find some reference in these sources, as it in fact does not. Elementary corroborative procedure might have suggested that Mr. Ganz be consulted on this point. "Where the little legend of our meeting in Germany came from," writes Mr. Ganz, "I do not know." As to the inference about a sudden change in Griffes's music, the songs mentioned were composed several years after his return to America and only after other piano and vocal works in a similar vein. But as, elsewhere in their text, Bauer and Peyser list *We'll to the Woods and Gather May* as one of his German songs, indeed one of " his first German songs," their misconstruction of his early output seems too complete for sustained rebuttal. The kernel of fact in their little anecdote may one day be uncovered.

John Tasker Howard in his not very usable monograph on Griffes hazards that "it was probably while studying composition with Humperdinck that Griffes conceived the ambition to be a composer. . . ." Mr. Howard's unjustified assumption becomes *fait accompli* in David Ewen's *Composers of Yesterday.* "While there [in Berlin] he came under the influence of Humperdinck, his instructor in theory, who — sensing that Griffes's importance as a musician rested more in the creative than in the interpretative field — succeeded in diverting the young musician towards composition." The *Dictionary of American Biography* falls in line. Griffes's own statement to the press that he " studied with Humperdinck, but never composition and very little of that with anyone " may be somewhat extreme, but it shows in what direction the truth lies. As a matter of record, it may be set forth here that Griffes had exactly eleven lessons with Humperdinck over a period of time extending from October 1905 to April 1906.

The best known, dearest loved, and most widely promulgated episode of the Griffes legend is the story of his death in abject poverty and want, or the story of a great unknown catapulted to fame after death. One is truly embarrassed by the wealth of riches from which to choose in illustrating this mawkish embroidery. For variety's sake it may be offered that Percy Scholes corrects the error in italics in the *Oxford Companion to Music.* The mythopoeic mind of music commentators has distorted even the original fabrication. Gallantry forbids naming the woman announcer who blithely declaimed that Griffes had met his death in a submarine. Other touches have been added. Mr. Howard tells that " before he passed away he received enough requests from various organizations for ballets, operas, and incidental music to keep him busy for many years to come." Before he died Griffes dictated a letter to Mrs. Elizabeth Sprague Coolidge regretting that his incapacity prevented his undertaking a work for her. That is all. The source of Mr. Howard's item would seem to be the *Musical Leader*, where it appeared in almost identical language with the original obituary notice. There is no foundation.

The same looseness has extended to even the most minor biographical details. " Fiction rarely interested him," says Mr. Howard. And " He rarely read fiction," amplifies Mr. Ewen. But Griffes loved good fiction and read it all his life.

". . . His copper-plate etching was so fine that at one time he was strongly advised to follow etching as a profession," says the *Dictionary of American Biography*. Griffes did experiment, and with mild success, in this medium. On one occasion he contributed an etching to the Hackley School annual. The engraver, impressed with this handiwork, pleasantly observed that if Griffes were ever in need of a job, he would be glad to employ him. This incident turns out to be the factual basis for the *Dictionary's* assertion.

In the matter of plain verifiable history there has also been the grossest carelessness. Dates of composition were hitherto unobtainable, but dates of publication needed only to be copied accurately from the published compositions themselves. Why there should be variance among the different encyclopedias and compendia is hard to see. Oscar Thompson's *International Cyclopedia of Music and Musicians* under *Five Poems of Ancient China and Japan* enumerates five songs that do not belong to that opus (and for some reason omits the piano *Sonata* from the list of Griffes's works).

The same applies to dates of initial performance. The string quartet, as a striking example, is given incorrectly in all sources. Carl Engel in Cobbett's *Cyclopedic Survey of Chamber Music* writes: " The *Two Sketches Based on Indian Themes* were first played by the Flonzaleys in 1918." The performance took place in 1919, and the composition was not the *Two Sketches* but two pieces consisting of an earlier string movement and one of the sketches. It was not till later that the second sketch was written and not till after the composer's death that the quartet was assembled in its proper form.

The confusion surrounding Griffes's manuscripts has perhaps reached its apogee most recently, in an incident of almost incredible slovenliness. Miss Irene Lewisohn, Griffes's patron and friend, in the summer of 1941 discovered a manuscript copy of the published piano *Sonata*, which she sent along with other manuscript material to Griffes's publishers, G. Schirmer, Inc. Mr. Gustave Reese of the publication department informed Miss Lewisohn in a letter dated July 3rd, 1941, that " Mr. [Carl] Deis has been able to reconstruct the 'Piano Sonata' and we are interested in acquiring it for publication." Under the date July 16th, 1941, Schirmer's then proceeded to enter an agreement with the Griffes estate for the acquisition of what was already one of G. Schirmer's most esteemed properties, the piano *Sonata* that they had published in 1921. The present writer, in Vermont at this time, wired his incredulity and received the following confirmation from the Griffes estate: " He [Mr. ——] seemed quite enthusiastic about the music, and thought it much more worth while than the other Sonata — a more finished piece of work, etc. He said, for instance, that Harold Bauer had never been able to work up any interest in the other Sonata but that he (Mr. ——) thought that he (Harold Bauer) would be very much interested in this one." The two sonatas were the same, and when this little travesty had at length run its course, Mr. Reese had to write a letter asking for a release from the contract. The inefficiency and fake in high places that dogged Griffes throughout his lifetime are still evident in this treatment of his work.

Enough has now been said to indicate the general unreliability of all that has been written and told about the composer. Rumors of another sort, hardly less tenacious in persistence, do not deserve the dignity of a refutation in this place and will not be dealt with in this book. It may also be stated here that the present biographer has not tried to violate the mystery of human personality, not tried to use Griffes as a means to psychology or sociology. The composer of the kind of music that was Griffes's unique gift to American culture and to the music of the world has a right to be understood in his own dimensions.

With all the glorified and romantic misrepresentation that has been described in the preceding pages, it was only to be expected that the pendulum of opinion should also be swung the other way. And this task was undertaken by Edward Robinson in a cheap piece of debunking entitled " The Life and Death of an American Composer," which simply repeats the earlier errors with unfavorable interpretations. ". . . His work as an etcher led many to advise him to follow that branch of art as his major activity." How many knew that Griffes did etching? " Some lessons in composition from Humperdinck induced him to consider composing as a career." Mr. Robinson is not above an invention or two of his own. " During this period [the years in America following his return from Germany] Griffes was not only able to compose regularly, but also to secure publication and performance of everything he wrote. . . ." Not the least remarkable of Mr. Robinson's accomplishments is that of bestowing good health upon the composer during his final visit to Boston. ". . . On the afternoon of November 28,

1919, he was present in Boston for the first performance of the work [*Kubla*], appearing on the platform to acknowledge the applause; and H. T. Parker, writing in the *Transcript* of the next day, could detect no signs of illness in him, but rather jovially noted his unassuming 'business jacket.'" Mr. Robinson, music critic, detects a jovial note in the style of Mr. Parker, music critic, and Griffes is made a well man.

It is not worth while to pursue any further the Griffes legend in either its favorable or its unfavorable ramifications. Enough has been said to obviate the necessity of repudiating it piecemeal through the pages that follow, for it was an entirely posthumous development and has nothing to do with the life as it was lived.

In one sense this Introduction is intended less in condemnation of the legend than in its extenuation. For there has been no real biography of Griffes available in the more than twenty years since his death. And even when Lawrence Gilman publicly called attention to this deficiency in a column in the *Herald Tribune*, no one was able to remedy it. This is not accidental. After Griffes's death and before his belongings could be cared for, his personal papers were left exposed for some time among his effects. There is reason to believe that these were ransacked and important material removed. All other papers and effects, including manuscripts, soon became so unbelievably scattered as to render almost hopeless the effort of putting together a true record of this life. (A definitive bibliography of Griffes's compositions will not be possible for some time.) That the present writer was enabled to surmount these difficulties is largely owing to the patience and good will of the many who have assisted him. He would like to record his deepest gratitude to all the friends and acquaintances of Griffes who have generously granted interviews, corresponded with him — even at great length on minor points — made available letters and similar autograph material that has come into their possession, and otherwise stimulated the completion of his task. Some have contributed only a single detail; others have contributed much. A few have been good enough to read portions of the biography. (The biographer alone, however, bears full responsibility for any errors that occur.) All have been sincerely helpful. It would be a pleasure to thank by name each of the more than two hundred persons who have assisted in this way, but for a variety of reasons this is not practicable. May they one and all find something of recompense in the pages that follow. Some of these collaborators have passed on during the progress of this work since its inception five years ago. In particular it has proved a bitter disappointment that Griffes's good friend Mrs. Laura Elliot, who offered such kind and unremitting assistance on the project, should have died just short of its completion.

The three names "Konrad Wölcke," "Robert Corby," and "Dan C. Martin" that appear in the text are fictitious, but the three persons are in all other respects historically delineated. To the two who are living and the family of the third, gratitude is hereby expressed for their co-operation.

Special acknowledgment must be made to the Misses Irene and Alice Lewisohn for permission to examine the scores of *The Kairn of Koridwen* and *Salut au Monde;* to George Morgan McKnight (deceased) for an early Griffes manuscript; to Mme Eva Gauthier for access to the Javanese songs by Griffes in her collection; to Miss Kate Pigott of Scarborough, England, for the loan of a journal kept by Miss Broughton; to G. Schirmer, Inc., for the opportunity of studying Griffes material in their possession; to Miss Caroline Beebe for a private recording by the New York Chamber Music Society of music Griffes arranged from his piano pieces for them; to Miss

Ernestine H. French for a transcript of some notes made by her mother during a visit to Berlin in 1905; to the attendants at the Loomis Sanatorium and the New York Hospital for help with the medical records; to the Elmira College Library for the loan of six German letters by Griffes; and to Gottfried Galston for permission to scan, and to quote briefly from, seven German letters that he is reserving for private use.

Professor Gwynn S. Bement, Chairman of the Music Department at Elmira College, very kindly provided an office and telephone to serve as a base of operations during sojourns in Elmira.

Thanks are due and gratefully rendered to the librarian of the Elmira College Library, who expedited dealings with the Broughton letters, the Harz flower collection, and other Griffes material belonging to the college; to Edward N. Waters, Assistant Chief of the Music Division at the Library of Congress, for information about the Griffes manuscripts lodged there; and to the librarians and assistants of the Harvard College Library and the New York Public Library. Miss Dorothy Lawton and her staff at the music branch of the New York Public Library were especially cordial in assisting with the collection of Griffes's books and music in their keeping.

A number of personal friends have shared in the heavy burden of library research and thus made it possible to take into account almost everything that has been written about Griffes during his lifetime and since. They have also been most resourceful in facilitating the arrangements and introductions that were incident to travel. But this is an obligation better expressed elsewhere than on the printed page.

A few notes may be appended here for the benefit of musicologists and students of American culture. Since almost every statement in an original work of this kind refers to some interview, document, or piece of correspondence, it would not be feasible to cite authority without recourse to some formidable footnote apparatus that would alienate the average reader. A fully annotated copy of the book will, however, be deposited with the Music Division of the Library of Congress or with the Harvard College Library.

Exact wording has been retained in all quotations from Griffes, but the spelling has been corrected in some instances, and the punctuation been made to conform to the general text. Obvious slips of the pen have been rectified instead of the customary reproduction with accompanying *sic*. Versed in German, French, and Italian, Griffes found it natural occasionally to write in these languages, and an English translation is given in most cases without any indication to this effect. A. Marguerite Griffes, expertly familiar with her brother's handwriting, has kindly offered advice on all passages of doubtful calligraphy. She has also generously provided transcripts of the whole sheaf of correspondence covering the German period, and these have been relied upon, for the most part, instead of the originals, where a youthful and unformed handwriting puzzles the eye.

General sources not revealed in the text may be listed briefly here. The quotation on page 23 is from an essay, " The Advent of American Music," by Paul Rosenfeld in the *Kenyon Review*, Vol. I, No. 1. The quotations from Foster and Nevin may be found in the biographies of these men by John Tasker Howard. The items concerning William Sharp are from *Fiona Macleod: A Memoir* by Mrs. William Sharp. The quotation from Louis M. Eilshemius appears in the biography *And He Sat among the Ashes* by William Schack. The Mahler incident is taken from Nicolas Slonimsky's *Music Since 1900*, which has also served as a reliable background text. The quotation from Busoni is in Edward J. Dent's biography of the composer. The first of the Arthur

Farwell quotations is part of a letter to Miss Juliet Danziger that was published in the *Musical Mercury*, Vol. I, No. 4. The Debussy quotation, to be found in Lockspeiser's biography, is borrowed from an essay by W. H. Mellers, the English music critic, in *Scrutiny*, Vol. VIII, No. 4. The Victor Herbert material is from Joseph Kaye's biography of Herbert. Several of William Treat Upton's opinions, from his careful and interesting study, " The Songs of Charles T. Griffes," have been drawn upon as present-day viewpoint.

The biography of a composer does not aim to substitute for the experience of hearing that composer's music. Without considerably expanding the scope of this work, it has not even been possible to include worth-while discussion of Griffes's compositions. (What others wrote of them, worth-while or not, is a part of the man's life and is accordingly set forth and summarized.) Exception has been made for the *Sonata*, of which a detailed analysis appears in Chapter XVII. The method used is based on that of Tovey as cleverly amplified with record collocations by his American disciple, B. H. Haggin. To Mr. Haggin the author is further indebted for a review of Bernard Shaw's music criticism (from which two Shavian references are lifted on page 120) that first sent him in serious quest of the riches to be found in that mine.

The American-Scandinavian Foundation (Hanna Astrup Larsen's translation of Jacobsen), Paul Rosenfeld (Appendix II), G. Schirmer, Inc. (passages from the *Sonata*), W. W. Norton & Company, Inc. (M. D. Herter Norton's translation of Rilke's *Letters to a Young Poet*), Mrs. Jane McIntosh (the description of the White Peacock), Alfred A. Knopf, Inc. (the paragraphs on Mozart's death from an Appendix of W. J. Turner's biography), and L. C. Page & Company (Rupert Hughes), have all generously granted permission to reprint sizable extracts from works copyrighted by them. Miss Irene

Lewisohn has graciously offered the right to reproduce one of Herbert Crowley's designs for *The Kairn of Koridwen*.

E. M. M.

March 1942

ILLUSTRATIONS

CHARLES T. GRIFFES

Chapter I

CHARLES TOMLINSON GRIFFES was born on September 17th, 1884, in Elmira, New York, and the tedious program his mother had followed in anticipation of the event came to an end. From the moment of conception, almost, she had lived on applesauce and rice, left off bread and meat, and read lovely books, seen lovely pictures, and thought lovely thoughts. But however the efficacy of this discipline might later reveal itself, the resulting child was not noticeably superior, at least in physical appearance, to her previous two, born without benefit of any such considered prenatal influence. Even the highly imaginative friend who had urged the procedure on her had to admit that. Whereas Katharine Griffes had been a charmingly grave and complaisant sort of baby, and Florence Griffes had at least been entertaining in her clamor, the new infant was plain, and neither submissive nor gay. He was quietly determined. And his nose was too big.

The ancestry that led up to this peculiar baby probably harks back to a distant Welsh origin but is here intercepted for inspection at its American phase.

A nuclear personage in the Griffes genealogy, Stephen Gates — according to a faded scrap in the family Bible — was born in the town of Huntington on Long Island in 1750 and lived there till 1773, when as a young man he went to Dutchess County to tend a run of mills that belonged to two brothers, John and Thomas Notherway. There he remained till 1775, when he moved with his family to Saratoga, three miles west of the historic Bemis Heights. In 1777 General Burgoyne arrived at Saratoga with the English forces, and Stephen Gates was ordered to military service with the American army or else be deemed a Tory and have his property confiscated. He therefore moved his family back to Dutchess County and after having made adequate provision for them returned and joined the army with Lieutenant Philip Rogers of Saratoga. Probably owing to his familiarity with the region, he was appointed a guide to the rangers, a scouting party, and so continued as a volunteer in the time of the general action at Stillwater. He remained in the field till Burgoyne's surrender, then, at liberty, went to his evacuated home, where his family rejoined him in January of 1778.

The sister of Stephen Gates, Abiah Gates, married William Griffes and had ten children by him, of whom the fifth was Nathaniel Griffes, born on October 4th, 1768. This Nathaniel Griffes married Esther Gates, the eldest daughter of his uncle Stephen Gates, and the product of this marriage was Stephen Griffes, the father of Wilber (*sic*) Gideon Griffes, the father of Charles Tomlinson Griffes.

In the lives of Wilber Griffes and his son Charles there are many striking parallels, none the less suggestive for their divergency in details. One of six children, Wilber Griffes early learned to make his own way in the world. His father had died when he was young, leaving to an eldest son the farm that had been their family's home for generations in the little countryside of Niskayuna, near Schenectady, New York. The widow proceeded with her daughter and youngest son

Wilber to Schenectady in order to secure whatever educational advantages she might for the boy. By careful management of living expenses and by outside occupation as a clerk, Wilber managed to contribute to the support of his mother and sister at the same time that he pursued his studies. An excellent student in the classroom and possessed of natural scholarly inclinations, he might have attended Union College on a scholarship, except that there was not enough money even for that when the time came. Instead there followed a job clerking in New York. He threw over this position when his sister married a man associated with the "gentlemen's furnishings" business, and he and his new brother-in-law entered into a partnership. The two men opened a store on Baldwin Street, in the broad, flat valley of Elmira, New York, a city rumored favorable to nascent industry; but nothing came of their efforts, and after the heartaches of a losing struggle "Waldron and Griffes" were bought out by a friend from Schenectady, who retained them as employees. Wilber was indeed valuable to the business. Although engaged as a shirt-cutter, he was also expected to wait on customers, and in this capacity he came to be relied upon by the beau monde of Elmira for the correct word in male apparel. He had, always, a sure taste and discrimination, an ability to say what clothes would look well on what clients. If his preferences were frequently a little on the plain side, this severity was perhaps needed to counterbalance the elegance prescribed by the fashion plates of the time.

The discontinuance of his formal education was the bitter disappointment of Wilber Griffes's life. A student at heart, he never altogether abandoned the attempt to requite himself for the opportunities life had not offered him. He was an incessant reader. And although the necessity of supporting a mother and sister in his youth, and the responsibility of main-

taining a family in his manhood, spared little enough time for
the indulgence of private aptitudes, he somehow found the
leisure for study. He loved to help his children with their
schoolwork, modestly cautioning them to "Do it your own
way" when his pedagogy seemed outdated. And he loved to
read aloud to them from Dickens or Thackeray or any other
of his reigning favorites. When he came to Elmira to live he
renewed his knowledge of German through the kind assistance of a local German minister. He also undertook the study
of piano, in spite of his age, and had been taking lessons for
some time, was indeed competent to render a composition entitled *Falling Leaves*, when in September of 1873 he married
Clara Louise Tomlinson.

Miss Tomlinson was no stranger to the rebuffs of circumstance. Her own education had been discontinued in order
that she might attend an invalid mother. Not, however, before she had undergone the rigors of an intensive and highly
checkered cultural program. She had started at the Misses
Galatian's private school, then studied a year among the
heterogeneous pupils of a Professor Roe, then entered Elmira
College as a "selective student." From the Misses Galatian
she had learned the "proprieties" indispensable to the equipment of the well bred; from Professor Roe she had acquired
a real and lasting appreciation of poetry; and from the college
she had carried away the technique of painting nebulous deer
staggering across a murky terrain. On the musical side, too,
her education had not been neglected. She had received a
piano for her tenth birthday. Progress in mastering the instrument was tolerably slow, however, for the girl was terri-
fied of her instructor, the organist at the Baptist Church, who,
anxious friends had warned, would rap her knuckles if she
committed any error. She had also a few lessons with the
organist at Trinity Church, a greater artist both in pianistic

Clara Louise Tomlinson

Wilber Gideon Griffes

interpretation and in methods of correcting stubborn fingers. Notwithstanding the infrequency of her lessons and the hazardousness of their achievement, Clara Tomlinson did attain a certain proficiency at the piano. She could sound out *General Grant's Grand March*, a stirring number that impressed her listeners and later afforded endless amusement to her composer son. She could also play the *Grand Duchess March*, brought home by her father from an entertainment he had witnessed in New York. And always, for so long as she was to have her piano, there reclined on its fluted racks two or three square albums of "Pianoforte Gems," eloquent mementos of her encounter with Euterpe.

Like the man she was to marry, Clara Tomlinson had quiet tastes, was fond of reading, and enjoyed a little circle of intimate friends. Like his, her life had been from the first swept up in the needs of others. On her had fallen the brunt of practical management in a household whose members were all busy with outside concerns. In particular, it was her lot to be subservient to, and complement the activities of, one of the most colorful women in the extraordinary community that was Elmira in the second half of the century, a woman who became the cornerstone of her own home when she married, and who exercised as great an authority over her children as she herself did — her mother, Delinda P. Tomlinson.

Among the residents of Elmira Mrs. Tomlinson fared as perhaps the most God-fearing and pious, certainly the most willing, Baptist in the service of the Lord. Her missionary ardor furnished the motivating drive to all her days. Yet with this religious intensity there was a surprising admixture of geniality and natural sweetness of disposition in Mrs. Tomlinson that made her liked even as her wide generosity made her respected. She was the daughter of John Rice, one of the Rices for whom Ricetown, New York, had been named, and of Margaret Crandall, from Pomfret, Connecticut. As a little girl she had been the means of her widowed mother's remarriage when she attracted the interest of a kindly old gentleman on her way to school. A born teacher, she pledged herself to propagating the Gospel as she conceived it. When her family lost their home, they had persevered nevertheless in their determination that Delinda should realize her aim of becoming a teacher. She had attended Miss Rockwell's academy for young ladies at Unadilla and later Miss Thurston's " female seminary " in Elmira. Then, armed with a list of the foremost families in Elmira, she opened a small private school, which she maintained till her engagement to Solomon B. Tomlinson, a promising young lawyer about town. Her marriage to " S. B.," as he was popularly known, brought an end to her professional career, but her missionary exertions continued undiminished. Even her husband's appointment as District Attorney and the birth of her two children meant no surcease in her activities. There were the weekly visits to the local jail to make certain the regeneration of the imprisoned. There were the neighborhood calls on the sick and unenlightened to provide nourishment and precept. There were the trips to the national meetings of the temperance movement to add the force of her own conviction. And not least there were the prayers for the state of her soul to buttress it in its faith.

In all this consecration there was nothing of the bigot about Mrs. Tomlinson. A fundamentalist she was: there was no real light to be found outside the words of Holy Scripture. Yet she professed only that which she sincerely believed and made no pretense of infallibility. When a thing was wrong, it was wrong, and nothing on earth might change that fact. She could not bring herself even to touch the deck of cards that her son once cached away, but carried them in the folds of her apron to the fire. On the other hand, if a good thing had been misjudged, reparation was a duty. She withdrew her daughter Clara from dancing school after two lessons in the plain belief that dancing was the Devil's invention. But when she later reversed this opinion she was nothing loath to confess her earlier mistakenness and, declaring that she had been cruel, re-enrolled the girl at once.

It was Mrs. Tomlinson who introduced her daughter to Wilber Griffes at a church social, and she who sponsored the match. Later, when " S. B." had lost his money through poor investments, and her own health was failing, she asked the young couple to make their home with her. And as Mrs. Griffes had once before cut short her schooling to nurse her mother, so now again she responded to the appeal. Mr. Tomlinson died in 1889, and Mrs. Tomlinson became a permanent member of the Griffes household and a second mother to the Griffes children. It was no uncommon thing on entering the Griffes home to be confronted by some frowzy-mannered tatterdemalion ensconced on the sofa in the throes of Biblical instruction: one of " Grandma's visitors." There was something unique and precious in everyone, and she never tired of awaiting and observing its manifestations.

For this reason her grandson Charles T. Griffes was her special delight. Named for her own son, a lawyer in Albany, he evinced so many startling traits that the latter never had. They were traits rare enough in the adult world; in a child their appearance was truly astonishing. Even when the boy was followed by a sister and then a brother it was still he who occupied the center of her interest. Among the five Griffes children he always remained her favorite.

Young Charles was in truth an unusual child. As he grew in years and his baby features assumed proportion, his nose came into harmony with the rest of his face. The big-nosed baby developed into an average, pudgy, round-faced tot. But he was an assertive tot, full of strange tastes and inexplicable preferences. When only two and a half years old he conceived an inflexible admiration for a most sinister picture in one of his sisters' geography books. It was an illustration of a vicious boa constrictor wrapped in deadly embrace about the body of a hapless doe. However often disquieted elders might seek to mollify the child with more suitable diversion, he was not to be sidetracked. He insisted on the " geog " book, and when it was ultimately brought forth, patiently awaited on their knee till they should find the picture he had in mind. It was compliance with an almost congruent fascination that brought him often in later years a rapt devotee before the snake pits at the zoo.

The young Griffes had an exceptional fondness for color, his favorite color being orange. Taken to visit his Great-Aunt Amanda, he could never disentangle himself from the old woman's embrace fast enough to be off to her garden, where the inviting rows of marigolds spread out in the gorgeous fullness of their " orantch." His delicate perception of color in its many gradations, from the green grasshopper that was " not ripe " to the little girl he had observed in a " watermelon pink " dress, won the respect of the Griffes family. He was soon consulted on all their artistic problems. The proper matching of segments for quilting, the correct flower arrangement for the jars and blooms at hand, the appropriate costume for the time of day and occasion, all fell within the scope of his judgment. Whether Katharine were to essay the hat with the roses or a leghorn with pansies hinged on his authority.

This trait assumes special importance as harbinger of the composer's preoccupation with color in its relation to music. ". . . A beautiful color is lovely in itself quite aside from any part it plays in the design of the picture," Griffes wrote in 1912 with reference to painting. Having so keen a visual apprecia-

tion, it was perhaps natural that like some musical Rimbaud —
and like several other composers in history — he should have
come to sense a tonality of color. Certain colors he associated
with certain keys in music. The key of E-flat, for example, was
yellow or golden. C major was an incandescent white light,
the most brilliant key in the tonality. It was his favorite key.
When a friend once expressed the opinion of a Prokofiev composition they had just heard that it sounded like a very dull
imitation of Haydn in the key of C, Griffes replied indig-
nantly: "Well, it isn't in the key of C. And how can you think
of the key of C as dull? To me it's the most brilliant key, it's
like a blazing white light. Many composers, consciously or unconsciously, have resolved the culminating passages of their
music, the revelatory finales, in the key of C." When he came
to the superbly evocative march ("You, whoever you are!")
in his setting of Whitman's *Salut au Monde*, it was in the key
of C that he cast it. A-flat had much the same quality for him,
but it was more tempered and removed from the absolute.

The unfamiliar tonalities of which acrimonious critics complained in some of his music were often the product of an artist's natural absorption in scraping and mixing precise colors.
"There is too much of the experimental handling of chords, of
the shifting of plans," wrote one critic of *Wai Kiki*. A more recent critique after recognizing the enigmatic character of that
song perspicaciously continues: "It is undeniable that in this
song — perhaps as in no other — we see Griffes's power in painting with elemental colors." It is small wonder that the composer should have kept by him for so long the text of Oscar
Wilde's *Les Ballons,* balked in his every effort to flesh it with
music. "The [*Ballons*] is a sort of old war-horse, which I have
worked at over and over again. The poem fascinates but defies
me," he wrote towards the close of 1914. How should it not
have fascinated and defied him with its "turquoise," "pearls,"

" silver," " rose," "amethyst," and " rubies "? In the end he left it unfinished.

Griffes as a little boy also liked to dress up, and he had many opportunities. There were the local pageants sponsored by Mrs. J. Sloat Fassett, society leader and wife of the Congressman, with Charles as a cherubic, if short-lived, page in one of the more spectacular. There was also the old chest of discarded clothing that inspired the Griffes children to invite their neighborhood friends for masquerades. It was a perpetually exciting old chest, and one never knew what character one might become in the oddments dredged up from its interior. On one occasion Charles might deck himself in the finery and chic of a Gibson girl. Or on another, he might become Faust, in a woolly cape of eiderdown lined with cerise satin and replete with swan's-down about the neck, and ruff and beads.

Sometimes the child's veneration for clothes manifested itself to a surprising extent. Presented with a broad-brimmed straw hat, he wore it all day long and would not relinquish it at bedtime, insisting that he wear it to sleep. (Its rust-colored band the four-year-old, with typically sharp color sense, identified as " mahogany.") Another time, when his mother altered one of his coats, Charles wept bitter tears because the marks showed on the sleeves where they had been let down.

One more outlet for his propensity to dress was the neighborhood plays, in which he sometimes participated. When the Griffeses moved in 1888 from the gray frame house on the corner of Main and Gray where Charles had been born (the present site of the Mark Twain Hotel) to 422 West First Street, they gave unwitting impetus to these dramatic activities. The new abode had a large deserted barn in the rear, ideal for theatrical purposes. Its vacant stalls contained dilapidated furniture and bowling balls that could be used as props, and the upstairs floor provided a perfect auditorium and stage. The children charged pins for admission. A neighboring boy wrote the plays, and Charles sometimes had a role.

Besides the barn, the new home had much else to recommend it as a background for childhood. It had eleven fruit trees in the yard — apple, cherry, plum, and russet pear — and a flower garden in front of the barn. Thick purple clematis vines covered the sides of the porch. It was a roomy house with large windows going down to the floor, and the Griffeses adorned it with noble pictures, from the large portrait of *Washington at Valley Forge* at the entrance to the old engraving of *Spirit of '76* behind the piano in the back parlor. The portraits painted by Great-Uncle Jabez, who had vanished in the Civil War, were consigned to the attic.

Charles's room was on the second floor, a large room at the left rear of the house, set apart as his private domain by two intervening bedrooms one had to penetrate before reaching his. In time he called it his " fort."

The Griffes family life was a happy one for any child. Mr. Griffes was fond of gardening and of hikes, and often took the children on long walks through the woods, where they gathered wintergreen berries, trilliums, pussy willows, milkweed pods (for pillows), daisies, brown-eyed Susans, and any other treasure that their father pointed out to them. To this early and impressive contact with natural beauty may be traced some part of Charles T. Griffes's unusual sensitiveness to it.

There were always new faces at the Griffes home. Sometimes they belonged to Mrs. Tomlinson's visitors, her cohorts and converts in the work of the Lord, and sometimes they belonged to visitors whom Mr. Griffes brought home with him from the Y.M.C.A. Into the latter category fitted a seventeen-year-old lad named Jack Raynes. A member of a musical troupe engaged to play at the Y.M.C.A., young Raynes was invited by the senior Griffes to his home and, having no time or place in which to change, appeared unforgettably in the full dress of his performance. His high spirits and bright humor soon won him a place in the family. For a long time he lived with the Griffeses, sleeping at night on their lounge. He was always ready to play the piano, could arrange and compose, and joined the church choir. Intermittently he vanished on out-of-town engagements, remembering the children with music on their birthdays and present-laden on his homecomings. Once, returning in the early hours of the morning from a trip west, he seated himself at the piano and banged out *Home, Sweet Home,* so announcing his arrival to the delighted consternation of the Griffeses. To young Charles Griffes, Jack Raynes taught all the popular ballads of the day and the Moody-Sankey hymns that were so sure-fire on the road. But notwithstanding these blandishments and friendly overtures, Charles was a little envious of the youth's niche in the good will of the family, and privately rejoiced when he left for good.

After Raynes's departure, there was a lapse in Charles's musical education. A brief period of study at the piano with Katharine, who was planning to become a music teacher, proved abortive and was dropped. The boy had always exhibited an unmistakable, though unconventional, musical talent; his failure was therefore disappointing. When eight years old he had once been sitting with Katharine beneath a plum tree thronged with orioles and had astounded her by his unusual persistence in trying to whistle an exact imitation of their cries. A year or so later he had been at the lakeshore, when from somewhere near by the strains of a violin floated across the water. Charles had gone to the piano and without hesitation or error played back the melody by ear. Confronted with a definite assignment and the niceties of formal instruction, however, this interest seemed to evaporate at once.

In the practice of art, the boy applied himself with more immediate success. His first efforts had been guided by Mr. William Giles, an old friend of Mrs. Tomlinson's, who designed patterns for a large shoe manufacturing firm and made violins. Mr. Giles it was who showed him how the grape center in the design of his earliest masterwork must be shaded. Next he went on by himself to boats, for a long time painting nothing else.

From these simple beginnings the boy turned to more ambitious projects and indeed showed considerable versatility in art. A glowering ink sketch of Dickens's Scrooge and a portrait of Marie Antoinette were the two big productions of this plastic period. The second of these occasioned him no little difficulty. It was a copy of the frontispiece in a bulky two-volume biography that he had borrowed from the library. Entranced by the colored reproduction that began the work he would pore over it by the hour trying to copy it to his satisfaction, and though he succeeded in capturing every color, to that of the tiniest jewel, he could not get the features. Time after time he renewed the book at the library, desperately wishing to own it. His interest in Marie Antoinette remained with him. No relic pertaining to her, from a lock of hair to a piece of antique furniture, would ever fail to evoke some response in Griffes.

Photography, too, attracted the experimenting artist, and he tried his hand there, sometimes elaborately posing his sisters and their friends in stilted tableaux for his benefit. Young as he was, they did not dispute his authority in these matters. Afterwards he pasted these pictures in an album and assigned them semifacetious captions, as: "At Night I Sit Alone and Dream," "To Have and to Hold," "Prisoners of Hope," and "All Alone."

It was not till he was eleven years old that Griffes first showed his real genius in music. At that time he fell ill with typhoid fever, and during the long period of his convalescence was compelled to hear Katharine at her practicing downstairs. She was studying something of Beethoven's that so affected the recovering invalid that he was beset with the desire to play it himself. Katharine obligingly resumed instruction and this time found a more receptive pupil. For her brother now demonstrated the most rapid advancement on the piano, mastering immediately whatever music was offered him. The simpler compositions of Mendelssohn and Chopin soon fell by the way-side, and he was demanding more exacting labors. This fervor and success in his musical accomplishment was accompanied by a genuine regret for lost opportunities. Often he would exclaim aghast at his previous folly. There was also a marked and noticeable change in the boy's personality, an increased maturity or sense of responsibility that illuminates, as will be seen, the nature of his inner life during childhood.

Soon the requirements of the overzealous pupil began to exceed the resources of his neophyte teacher. She was obliged to consult her own instructor, the "Professor of Piano Playing" at Elmira College, who advised what pieces to assign and marked the fingering on them. In this way, by proxy for a while, Charles continued his studies, till it was decided that he had better study with Katharine's teacher in a manner less indirect. So at about fifteen years of age the aspiring Griffes was introduced to the woman who was to have greater influence than any other on the subsequent course of his life.

Chapter II

IN A LETTER to his publishers after the composer's death Mary
Selena Broughton wrote: "I was Mr. Griffes's first teacher and
always maintained that he had very unusual talent." The sentence is as indicative in its understatement as in its content of
the woman who wrote it. Miss Broughton was Griffes's first
teacher. She was also the earliest supporter of his talent. Yet
she was something at once more important and more personal
than these.

From the day of her arrival in Elmira sometime in the year
1891 Mary Selena Broughton had remained an enigma to its
curious citizens. They were principally of two minds about
her. To most she was a brusque, outspoken, independent
woman with not a human feeling in the world except a fanati-
cal loyalty to her native Britain. Nor did her personal appearance detract from this impression. She was a tall, spare woman,
as renowned for her atrocious clothes as for her inability to
wear them. Her long, narrow face was sharply angular with its
high cheekbones and pointed chin. When she spoke she was
all teeth. When she laughed the effect was a whinny. "Young
man, I want that chair," she would snap to the nearest seated
youth on entering a room. Her bluntness impinged on cruelty.

If she believed a person's opinions to be nonsense, she said so at once, sparing no one. Her own opinions were pronounced and final, and expressed with so great an air of self-possession as to discourage all dissent. Chief among them was the conviction that the British Empire was the greatest in the world. On this subject there was no room for argument of any kind whatever. Her criticism of Americans was based on their lightheartedness, for they could make a joke of anything. " Someday," she would glumly predict, " they'll get a knock and learn."

Yet there was another impression of Miss Broughton, had by a few close friends who could reconcile these forbidding aspects with human frailties. If she pierced the innocent bystander with gimlet eyes as she passed but did not smile in greeting, the oversight might better be attributed to her nearsightedness than to snobbery. If there was something almost intolerant about her self-assurance, that was because there lay a girlish disappointment with people beneath it. If she was opinionated, she was also a remarkably cultured and educated woman whose opinions might be heard with profit. She admittedly cut an old-world figure when decked out in something like her stiff, brocaded Dresden gown, with its ruffles and roses so much too big for the Dresden pattern. But she had few clothes, and there was something placid and almost delicate about her when she took pains, as for example when she appeared in the simple white frock with the loops that she had purchased at Redfern's. Her intimate friends could point to her generous loyalty as refutation of the charge that she was unfeeling. Moreover, she had a very alert sense of humor, and they accordingly saved up their best stories for Miss Broughton. For they knew that she was a young gossip at heart, who dearly loved a good joke. The reconciliation of the reticent personality with the formidable exterior was also easier in the light of her past.

Miss Broughton was born in Picton, New Zealand, in 1862, some thirty-seven years before her meeting with Charles T. Griffes. Her father was Lieutenant Brian Herbert Sneyd Broughton of the British Consular Service, who was drowned shortly before his daughter's birth. His boat had capsized when he was out sailing, and when it later drifted back to harbor his jacket was found in it, but the body was never recovered. Some believed that he had been devoured by sharks. Miss Broughton often showed a picture of her father as a little boy seated on Wordsworth's knee. Her mother, of Irish gentlefolk, played the harp, and owing to Miss Broughton's unexpected arrival on earth, the baby was born in a harp case. Left an orphan in girlhood, Miss Broughton was educated by a governess at the house of some relatives in Auckland, New Zealand. She next went to England to live with relatives in Ambleside, Grasmere; then to Berlin, arriving the day that Friedrich III died, to study piano with Karl Klindworth, pupil of Liszt and fellow student of Hans von Bülow.

A sad love affair with a tubercular young Englishman furnished the tragic motif to Miss Broughton's life. Ever afterwards she nursed a feeling of bitterness towards his sisters, whom she blamed with the ruination of her life. They prohibited the match. With their selfish anxiety to retain their brother's dependence they had cared nothing for her own unhappiness. Inasmuch as Miss Broughton was herself an arrested tubercular, it is entirely possible that the relationship was doomed from the outset. On her many trips to England, after settling in Elmira, she always visited her lover's sanatorium and so knew afresh the torment of her original misfortune. The whole affair was secret and unsuspected in Elmira, but Miss Broughton's private instructions, complied with upon her death, that his letters (and the New Zealand flag) be interred with her, emphasize its importance in her life.

As a girl Miss Broughton never cared much about music. Had she followed her own bent she might not have entered on it as a career. Still, it afforded one of the few respectable means by which a woman of her " class " might earn a living. While she was studying in Berlin, Klindworth received a contract for a piano teacher from the Music Department at Elmira College (the first American college to award the bachelor's degree to women). Miss Broughton signed and overrode the horrified protests of her family by reminding them that a lady always fulfilled her obligations. They therefore consented to her accepting the position for a year.

She was not immediately welcome at the college, which had asked for a man. Nevertheless they were willing to await what she could do. Her first recital resolved all doubts. Attired in a hideous gown, variously described afterwards as red plush and rose velvet, she flicked aside her long train and strode out upon the platform. Her short sleeves and low neck were calculated to set off her gawky figure to worst possible advantage, and her pile of light hair bespangled on the trellis of a Spanish comb added unnecessary height to her elongated face. Then she played, and appearances were forgotten. On Miss Broughton's ability as a pianist there is singular unanimity of report. It was snappy, brittle, clean, accurate playing, with no loose ends. Her phrasing was concise, her staccato crisp to the point of being bitten off, and the tone produced by her thin wiry fingers sharp, not deep. There was no retarding anywhere in her strict tempo. In matters of exactitude she was unbeatable. Hearing the accomplished harpsichordist Wanda Landowska play Rameau's *Coucou* in Berlin, Charles T. Griffes wrote his teacher: ". . . she played [it] very beautifully, only not with quite such a good Coucou in the right hand as you." Her performances, though sincere, honest, and painstaking, lacked warmth. She seemed anxious, almost, not to reflect anything of herself in her waltzes. It was only when she played Chopin's *Marche Funèbre* late into the night by herself in the chapel that eavesdroppers might detect some personal feeling.

Fright was Miss Broughton's limitation. Calm and confident as she appeared to her audiences, she remained in a state of high nervous tension from the moment she ascended the platform. Her two or three recitals a year, attended by people from Buffalo and Syracuse as well as Elmira, summoned forth the utmost of her courage. When she finally abandoned music and locked her piano for good, she proclaimed that a great stone had been lifted from her.

Miss Broughton was a distinct addition to Elmira society, despite her impatience with the flippancy of American life. If her estimates of people on their own merits and her perennial gathering of baskets for the poor often brought her dangerously near *hoi polloi*, nevertheless her British punctiliousness about dressing for dinner and her insistence upon tea at exactly four o'clock carried a remote and authentic flavor. She made a ready addition to any dinner that included asparagus or strawberries; and once a year, on Christmas, she permitted herself a glass of champagne. One soon became accustomed to her unconventional table manners. When Miss Broughton hotly demanded: "Is there any reason why I can't have that salt?" there was a general skirmish in the direction of the salt. To friends she confided her connection with the Countess von Arnheim, author of the pleasant and phenomenally successful *Elizabeth and Her German Garden*. Later she revealed her cousinship to Kathleen Beauchamp of New Zealand, writing under the pseudonym of Katherine Mansfield. On her expeditions to England, she regularly visited Miss Mansfield, who referred to her as "beloved Lena."

This then was the woman to whom Charles T. Griffes was brought for piano instruction in his youth. The results could scarcely have been anticipated. From the first Miss Broughton conceived a partiality for her talented charge. He became her protégé, the favorite student upon whom she lavished a wealth of care and devotion. In him she experienced more than the satisfactions of a sacrificing teacher — even a sort of vicarious maternity. She corrected his informal speech and appearance, suggested books to read and discussed them with him, encouraged a variety of interests, lauded his paintings, and fostered his composing. She was a sharp and omniscient taskmistress. On his side the boy accepted these exhortations and admonishments gladly. For he welcomed the authoritative interest. " Do not imagine that I am offended when you correct me," he afterwards wrote her from Berlin, " for I am not at all. In fact I should be very glad to always have you correct me if I use any incorrect words. I laughed when I saw that you had cut out my spelling of ' disappointed ' and pinned it on the letter. If I continue to use it, it is not because I do not believe that you are right, for I know you are." He concluded: " Lecture all you want to, and I will try to correct myself."

The air of deference that the usually positive Miss Broughton accorded her protégé's opinions astonished her pupils at the college. They joked over the amount of time she spent with him. It was hard to see what she discerned in his playing that merited such sedulous nourishment. It was certainly not rhythmical as they expected it to be rhythmical. His hands were rather too small for any great technical advancement. Also he had an unnatural preoccupation with harmonic structure and a tendency to read eccentric design into his pieces.

The music that Griffes learned from Miss Broughton was the same that he heard at concerts and at home. Liszt, Chopin, Wagner, Raff, Grieg, Schumann, Brahms, Mendelssohn, Beethoven, Weber, Schubert, Moszkowski, and so on, were the names that appeared on assignments, on the programs of Elmira, and indeed on those of the entire country. "To the United States," one critic suggests, "romantic music had come in company with the gentler immigrants of the middle and late nineteenth century. It was connatural with them; they supported its interpreters; and they found no native tradition of musical art to balance it. English culture had pretty thoroughly ceased producing high musical expressions after the revolution of 1688; and the Anglo-Saxon immigrants had produced almost none of their own — not at all fortuitously, since music is the social art and necessarily slow of development in pioneer communities. The descendants of the Puritans accepted romantic music . . . for the most puritanic of reasons. . . . Not liking the stuff, they felt the fault within themselves and decided they ought to like it. Probably its abundant sentimental facets also helped endear it." It might further be added that its erotic temper offered outlet to expression of a kind not readily assimilable in their society.

One individual preference young Griffes stoutly maintained: Bach. It was his own enthusiasm that secured him assignments in *The Well-Tempered Clavichord*. It was mainly that enthusiasm, together with a certain mechanical interest, that supported him through the organ lessons he began with Mr. George Morgan McKnight. But an instinctive dislike of the instrument prevailed, and he discontinued after a while.

There was music in Elmira. There were the Trinity Church choir, directed by Mr. McKnight, the summer operas at Rorick's Glen, and the recitals at the college. There were also visiting performers, like the Kneisel Quartet and Godowsky and celebrated singers of the day. Charles was an inveterate follower of such functions. Lacking friends, he would sometimes importune a kind adult acquaintance, like Professor Howard Conant, principal of the high school, to accompany him.

His own first public performance came about unexpectedly.

Mr. Herbert Lansdale, secretary of the Elmira Y.M.C.A., was in constant need of an accompanist for the regular Sunday afternoon men's meetings. For it was a problem of these meetings to obtain good music without any expenditure of money. Lansdale had come from Baltimore, a musical city, and had been musical director in church work there. He had also attended concerts regularly at the Peabody Conservatory of Music, and his canons were higher than those of the average Y.M.C.A. secretary. He therefore found it a difficult task to secure good enough accompanists for his Y.M.C.A. chorus and for the guest soloists who would donate their talent on the condition of his providing an accompanist. One Sunday when the situation became more desperate than usual, a young man present bethought himself of Griffes. "Why don't you try Charlie? " he suggested. Griffes was asked but refused, explaining that " he had never done such a thing in public." Petitioned on all sides and moved by their need, however, he finally gave in and proved a great success. Thenceforth he played every Sunday at meetings, also volunteering as Lansdale's accompanist at Young People's Services.

His association with the Y.M.C.A. secretary ripened into friendship. Before long he conferred upon the man the office of father confessor to his problems. As they lived in the same neighborhood, Griffes would stop at the Y almost every afternoon so they could walk home together. Paramount among the problems that vexed him was " How am I going to make a living? " Most of the boys of his age considered him unlikely to earn a livelihood because he wasted so much time on music. Understandably enough, there was some opposition in the Griffes family, as well, to the incipient crystallization of his ambitions. These surrounding doubts privately unsettled the boy and bred misgiving. He had a certain practical side that could not look out upon an indeterminate future with equanimity. Even then he had begun those small personal expense lists that he was to keep ever after, dispensing not so much as a stamp unmindful of its place in his budget. Lansdale could only prescribe fortitude.

There was another problem troubling the boy at this time, and one central to the increasing perplexities of his everyday life. He could not take it to the Y.M.C.A. secretary or, indeed, to any other adult of his acquaintance. For it was one with which he must deal alone throughout his life. It was the problem of his difference from the other boys he knew. Writing of his homosexuality in later years, it was on this aspect, his early ignorance, that Griffes laid stress. To whom might he have turned for enlightenment in his difficulty? He had no intimate friends of whom he might ask his questions, the very difference at point seemingly precluding the necessary rapport. Victorian prudence everywhere intensified a natural dilemma. Consequently, as Griffes later expounded in a letter to a German doctor, he was handicapped in the discovery of even an ordinary sexual background.

But whether Griffes's early ignorance of these matters operated as a factor or as a result in his homosexuality is by no means certain. Indeed, this entire side of Griffes's personality must remain in large part unclear. For any efforts to comprehend the situation are complicated by the fact that Griffes himself, through reading and experience, built up several theories of his own and so acted upon them as to create, by the consequent modifications of his behavior, the question of what in his conduct was directly symptomatic and what merely expressive of his own analyses. He read much in the new psychology and in biographies of eminent homosexual figures of the past. He had little patience with the sham that surrounded the subject. Of one typical gathering-place for homosexual contacts he wrote: " It always angers me that one cannot meet these people anywhere except there, but they always seem to be afraid." His letters and papers contain many and copious discussions of the subject. This material is for the most part of such purely clinical interest, however, that there would be small excuse for its reproduction. A psychiatrist would probably offer as a general stricture on Griffes's method in these writings (especially his explanation of the lure of uniform) the fact that he too often elevated contributory factors to the status of decisive conditions.

Where systematic analysis is impossible, and indeed out of place, description and simple understanding are not. One or two things are clear. First there stands out the overwhelming urgency of the passion that motivated the composer. Rilke has suggested that "artistic experience lies so incredibly close to that of sex, to its pain and its desire, that the two manifestations are indeed but different forms of one and the same yearning and delight." American music affords no more forceful illustration of this thesis than Griffes. Immersed in creation, during the periods when his need achieved a satisfactory balance with fulfillment, he could be profoundly detached. Yet any disturbance of this psychic equilibrium produced the most disastrous upsets, in the practical management of his daily life no less than in the delicate mechanics of composition. (It was a state comparable to that which Tchaikovsky labeled "sensation Z.") His years were to be perforated by the emotional crises precipitated in this way, though he at length found a partial escape in the permanence of his final affection. But of simply repressing the problem altogether there was never any possibility. When tortured so that neither music nor literature nor anything in nature or art would serve to deliver him, then "After all, that is the most powerful remedy," wrote Griffes.

Another thing that is clear is that Griffes's homosexuality dated from childhood, a fact he himself affirmed in one place.

Incidents such as those mentioned by him in this context probably have no real cogency. There is, however, clear evidence of
a determinative connection with a certain older man during
childhood. Moreover, the quality of his predicament was something that conveyed itself to all his associates. This boyhood
uncertainty cannot be overlooked, for it is in striking contrast
to the manliness that characterized his later years. It is surely
significant that the characteristic vanished almost commensu-
rately with the increase of his factual knowledge on sexual de-
viation. By the time of his return from Germany in early manhood there was little trace of the invert about him. His modest
and unassuming demeanor, as well as his quiet strength of character, betrayed nothing of the turbulent schism within. Nor
were many friends, except those he chose to inform, to divine
its presence. It is known that several women took a romantic
interest in him during his lifetime, and one at least proposed.

Miss Broughton, though probably ignorant of its route, was
not unaware of the difference that set apart her prodigy from
the society of other boys of his age. Once when a faculty colleague broached the subject to her she said nothing in reply.
In the same tolerant and discreet spirit she forbore to discuss
the matter with Griffes and wisely refrained from venturing
any criticism that might injure him. It was perhaps regrettable
that he should be taking piano lessons at a girls' college. But
his nativeness in music gave him an assurance in facing the in-
different world of the other boys. He had something of his
own to compensate for the lack of their petty joys. It was a
compensation, as already noted, that quite suddenly assisted
him towards maturity and enabled him to face the prospects
of growth.

Griffes was not entirely lacking in social life. There was always the companionship of his family and their many friends.
For the rest, he affected a conscientious scorn of others and

evolved a rationale that was partly grounded in truth. There were not many boys who shared his artistic interests. He was far in advance of those who did. And he preferred his hours of reading and long solitary walks to the gregarious banter of a neighborhood gang. So much was true. But the picture was less than complete. For this was a recluse who found it necessary to practice in the Y.M.C.A. at a time when there were two usable pianos at home (Katharine had acquired one to meet her teaching needs). Nor was it by chance that his practice always coincided with the noisy recess hour when the lads were returning from basketball practice. *Anitra's Dance*, by Grieg, he adjudged an obvious bit of tripe designed for popular approval; yet it was this very bit of tripe that he labored upon so assiduously at recess hour. To this supposedly dim-witted audience he confided some of his choicest and most personal observations — for example, that Russian music always ended as though there were more to follow. The occasional unhappiness that tinged his isolation may be inferred from the spasmodic moods of fraternity that resulted in such discrepancies.

His experiments in sociability also included an unsuccessful episode in smoking corn silk with other boys atop the hen coop behind Mr. Welch's barn.

These moods were, however, intermittent and short-lived. He withdrew from Miss Webster's dancing school after a few lessons on the excuse of a distaste for dancing. At Public School No. 2 and the Elmira Free Academy, where he played bored accompaniments to the marching in assembly, he made few friends. A boy next door to the Griffeses, losing a cherished bantam hen, charged Griffes with abducting it from sheer spite. Something of the overbearing and scornful aspect he presented to outsiders may be gathered from such an accusation.

The boy's unsociability attracted no particular notice in the Griffes family. Uncle Charles, to be sure, complained of his nephew's taking no part in athletics on the ground that he might not grow. When his mother asked him on one occasion why he displayed so little interest in girls, the boy replied in earnest: " I have resources of my own."

It was true. In later years, when his developed personality and unusual endowments won him the friendship and eager society of many and when he no longer required the defensive rationale of scorn, he showed this same capacity for reliance upon resources of his own.

There was school, with the fascinating class in psychology being conducted experimentally by Mr. James Bissett Pratt. There were his rambles in the woods and his painting and drawing. There was the world of books. The novels of Dickens and Thackeray, George Eliot's *Romola*, Eugene Field, *Swiss Family Robinson*, Mark Twain's *Roughing It*, Stevenson's *Will o' the Mill*, Coleridge, Keats, and Shelley, offered bright reward. There were even more books accessible to one like himself who read French and German. Poems like *La Tombe Dit à la Rose*, and indeed all the works of Victor Hugo, justified the effort.

One literary favorite already presaged a skepticism with his Baptist upbringing, and his natural affinity with the Orient. In Christmas of 1901, Griffes acquired a copy of *The Rubáiyát*, which he read with excited discovery, scoring and marking the verses in his absorption. The lines " Drink! — for, once dead, you never shall return " and " The Flower that once has blown forever dies " he appreciatively underlined. Some vestige of the epicurean meditation may have lingered in Griffes's consciousness during those later years when his activity-crowded days and nights compelled the apprehension and wonder of friends.

More than nature, art, and reading, there was his music. His skill at the piano had now developed to a point where the proud

Miss Broughton felt that she had nothing more to offer. She therefore resolved upon his studying abroad in Berlin and, appreciating the impossibility of such an expense for the Griffeses, undertook to send him herself. Mr. Griffes's offer of a note to cover the risk met with indignant refusal. The boy was a good investment and would himself eventually repay her. Uncle Charles also volunteered to help with the expense.

Griffes was to be graduated from the Academy in June of 1903 and could therefore leave in the summer of that year. His parents may have felt certain initial qualms about entrusting one so young to an independent life abroad, but these were dissipated by the irrefragable argument that study in Germany was the only recourse open to those musically gifted. There was no question of that. Moreover the boy was gifted. He had been earning already by occasional engagements, like that on February 14th, 1901, at the Women's Musical Club. Only a summer back, in 1902, he had been paid with two other boys to play dinner music at a hotel on Keuka Lake. He had played the organ for the Lutheran Church all last year. That very summer another bid, to the Methodist Church in Southport, had brought an announcement in the newspapers: " Charles Griffes begins work as organist of Centenary Church today, taking the place of Louis Reynolds, who is going to New York."

Charles was himself pleased by these auguries of success. His engagement at Keuka Lake had won him an appreciative friend, Miss Marion Logan. The potentialities of music were also enormously augmented by a few lessons in harmony and counterpoint that Miss Broughton had offered. To Miss Mabel Daggett, teacher and friend at the Academy, he now boasted that he was going to be the greatest composer in the world. He had, actually, made a few hopeful steps in that direction. One of his college recitals included a derivative piano prelude of his own, which brought forth the prophetic comment in the news-

Early manuscript

papers next day that "there is no doubt that the future holds for him an enviable success, which will probably include composition as well as execution." The same review justly noted: "His attainment is something unusual to one of his years, who has, during his entire time of study, kept up his school work."

A farewell recital on May 21st, 1903, numbered among compositions by Chopin, Mendelssohn, Daquin, Liszt, and Brahms, two by Charles T. Griffes. The departing musician was assisted by Mrs. William Barron, soprano, Mr. Frost, tenor, and his erstwhile organ instructor, Mr. McKnight, baritone. To Mrs. Barron fell the two Griffes compositions, romantic settings of French texts by Sainte-Beuve and Victor Hugo. They were *Sur Ma Lyre, l'Autre Fois* and *Si Mes Vers Avaient des Ailes,* respectively, and bore the date of composition 1901.

As the time for sailing drew near, the boy launched into a frenzy of preparation. With last-minute misgivings about his knowledge of German he exchanged English lessons for German with the baker's son. There was parting advice to be heeded; farewells must be made. Yet it was not painful to be leaving Elmira, and there was excitement in visualizing a new environment.

For Charles T. Griffes's Elmira was not the Elmira of history. His grandfather "S. B." had belonged to the renowned Southern Tiers. His mother well recalled the tattered Rebel soldiers in the Elmira prison camp. But Charles preferred to contemplate the past only as it manifested itself in some curious or striking token: the bit of prim needlework stitched by his great-aunt in Niskayuna; cut-glass candelabra with rainbow-hued and detachable prisms; Great-Aunt Esther's Chelsea china set, austere, with small bunches of lavender grapes delicately congealed to its sides; an old snuff box, the dignity of its original ownership still implicit in its square design.

Nor was Charles T. Griffes's Elmira the Elmira of Mark

Twain. Twain himself, with his white flannel suits and worried expression, was a familiar sight to the Griffeses. And Charles was a frequent and welcome visitor at the home of Miss Alice Jane Roberts, where the best local minds reflected the liberal culture of Thomas K. Beecher, Elmira's most famous minister, in the same lively aura imbibed by Twain.

Charles T. Griffes's was, rather, the Elmira of "lonely forest pathways" and solitary retreats, of thoughtful reading and long hours of practicing. Yet too much emphasis cannot be placed on this period of the composer's life. In any understanding of his subsequent character and career it is of cardinal importance. Essentially Griffes always remained the boy from Elmira. In his flabbergasted perambulations about Manhattan he was always the small-town boy in the big city. His carefully nonchalant endeavors to take in stride everything it presented only betray a naïve eagerness to simulate cosmopolitanism. The little English compositions he sometimes wrote in his letters and notebooks smack more of the diligent schoolboy's ideal than of the cultivated gentleman. In the recurring slight provincialisms of his vocabulary and grammar he spoke always as had the boy in Elmira. In his abashed pleasure before the luxuries of wealth he was always the boy who had marveled so at the paper frills round the lamb chops at Truman Fassett's birthday party. And he was ever the boy from Elmira in his peremptory dismissal of that city as the benighted sticks and its inhabitants as unenlightened backwoodsmen.

In other respects as well he remained the same. The happiness in nature, the profound, almost tragic sensitivity to beauty in whatever manifestation, the musical genius, the candid and undeceived conscience, were all as apparent now as they were ever going to be.

Chapter III

There was once a Geigenspielerín
Who took some lessons in Berlin;
And being sentimental, too,
Her favorite piece was *Simply You.*
Now, hearing music — as she does —
And practicing till our ears just buzz,
We hope her taste will soon improve
And gradually get on an upward move.

THUS SANG the young Charles T. Griffes in one of his few attempts at verse, an amorphous piece composed in Germany. The meter was undoubtedly bad, and the rhymes forced, but the case described was not untypical.

From every quarter of the United States and Canada students were flocking to Berlin to nibble at the musical culture, rich as fruitcake, that nourished imperial Germany. Edward MacDowell's return in 1888 to the United States, where a career as American composer and musician awaited him, had not served to mark a new epoch in American musical history. When Griffes sailed on the *Grosser Kurfürst* on August 13th, 1903, he was still part of a general drift that had characterized the latter half of the nineteenth century and was to carry over into the earlier part of the twentieth.

The young Americans were avid to ingest the German atmosphere. Together they traipsed through Unter den Linden and the Tiergarten, fingered the displays at Wertheim's, and gawked at the innumerable royal processions. Then they repaired to their various pensions, where they clamored impatiently for admittance, explaining to their astonished chambermaids that they had eaten (*gegessen*) their keys, when they had merely forgotten (*vergessen*) them. There they scraped, banged, and shrieked, with merciless disregard for intervening tenants, until their hours of practice had been consumed. Then there were concerts to attend or concert rehearsals (which were " cheaper and just as good "). Their irate landladies were compelled to provide early suppers for them so that they might be on time. They were also in continual attendance at all the plays and operas, or opera rehearsals (which were " cheaper and just as good "). They scrupulously honored the multifarious and unaccountable German holidays as each unfolded on the calendar. They visited Mendelssohn's grave so often that the old Jewish cemetery in which he lay buried took on a cozy familiarity. Their exasperated music masters, whom they adored, rapped their knuckles, exhorted them to " go back to Cincinnati and darn socks with your mother," and often exorbitantly overcharged them. But this was their chance to " get culture," and they knew it. A return to America, the musically barbarous, lay at the end of the road. So most of them divided their money into two sums: expenses and tuition, and concert money. If they survived the heavy and unvarying menu of pension fare and the exertions demanded by long hours of practice they might one day offer prospective pupils the guarantee of having been trained in Germany.

For many the effects of this pilgrimage proved disastrous. They were doomed forever after to speak musically with a decided German accent. At their freest and most lyric they would remain basically derivative. And in the young industrial civilization to which they returned their expression was faded and hopeless, a bloom that would not take life transplanted from its native soil.

For others, the more resilient, this training was salubrious. They outgrew its localism, cast off its alien restraints, and profited by the discipline. They had been exposed to a rigorous apprenticeship in music and had had inculcated upon them a thorough understanding of its groundwork. Whatever might be their future development, they would meet thereafter at least the minimum requirements of sound craftsmanship.

To Griffes, who had traveled little, the journey would have been treasurable apart from its musical opportunities. He had been accompanied by his sister Florence from Elmira to New York, where the two were joined by their Uncle Charles. As a highlight of the occasion he treated them to a trip to Chinatown, Griffes's first encounter with this future rendezvous. But the expedition was dramatically terminated. From a shadowy doorway a shot rang out, a figure darted close by pursued by two others, and the uncle hastened his charges to less glamorous but safer quarters.

The next day Griffes was seen to the boat by Florence and his uncle, and after the novelty and excitement of an ocean voyage arrived in Berlin on August 25th, 1903. Miss Broughton, sojourning on one of her summer trips abroad, met him there. She introduced him to her friend and countrywoman, Miss Kate Pigott, who held a position locally as governess, and the three explored Berlin together. Determinedly and passionately attuned to the new environment, Griffes let nothing escape him. This was his education. From the moment he had set foot on the ocean liner he had been jealous and retentive of every detail the voyage had to offer. So now. One such detail, seemingly insignificant, had future importance. Miss Broughton, Miss Pigott, and he visited the Zoological Garden. In a letter dated September 1st, he mentioned something he had seen there. " Among the peacocks was a pure white one — very curious." The image, subsequently almost forgotten, lodged itself deeply in his consciousness, its proper associations meanwhile accruing till that time when its potentiality should become apparent.

All Griffes's ideas of Germany had been gleaned from *The Boy Travelers in Northern Germany* and Jessie Fothergill's *The First Violin*. These sources proved somewhat inadequate. For as he later wrote: " I must admit that most everything here is almost the opposite of what I pictured it before I came, but still it is by no means a disappointing kind of opposite. To be sure, life here is as real and matter-of-fact as it is any place, and one gets so accustomed to it that he forgets that it is anything out of the ordinary to be over here."

Miss Broughton was of inestimable help in accustoming her pupil to Berlin and the stringencies of a full-time musical life. But she soon departed for Elmira and the fall term, and he was left on his own. Making friends was easier than he had expected. True, there was still something almost soubrettish about him that annoyed some of his fellow students. To them he was never anything but an insufferable prig. He was fussy about his surroundings and constantly changed pensions. (During his four years in Berlin he lived at Kurfürsten Strasse 48, Goltz Strasse 28, Lützow Strasse 44, Motz Strasse 64, and Motz Strasse 16, accustoming himself to landladies Werner, Scheffel, Pfeifer, Hilpert, Wesche, and Behrend successively.) His pride was incomprehensible. What did he mean by his airs? He seemed to consider it a privilege even for anyone to call him by his first name. " It seems to me that those people at the Lutheran Church must be getting extremely familiar suddenly to call me as Mama mentioned. There were only a very few who went so far as to call me by my first name and not by my wish, I am sure." But this vehement assertion of pride was partially the obverse of a real lack of self-confidence before the discouraging abundance of talent with which he was suddenly surrounded. It was the continuation of his defense mechanism at home. And it was the rather pathetic expression of a frankly acknowledged insecurity that he felt in his own background as a young American confronted by the more highly developed Continental society. "Every time I stop to think of it, I begin to tremble for fear I have done or shall do something which isn't in good taste. I don't worry about my English because I am sure it is as good as anyone else's here, but it is little things."

Petty and superficial, honest and anxious to learn, he was also interested in people. And the pension showed itself congenial. The cosmopolitan pensionnaires recommended music and reading that he might not otherwise have happened upon. Soon with that almost inebriate eclecticism of which he was peculiarly capable he was simultaneously reading Dante's *Divina Commedia* and Elinor Glyn's *Reflections of Ambrosine* and finding both enjoyable. He made several good friends — Dr. Landau and family, by whom Miss Pigott was employed; Leslie Hodgson, Harold Henry, and Douglas Bertram, pension neighbors and fellow students in the theory and practice of music; and dearest of all, the Shooberts. Mrs. Shoobert, a widow, Australian born, had lived in San Francisco for many years. She and two of her four daughters had come to Berlin so that the girls might study. The elder Miss Shoobert, Fanny, played the piano, and the younger, Lillian, the violin. It was with the latter, a lighthearted, witty, and attractive girl, known to her friends as " Babe," that Griffes found a particular affinity, and his friendship with her was a boon that stuck through the years. It was she who figured as the heroine of his crude little verses about Berlin and musical taste. And with her he studied violin awhile, to improve his knowledge of the instrument.

The Shooberts' arrival had been inauspicious enough. " Three more Americans from California have come to Frau W——'s — isn't it awful? A mother and two daughters, one to study violin, and one to study German. And they practically can't speak German at all. It is horrid, but I suppose we shall have to stand it." But the three Californians had no intention of dispelling the precious German atmosphere. They entered splendidly into the spirit of things and became Griffes's eager confederates. They accompanied him to concerts, dragged him to royal processions, and applauded his student efforts in both composition and performance. They introduced him to a new gaiety, a more sophisticated social comradeship than any he had known. When they greeted one another gustily with the password *"mein lieber Schwan"* (after the swan in *Lohengrin*), when they designated prunes as "sea-urchins," when their whim inexplicably assigned him the nickname "Cuss" (after the duck Cusmoodle in *Lovey Mary*, which they were all reading), he felt his former limitations among people dissolving. He even began to reciprocate after a fashion, and a caustic give-and-take soon developed between him and the Shooberts. Before the year was over, he was writing: "I feel as if I had always known them."

Although not a regular Conservatory student, Griffes was enrolled at the Stern Conservatory — directed by Gustav Holländer — during his first two years. Dr. Ernst Jedliczka, his piano teacher, was the well-known professor of piano and former pupil of Nicholas Rubinstein and Tchaikovsky. Philippe Bartholomé Rüfer, with whom Griffes studied composition was the composer of two operas, *Merlin* (1887) and *Ingo* (1896), as well as many instrumental and orchestral works. And Max Julius Loewengard, his theory instructor, was a former pupil of Raff's and author of textbooks on music.

It was an invigorating period. The concerts, the lessons, the theater, the expanding social life, all contributed. Musically, there was the joy of hearing and the even greater joy of participating. And most singular of all, inside himself Griffes now began to feel something of his own yawn and stretch and awaken.

In letters glowing and exuberant he wrote of this new life to his family and Miss Broughton. The style was an execrable jumble of himself and Miss Broughton's pet terms, not always pleasing to his former teacher, who chided him for his " provincial " language. " My language must be very bad indeed to occasion five pages of lecturing." They were letters meant, he explained, to provide a record of his German years. Sometimes they are obviously puerile and jejune, as for example in this description of Coquelin as Cyrano: " The play is real pathetic, I think, for nothing comes Cyrano's way; he says himself that he can't even die honorably." At their best, as in the sharp-witted account of the birthday celebration honoring the Kaiser, they offer priceless vignettes of the musical life of the milieu. In sum, however, and even greatly abridged and condensed, they provide just what they were intended to: a chronicle of the young composer's own artistic development. Unless otherwise indicated, the extracts that follow are from letters addressed to Mrs. Griffes. They cover the first year.

September 1st, 1903
     Composition lessons at the Conservatory are $50 extra, but Miss Broughton says for me to take them just the same.

September 6th
     I went and played for Dr. Jedliczka Thursday A.M., and we were very much relieved when he said he would

take me, for he had already said his classes were full. He said some very nice things about me and seemed pleased with my playing — I played the [Mendelssohn] *Prelude and Fugue*, you know. So I have my piano lessons Mondays at 11, forty minutes each time; but you can come any time you want to and listen to the others, and that is what they mean by class lessons.

September 9th

Just before I went he [Jedliczka] said that next lesson I must show him that I was industrious, and an American; he says lots of things like that which sound so funny. He was also kind enough to say to the other pupils in the room as I went: "He is very gifted." It is rather discouraging at first to find so many pupils in the Conservatory who can play just as well and lots better than you can. There are some very talented pupils there, who are fine already.

Last night I was invited to the Landaus' again for supper and the evening. During the evening of course we had music, and I had the pleasure of being obliged to accompany Dr. Landau at sight in two terrific sonatas and a Mozart concerto. It is fine practice though, for he is a good player. He wants me to come to their Quartet Evenings each Tuesday night after they begin. It is nice to go to places where they are familiar with all the best music and are accustomed to playing it.

September 10th

[TO MISS BROUGHTON] — He [Jedliczka] said lots of funny things, or that at least sounded funny; whenever he wanted to show me about something, he seemed to address me as "Gentlemen," and if I didn't give a note its full value he would always say: "Don't swindle." He is very particular that you play with loose wrists. I am so afraid I will unconsciously get the harsh and bangy tone so many of the Ger-

mans seem to have. Even Dr. Jedliczka the other day in the
lesson before mine got some tones which were extremely harsh
and hard, but of course the bare room made them sound worse,
and then he was perhaps exaggerating in order to make the
young lady understand more clearly.

This A.M. I had ensemble and composition. . . . The composition lesson, however, was very exciting, for you should
have seen how Herr Rüfer tore my poor little *Si Mes Vers* to
pieces. In the first place he corrected my division of syllables
and said that "*fuiraient*" could not be made into three syllables as I had done; and then he said that in those words that end
in "e" like "*comme*" I ought to put in another note on the
same line or space for that last syllable. I had lots of consecutive
fifths in the accompaniment, for I hadn't thought of their being
wrong in piano music, and every time a seventh wasn't resolved
to the next lower tone it had to be changed—so that there are
quite a few changes of a note or two. Most of them suited me as
well as the original, but I didn't hesitate to say so if they didn't.
For instance he said that modulation at the end into A major
for one bar was "*unbeholfen*" and "*unnatürlich*" and said
that something like this would be better [a suggested alteration
that Griffes labels "terribly ordinary and common"]. I immediately said: "*Ach, das gefällt mir gar nicht,*" and so he
didn't change it. I should much rather have it as at first even
though it might be *unnatürlich*. . . . Since you and Miss Pigott have spoken of their [Griffes's songs] being so French I
have come to the same opinion myself. Dr. Landau thought
they were more English. The Germans go in for a heavier and
more solid style, I think, don't you?

September 18th

[TO MISS BROUGHTON]—My composition
lesson Thursday was a little more encouraging than the first.

Herr Rüfer said my chorus was "*gar nicht schlecht, aber ganz gut*," which was very comforting. I was rather disgusted that he found so many consecutives in *Si Mes Vers*, so in this one I was determined there should not be a single mistake. I was very glad to show him that I could write without mistakes when I wanted to. He made a few changes which I think myself were improvements, and said: "*Es gefällt mir besser als das Lied*," and for next week I have another mixed chorus and a *Männerchor* to write.

September 24th

The church bells here have such an odd tone, very deep and heavy, and in this neighborhood we always hear two bells of different tones which ring alternately in quick succession. It is an almost weird tone to me, but I like it extremely.

September 28th

I don't think there are any singers in Europe as fine as the Metropolitan stars. These people here in the Royal Opera House are made members for life, and they have to sing too often. The soprano last night at first had a beautiful voice, so they say, but now it shows very plainly overwork.

October 1st

For next Thursday I have the task of writing my Minuet over for string quartet — two violins, viola, and violoncello; and I think I shall have some fun trying to do it. But of course I can't expect to do it so very well the first time.

October 18th

[TO MISS BROUGHTON] — At my last composition lesson I screwed up courage and told Professor Rüfer I still had two French songs which I should like to have him correct, so he said to bring them along. I didn't find it so awfully hard to arrange my Minuet for stringed instruments, after all; last week I wrote another Minuet, writing it immediately for the stringed instruments this time. For Thursday I am to bring the theme for an Adagio, so before the year is out I shall no doubt have written a whole string quartet or two. I think I had better finish out the year with him.

October 25th

Thursday night we went to the Berlioz *Requiem*, and I wouldn't have missed it for anything. It was the most majestic and overpowering thing I ever heard. There was an immense chorus—four hundred, I heard—and magnificently trained, and a big orchestra; and beside this there were four brass orchestras—trumpets and trombones—in the four corners of the hall in the gallery. These other orchestras came in part of the time, and it was just like an immense band. It is certainly a unique composition, and I am awfully glad to have heard it.

October 30th

We had such a lovely walk home this A.M. through the Tiergarten. The leaves are all turning yellow and brown, and you can't think how beautiful it was to see the trees this color and the ground covered with the leaves. The only thing was that there were none of the lovely red ones we have in America.

November 1st

[TO MISS BROUGHTON]—I am to play the Andante, the Scherzo, and the Rondo of the Schumann *Sonata* [in G minor] at the next Vorspiel in about two weeks; I was so afraid he would want me to play the first movement, and I am not at all sure of that. . . . A German girl is going to play it, I think; he always divides sonatas up like that.

I have been trying to write a theme for an Adagio. First I wrote one that he said was too short and incoherent, and then for last week I wrote it over again, making it longer and more flowing, as I thought; but this time " *es könnte weiter bis in die Ewigkeit gehen und kein Ende finden.*" It was like some kind of a worm — I didn't get just which; but at any rate it wasn't a very complimentary comparison. So I have to do it again, but this time I am going to make an entirely new one, for I hate that other old one. I hope this new one will have some redeeming feature. Professor Rüfer says: "*Sie haben Talent*" and "*Sie haben hübsche Gedanken, aber —*" and he went on to say something which I suppose meant that it must be trained.

You are awfully generous to invite me to Paris next summer, but I think it would be sponging on you altogether too much. Sponging is not a very polite word, but you are doing so much for me already that I feel that you ought not to do any more.

[He has heard] an unvollendete *Symphonie in D moll* by Anton Bruckner. This Bruckner piece was *ganz modern und nicht sehr verständlich*. It savored too much of Wagner (no insult meant to Wagner) and seemed to me copied too much after him. The Adagio was practically a long series of modulations with no especial melody; the composer seemed to be seeking out the most unusual chords and modulations. The Scherzo, however, was beautiful and couldn't help but please. The work is regarded very highly, I guess, but I didn't enjoy it an awful lot.

November 18th

[TO MISS BROUGHTON] — The Vorspiel came off last Tuesday A.M. [November 17th], you know. My number was about the fourth, and it went very well. At the end he said "*ganz schön*," but he says something like that to about everybody. I had to play only the last three movements finally and was very glad; a German girl did the first movement, but I didn't hear her as I was five or ten minutes late. She must have played the first one, and I suppose he wanted mine to come right immediately after, but I thought they wouldn't begin promptly so didn't hurry. As soon as he spied me in the back of the room he called out from the front: "*Haben Sie gut geschlafen?*" Of course everybody looked around and laughed.

My third attempt at an Andante theme proved at least passable, in fact "*gar nicht schlecht*," so I am progressing slowly through it. My first second-theme wasn't just right, so I wrote it over again, and this time it was all right; now I begin to develop the themes, which will be more interesting and easy. After I get a little farther perhaps I will take something to Dr. Landau. However, at this stage I wouldn't venture to. That night of the company when we played the Mozart quartet Dr. Landau said I was a Mozart player — which was a fine compliment, I think.

November 29th

You and Miss Broughton both seemed to be quite worried about my swiping rolls at breakfast, but I suppose you have been relieved of your anxiety already for quite a while, for I didn't do that but a very few times.

December 6th

[TO MISS BROUGHTON] — I have about finished my Adagio for the string quartet, and I think it will be quite respectable; I should very much like to hear how it sounds if I could do so without anyone else's hearing it. After the Andante I begin the first movement, and there I am to have some fun, I know. It seems as if I am going terribly slowly, but I suppose the first string quartet must necessarily be a rather slow process. My Andante is in B-flat and one of my Minuets, so I think I shall make the first movement in G minor. I think it is getting easier now to sit down and write something in spite of lack of inspiration; perhaps I am not quite so particular as at first.

December 7th

Last Tuesday night Miss S——, Mr. Henry, and I went to *Manon Lescaut* at the Opera House, and I enjoyed it as much as anything I have yet heard. I even forgot I was standing. Geraldine Farrar, the only American in the company, sang the principal part, and she was perfectly charming. . . . She has a fine voice and acts well, too; she is about twenty-three now, I think, so of course she isn't what she will be later.

December 20th

It is so pitiful to see the poor people at Christmas time; of course I never lived in a big city before and never noticed so much. All along on Leipziger Strasse were so many children of all ages, trying to sell little things like toys and matches. It looks so pitiful to see old women doing such things, too. Miss W—— says there isn't near so much poverty as in the East Side of New York, and no doubt that is true.

January 4th, 1904

[TO MISS BROUGHTON] — Do you know any of Hugo Wolf's songs? Everybody here seems to sing them now. . . . They are beautiful. There is an exquisite one called *Heimweh* which Lilli Lehmann and also that Sydney Biden sang, and each of them had to sing it over again.

January 18th

After I got home in the morning I spent the rest of the time trying to do some composition; I worked until dinner, but I couldn't get anything to suit me at all, so there I was no farther than when I started. That is the worst thing about composition; I feel that I have to write a certain thing at a certain time whether I have any ideas or not. And sometimes I work an hour or more on it without hitting upon a single idea that suits me; and then perhaps in the end I will write the whole thing in ten minutes at some time when I am not trying at all.

Thursday night I heard a dandy concert by Pablo de Sarasate, the Spanish violinist. His bowing is something wonderful, and he seemed to throw off tiny notes by the thousands from the bow without any effort. They were like raindrops, so fast and clear.

January 31st

[TO MISS BROUGHTON]—I met [Richard] Strauss in the street a day or two after the concert. He is very thin and pale — sort of a wan and unhappy expression on his face; I don't believe he smiled once during all the applause given him at the concert. He seems to direct quite a little with his left arm quite motionless at his side.

I am working on the first movement of my string quartet, and am writing now on the " *Aus Arbeitung.*" It is extremely hard but, as he says, it is better to do it thoroughly and correctly, and I think I shall have learned a good deal when I have finished it. I shall certainly never forget the sonata form, and as that is the basis for almost all other forms, I shall have a little start. I wrote three different modulations from the original key, G minor, to the second subject, B-flat major, before I got one to suit him. He says I do not yet modulate naturally and easily; it is so hard to write a good modulation of from sixteen to thirty bars and to have everything come naturally. I think perhaps I shall let Dr. Landau's quartet play at least one or two movements of it; it would be a great help to me. Professor Rüfer asked me the other day if I had any way of hearing it played. The younger Miss Shoobert has suggested that she teach me enough violin so that I shall not write things for the various instruments that are very awkward or impossible to play. In the Andante I had one passage for the second violin which was impossible. I think her suggestion was very good, and I shall be glad to do it.

February 5th

It is funny how great a sense of regularity the Germans have. If they have a shelf with ornaments on it, there will be one central dish in the middle, then one of a set of two vases on each side, and then still another set of twins perhaps, making each side exactly alike. There must be two of every kind of vase or ornament in the room so that they may radiate from a central object. The Landaus have a shelf in the dining room on which I think there must be about three or four sets of twin vases beside the central one.

February 15th

Most of the evening we had music, and among other things Miss C—— sang *The Rosary* to her own accompaniment. We all roared inwardly when she began that, for it and a few other songs such as *Violets* . . . are standing jokes. I have heard so many of the fine German songs — in fact only them — since I have been here that those sentimental American songs seem terribly silly.

It seems to me I never saw such people as the Germans for trying to impose upon others and get the best of them. You have to just look out for yourself and not care whether anybody else is provided for or not. It is very disagreeable sometimes.

February 26th

[TO MISS BROUGHTON] — His [José Vianna da Motta's] last two numbers were abominations among abominations — a *Polonaise in C minor* of Liszt and another piece of his called *Die Schlittschuhläufer*, in motives from Meyerbeer's *Prophet*. They were positively the limit of everything common and vulgar. The *Polonaise* was the most insipid and sickening thing I ever heard; the middle part might have been appropriately named "Love's Message" or some such silly title. *Die Schlittschuhläufer* was so gaudy and tawdry that it was actually funny. The melodies were regular music-hall style, and the whole thing was full of glissandos and all such tricks.

March 20th

I was at the National Gallery one Sunday a while ago, but that time I saw only the pictures on the first floor. This time we were on the other two floors most of the time. There are two or three beautiful pictures of the modern impressionist school; the impressionists give their attention to the general effect rather than the details, and their pictures always look rough close to them.

March 21st

[TO MISS BROUGHTON] — I suppose you have heard all of the Wagner things several times, but you see I have heard so little of him and almost nothing from the *Ring*. The more I do hear, the crazier I am to hear still more. I can hardly wait to have a chance to see those operas that I haven't seen yet.

I scrambled through all right at the Vorspiel [on March 18th]; Jedliczka said the *Variations* [the Beethoven thirty-

two] were not bad, but that I played as if I felt sort of nervous
—though I didn't feel consciously any special nervousness. I
remember you said the same thing about my last concert at
home.

April 25th

[TO MISS BROUGHTON] —I don't want to tell
you whether I think I have improved much and where, but I
feel that I have, and I don't feel myself that the year is wasted.
I am sure also that I have improved in composition a good deal,
and I have a much better idea of how to go to work. If I can
get a chance I want to ask Professor Rüfer if he thinks it will
be really worth spending the money on next year.

May 7th

I don't know exactly where to begin about my
things, but I guess the money is most important. You know I
brought over $370 in checks, $250 of Miss Broughton's, $120
of concert money, and then Miss Broughton made me a present of $50 extra, you remember. Then she, has just lately sent
me $100, and I wrote for fifty marks or about $12.50 more before July 1st. That will make in all $532.50 which I shall have
had from September 1st to July 1st, for I didn't break into the
checks until the 1st of September. Of that of course $150 has
gone for tuition, also about $5 more for the entrance fee and
the *Garderobe* or cloak-room of the Conservatory; then $250
for rent and $25 for piano rent, leaving $102.50 for other
things. I divided this up among the ten school months from
September to June, and it left me a little over $10 a month for
concerts, and extras, you see. . . . I have kept within this
$10.50 limit each month so that each one has been the same. I
suppose I might have done with less, but still I do not think I
have been extravagant or spent any uselessly. . . . I am afraid

it will come to about $600 for this year. By July 1st I shall have had $412.50 from Miss Broughton, including the $50 which she said was to be a gift. As for next year, I don't know whether it will be cheaper or not.

May 30th

I told you, I think, about Dr. Jedliczka's illness. Now the physicians have decided that he must not give any more lessons, but must go away and stay until September. So during June we have the privilege of taking of another teacher in the Conservatory. We Americans have decided upon a Gottfried Galston, a young Leschetizky pupil, who has just taught in the Conservatory for a few months.

I forgot to tell you that Thursday night I heard *I Pagliacci*, a modern Italian opera, at the Opera House under the personal direction of the composer, Leoncavallo. Leoncavallo has been writing an opera for the Emperor, and he was here last week to bring it. And among other things he directed the performance of his *Pagliacci*. It is a perfectly charming opera. After it they gave *Cavalleria Rusticana*, and I am glad to say that I have at last heard it after all these years of its popularity. However, I don't think I should care to see it again, for it was terribly flat to me. I suppose there must be something in it, or it wouldn't hold its popularity so long, but it is a mystery to me what that something is. Some of the music is rather pretty, and it is sort of showy for the voice, but to me it was too flat for anything after *Pagliacci*.

June 13th

I have been so excited since yesterday that I don't know what to do, for I just learned yesterday A.M. that I am to play in the Beethoven-Saal next Sunday morning at one of the closing concerts of the Conservatory. . . . Yesterday A.M.

I was at the Conservatory with Mr. Henry and Mr. Bertram, and as we came out Mr. Bertram asked the Secretary if he was to play at the first one, and Herr B—— said not he but I was to play at the first one, on the 19th. Of course I was dumfounded, but he showed the printed program, and there was my name and what I was to play. . . . There are about six or seven of these concerts at the end of the year, in which the better pupils of all the teachers take part and which are held in the Beethoven-Saal, one of the big concert halls here. There are about ten or twelve pupils of Jedliczka who play this year, I think. Miss Broughton will get here just in time to hear me, which is nice in some ways and not nice in others. . . . I can perhaps do it if I do not get rattled and lose control of my fingers. But I did not play this same piece well at the Vorspiel just because I didn't have perfect control of my fingers, though I didn't realize myself that I felt nervous. . . . I suppose Holländer thought of course I knew it from Jedliczka or someone, and probably Jedliczka thought I knew it from the Conservatory. And I myself never thought of asking or looking it up, as I thought it settled that I wasn't to. And so it might have gone on until two or three days beforehand when they would perhaps have posted up the program on the bulletin board, and I would see my name down and finally have about one or two days to get ready in. I shudder when I think of it, for it was just a mere chance that I was at the Conservatory yesterday and another mere chance that Mr. Bertram asked them when he was to play.

June 19th

> I am so relieved to think that Sunday P.M. is at last here, for you remember this A.M. I played in the Beethoven-Saal. I got through really much better than I expected and felt fairly well satisfied. It went better than at the Vorspiel in Feb-

ruary or whenever it was. I was recalled twice like all the rest. I wasn't nervous much — in fact, not nearly so much as for the common Vorspiel in the Conservatory.

Miss Broughton seemed rather pleased. But right here I must impress upon you at home that you *must not* imagine there is any wonderful improvement in my playing. Miss Broughton says she couldn't make you understand that she wasn't especially anxious to hear me play and wasn't expecting anything very different from last year. If you or most anybody else should hear me now I haven't the least doubt but that it would sound just the same to you as before. Katharine might notice differences, but I don't think the rest of you would find any. The ways in which I may have improved would be unapparent to most people. The majority of people — I think you are more reasonable — imagine that one has only to come over here for a year and take a few lessons of some celebrated teacher and he will come back a finished artist. They seem to think it sort of soaks in or some such crazy idea. In a year, one gets lots of ideas, etc., but hasn't had time to work them out.

Chapter IV

ENGROSSED in getting "lots of ideas, etc.," during his first year abroad, Griffes suffered little from the ubiquitous distraction of his homosexuality. The figure of the earnest music student completely taken up with the study of music was a familiar one to the pensionnaires, and Griffes's protestations that German girls were physically unattractive and did not know how to dress roused no special curiosity. His additional argument that he could scarcely afford the luxury of frolics was only too patently true. They knew how scrupulously he managed his expenses. They had all at one time or another observed him jotting a record of his most infinitesimal purchases into a little account book. No item from the price of a newspaper to the payment of tuition escaped its final reckoning in that little brown book. To one thus circumscribed by financial circumstances inattention to the opposite sex might well be a necessary attitude. Indeed, Griffes himself might almost have been deferred full revelation at this period of his life: it was only the proximity of Konrad Wölcke that brought matters to a head. His close attachment to Wölcke, growing to prominence during his second year in Germany, dominated throughout the remainder of his stay and endured in influence far into his life.

In later years he would sometimes leave Konrad's picture on his dresser as an experiment to test whether the bond still held. Looking back in 1914 it was the thought of Konrad that made him refer to the years of his German apprenticeship as "that fatal time in Berlin — fatal and yet not fatal."

Konrad Wölcke, the eldest of three sons in a comfortable middle-class German family, attended classes in civil engineering at the Hochschule and lived in pensions with his widowed mother. He was a stocky, blond, handsome man, military in appearance, and of a ruddy complexion. Frau Wölcke, a tedious invalid, selfishly monopolized the time and energy of her son to such an extent that he was allowed almost no personal life away from her. He did not rebel. His passive submission to her will was commented upon by all who met him. It was something that transcended even the traditional German respect for maternity into realms where psychiatric interpretation became more appropriate. And its end product was an emotional cramping that left him not averse to a romantic relationship with a younger boy.

At first Griffes merely regarded Wölcke as one of his less interesting neighbors. "Mr. Wölcke, a German whom Miss Broughton will remember as the one who was very polite to his mother . . ." He laughed at the man's ludicrous attempts to render arias from *Die Meistersinger* and at his calm deduction of "popcorns" as the logical plural of "popcorn." Then by degrees he took note of the older fellow's persistent attention. Wölcke palpably realized in one person everything of which Griffes then stood in awe. He was chauvinist about Germany, stanchly prejudiced in favor of German music, and skeptical of the "Anglo-Saxon" sensibility. He asked the boy out on walks, called for him after concerts, and conversed with him like a fellow German. (The last meant a great deal to Griffes, who even begrudged himself the English newspapers his Uncle Charles sent him, for fear of hampering his progress in German.) As a student at the Hochschule, Konrad was able to purchase concert and opera tickets at greatly reduced rates, and the seats were always excellent. Griffes was thus spared the tribulation of standing in line two or three hours to get suitably priced tickets. When Konrad went along to concerts, he usually happened to own the scores of whatever compositions were being performed, so that they could follow the music. Konrad also owned an interesting library. Griffes could borrow the original German of the two volumes of Mendelssohn's letters that he had once got in English from the Park Church in Elmira.

Recurrent mention of Konrad in letters home finally provoked some inquiries. Griffes's reply was heartening: ". . . I have in him a friend such as I never dreamed of finding in Berlin, and one who I think will stick by me. You ask how he looks and about him. But I can't tell you much except that he is decidedly German in character — and therefore very different from Americans — and wears his hair in a pompadour, according to the German fashion. He is twenty-eight now, but he never seems half so old as that to me." A later amused interrogation elicited something more. "I am sure that if you laughed before at the frequent mention of him in my letter, you will roar at this one. But really he is the only person with whom I have been doing anything special, and if I don't write about that there is nothing." The disparity in their ages seemed to make little difference. "I suppose you wonder sometimes that we seem to be so congenial to each other and so much together in spite of the eight years' difference in our ages. But I don't know whether we meet in the middle or not. Konrad never seems a bit old or dignified, and with me, some people think I am older and others younger than I am, so how it really stands I don't know." (Despite a small premature loss of hair, for which he was then consulting a doctor, Griffes was usually taken for just sixteen.)

The Shooberts' eventual departure from Germany threw him more than ever in the company of his friend. Konrad's influence over him became the decisive factor in his German life. As in everything else, Konrad held definite and confirmed opinions on music. "He is a crank on the subject of opera and the orchestra, in fact music in general." Chiefly he worshipped at the shrines of Richard the Great and Richard the Lesser, Wagner and Strauss, with the preponderance of favor disposed to the former. Wagner's *Die Meistersinger* he proclaimed "the greatest German work which there is," which more or less distinguished it as the acme of world culture. His able, authoritative judgments on music both as created and as performed commanded the reverence of his youthful admirer. Griffes was certainly not unprepared to counter with views of his own. Miss Broughton, in a lecture delivered in 1921, declared that "the accessibility of my books and music laid the foundation for the excellent training which he received later in Berlin." Among other things, they had read and discussed Huneker together, Griffes relishing an animadversion of Huneker's on the "Zāl" of the East. In their correspondence valiantly if uncertainly conducted in French, Italian, and German, as well as English, they continued the interchange. With this background and his own insight he retained enough contact to express at least a personal wish not to compose like Wagner. He scoffed at the banality of the prize lied in *Die Meistersinger*. Certain individual tastes he reaffirmed. ". . . I am interested especially in the old music, and still more so when it is performed on the instruments for which it was written." But in the main Konrad triumphed. For as Griffes stated years after in a newspaper interview: "When I went to Germany I was of course ready to be swept under by the later Wagner and Strauss. . . ." German music became the great oasis in a musically barren world. Where Konrad's pronouncements and endearments proved insufficiently convincing, his extravagant gifts of German musical scores served as concrete illustration. "Sometimes I wish I never had to go back to America," wrote Griffes. In Germany music was part of life, unlike " America, where music in a company is generally just to give people's tongues a little time to rest, and often not even that." As to American music: "I must say that most of the American songs seem pretty empty and shallow after the German ones."

Konrad's direction of the boy's musical ambition was astute and sympathetic. He recognized that Griffes's creative talent was more important than his ability as a pianist. Indeed, he quite disparaged Griffes the pianist all the while that he fostered and encouraged Griffes the composer. ". . . Herr Wölcke, who I don't think ever thought much of me purely as a piano player . . ." " Konrad said that for the first time he had the feeling that I might after all become a fairly good concert pianist in spite of my small and unfavorable hands. I was very much pleased, for as I have written you, he always maintained that I had very little if any pianistic talent and that my hands were quite too unpianistically built." This criticism together with vicissitudes at the keyboard excited an honest self-appraisal: " The E-flat one [Chopin *Étude*] is a little beauty, but I don't know whether I could ever do it well with my small hands. My hands are a fearful nuisance; I should like to exchange them for a decent pair." It was Konrad's serious elucidation of the limitations and potentialities in him that brought the future composer to a more complete understanding than he would otherwise have attained at that time. The carefully thought out letter to his mother dated February 2nd, 1905, bears Konrad's mark in every sentence. "I realize now that I knew absolutely nothing about music in general when I came over, and that though I could perhaps play a little better than some other people in Elmira, it was very small indeed compared to really finished playing. Last year I began to realize what a lot there was for me to know besides the piano, and especially if I wanted to do anything with composition and the other branches. . . . I feel this almost more in the composition than in the piano playing. For instance, I am beginning orchestration now and by June will have finished an overture and have learned a good deal. But in this short time and this one thing I shall not have gained enough facility in writing for the orchestra so that I could go ahead and attempt anything alone. . . . A composer nowadays has to be able to write for the orchestra. The Americans are under a great disadvantage; unless they happen to live in New York where things are given and have money enough to take them in, they generally know only their own instrument and its literature, at most. With me, who never heard an orchestra in my life but three times in Philadelphia and twice in New York and who didn't know one instrument from another, it takes a long time to get even a slight knowledge of the different instruments and of what can be done with the orchestra. And then I am just making a beginning in really getting acquainted with works outside the piano literature. The first part of last year I didn't realize or think much about how much I didn't know, the latter half I began to see it, and this year I see it still more. And I think a large part of it is due to Herr Wölcke; he saw still better than I what I didn't know and what I ought to know. . . . I don't want to become merely a piano teacher. And I feel sure that I shall never become a great concert player and virtuoso, for I realize now that to be such one has to begin much earlier than I did and has to devote much more time to it than I ever did at home. So I want to be an all-round musician who can do something else besides teach and play the piano. Not that I want to play any other instrument than the piano, for it would always be my specialty. But I want to know music in general, and especially if I want to do anything with composition, I feel that I ought to have a good foundation." Griffes was here pleading for a prolongation of his study abroad, but the letter reflects a new and more distinct orientation. His indebtedness to Konrad would have been evident without the explicit acknowledgment. It was Konrad who pointed out to him unmistakably that his musical future lay in creation. It was Konrad who criticized his songs and informatively corrected his instrumental compositions. It was therefore to Konrad that he owed his musical maturity. He would have come upon this development by himself. Everything in his past and in his temperament points to that. But Konrad's influence acted as a catalytic agent.

In a letter in foreign English to Mrs. Griffes, Konrad helped prepare those in America for this shift in the professional aspirations of "my dear little Cossi." (Konrad converted the nickname from Cuss to Cossi.) "I have noticed," he wrote, "with true joy from the bottom of my heart, which you will also feel and understand as his mother, that he has made such progress as an all-round musician in the last year as I have never before had the opportunity to observe in a person. . . .

"I see how his playing always becomes freer and how his warm feelings unconsciously always come out more and more in his playing; and how all those acquaintances of mine who are really musical feel and notice it also, and always like to hear him. I see how he has more understanding and interest in the orchestra than he dreamed of yet a year ago."

Not alone in the resolution of musical problems did Konrad enroll his German solidity. It became the beacon light that illumined everything about those last years in Berlin. Griffes wrote: ". . . I trust his judgment pretty well as he is much more observant of everything and demands a great deal more than I do." It was almost a privilege to enjoy the affection of one so distinguished. Konrad took him to the Hochschule to show him his drawings. Together they observed birthdays and holidays, celebrated Konrad's departure from the Hochschule and Griffes's first German concert performances. He began swimming lessons because Konrad thought everyone ought to know how to swim. On hot spring evenings they took long cool trolley rides to Grunewald. They attended the circus, a treat that Griffes had loved from earliest childhood. They visited the grave of Konrad's father and brought flowers. They splurged on a taxi, Griffes's first ride in an automobile. For birthday presents Konrad accepted only original compositions or the playing of specially requested and memorized works. Konrad also frequently coaxed him into piano duets and provided a lame but energetic partner. They rosily envisioned a blissful reunion in America some day. Konrad gave him the score of *Tristan und Isolde* and inscribed on the flyleaf:

> *Bleibe mir, wie Du bist;*
> *so wirst Du es sein, wie*
> *ich wünsche, dass Du mir*
> *immer bleibst.*

He did not respond wholeheartedly to the friendly importunings of an attractive Norwegian girl who entered the circle of his Berlin acquaintances. And he grew resentful of Frau Wölcke's excessive demands upon her son. " Frau Wölcke has gotten so in the habit of expecting him to do everything for her. . . . It exasperates me fearfully sometimes to see how absorbingly selfish she is and how Konrad gives in to her slightest whim."

Hitherto there had been considerable mystification in Griffes's comprehension of his sexual nature. His friendship with Konrad lifted the veil from his eyes. When on his departure from Germany Griffes presented his perhaps most ambitious musical production of that period, a *Symphonische Phantasie*, to Konrad, it was, significantly, as the child of their relationship that he dedicated it. "*Dem einzigen Freunde widme ich diese Partitur, das Kind unserer Freundschaft, in unvergänglicher Liebe* — Cossi."

Germany and Konrad wrought their inevitable result. Mrs. Horace C. French of Elmira, arriving in Berlin with her daughter Ernestine, could scarcely discriminate her townsman from his German associates. She described in her notes, September 25th, 1905, ". . . the dear Frau Wölcke — rather hard of hearing but interested and sympathetic, and very devoted to her son, Herr Wölcke, who was our first real acquaintance with the genus of German young man. His complexion was like the 'wild, wild rose' and his eyelids drooped and his hair was dressed à la pompadour, and his speech faultless. . . . Next to him sat Charley Griffes, an American young man — even an *Elmira* young man but so imbued with German customs and language as to seem equally foreign with the others."

Griffes had originally planned on two years of study. Then Konrad's advice and his own urgent entreaties had extended the period another year. For it was true that the young musician's talent was just unfolding and that he needed additional guidance. Miss Broughton managed to scrape up the necessary funds. The death of his father on November 10th, 1905, did not bring him home. There was little he could have done, his education as yet incomplete, to alleviate the family's financial burdens. Wilber Griffes, foreshadowing certain features of his son's death in his own, had been abed with grippe for some time, had forced himself as family provider to work again, immediately relapsed for two days, and died. Uncle Charles took over the support of the family.

To Griffes the loss was somehow intangible. Partly it was

because, as he himself recognized, it was impossible to accept the fact of death at so great a distance from its occurrence: ". . . it is hardly possible for me to realize it all over here. I read about it, but yet I can't think that it is any different from when I left." He therefore attended a concert the next day after receiving the news, first evolving a crude rationalization to excuse his behavior. None was necessary. It was the fault of neither father nor son that an intimate relationship had not existed between two such separate personalities. Konrad did not understand, but instead construed the occasion as one more for extending Griffes's dependence on him: ". . . he has done everything in his power to keep me from feeling lonesome and to make me feel that he was going to do everything possible to try and make up to me the loss a little."

It was necessary to return to Elmira that summer. Griffes appreciated that a bereaved family would expect at least so much attention from him. But the idea of returning to America for good was still unthinkable. Konrad strongly counseled another year, and he himself desired a fourth year as he had never desired anything before. Miss Broughton's generosity had now, however, exceeded her funds. Prospects were glum, when suddenly Konrad volunteered to provide the money, and the offer was gratefully accepted. Griffes could also help himself by such pupils as he might be able to attract and by those Konrad sent him. Playing engagements and occasional checks from home would help out too.

His visit to Elmira in the summer was reassuring to all, after the shock of his foreign manner had been encompassed. The returning student landed with two German immigrants whom he had met on the boat and for whom, with typical goodheartedness, he felt a personal responsibility. It was necessary to see them safely to their Brooklyn destination before his conscience was appeased. Then he was hauled off to the clothiers by Un-

cle Charles to impart some faltering semblance of Americanism
to his German appearance. When the German clothes were replaced by more seemly apparel his true changes might be more
accurately remarked. He had grown, his features were more
mature, he was less the precocious child. He had developed a
mustache on Konrad's advice that it would make him look
older, thereby facilitating his chances of securing pupils. His
matter-of-factness and bravery in recovering a stolen watch
for his mother that summer showed a new adult competence
in practical affairs. His piano had improved. On July 24th he
gave a solo recital at the College, which included two compositions of his own, *Si Mes Vers Avaient des Ailes* and *Nocturne*
from *Suite for String Orchestra*, as well as his own arrangement of Strauss's *Wiegenlied*. To Konrad he dispatched copies
of the favorable review that he received and shortly followed
them in person.

So Griffes studied four years in Germany. Dr. Jedliczka
died in August of 1904, and Griffes learned the Leschetizky
method with Gottfried Galston. Loewengard having departed
for Hamburg in the same year, he began theory with Wilhelm
Klatte, one-time répétiteur under Strauss at the Weimar Opera, coauthor of the earliest sketch of Strauss, and music critic.
Engelbert Humperdinck, the famous composer of *Hänsel und
Gretel*, succeeded Rüfer as his composition teacher. The man's
name alone would prove valuable in America.

His three summer vacations had come as mere breathing intervals in the strenuous routine of work. The first summer Miss
Broughton had come over, and they and Miss Pigott had traveled in the Harz Mountains. Griffes had painted delicate water colors of castles and landscapes while his spinster compan-
ions read or did needlework in the shade. All three had collected
mountain wild flowers, which they carefully pressed and preserved. The more perishable specimens were copied for good

measure. (Years later Griffes was so haunted by the tranquillity and color of those days in the Harz that he tried to whip his letters of the period into some kind of monograph.) The following summer he spent in worshipful happiness with Konrad at Rügen, a little island on the Baltic. The third summer was the visit to America. In his last summer, 1907, he came home.

What outlook might have emboldened him as he surveyed the future? For four years he had practiced and studied. All that an intensive and prolonged theoretical training could impart to a novice he had gratefully accepted. What if he had, perhaps, been unduly conditioned by his masters and the milieu? He was young, and eclectic by nature. He would outgrow the specific. In the approaching radical era of modern music, when so many of his contemporaries were to function as simple neoterics, vacuously rejecting a heritage they had never bothered to possess, Griffes would bulk as one composer who retained a mastery of the traditional craft. Whatever the course of his expression, it would rest upon a firm foundation of knowledge.

Or perhaps Griffes may have recalled those prophetic verses that Konrad had inscribed in the score of *Siegfried* that he had given him:

In des Herzens heilig stille Räume
sollst Du fliehen aus des Lebens Drang,
sollst im holden, schönen Reich der Träume
schaffen uns manch' lieblichen Gesang,
sollst in frohem, stolzem Glück gedenken
all die schönen Stunden, die vereint uns einst.
Sollst dein liebes, warmes Herz der Menschkeit schenken,
Die dich liebt, wenn oft Du's nicht vermeinst.
Sich dann wird dein Leben segen werden,
Dir und allen, die Dir lieb und nah,
und es wird Dir scheinen schon auf Erden
durch die Kunst das Höchste offenbar.

(To the holy quiet resting place of the heart
You will flee from the press of life,
To the pure, beautiful realm of dreams.
You will create for us much lovely music,
You will remember in gay, proud happiness
All the beautiful hours which once united us.
You will give to mankind your dear warm heart,
[To mankind] which loves you, when often you do not know it.
See, then your life will be a blessing
To thyself and to all, who are near and dear to you.
And it will appear to thee already upon the earth
Through art, the highest things made clear.) [1]

[1] A translation by Miss Broughton. The last line might better be translated " the highest things revealed."

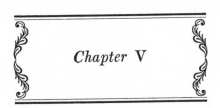

Chapter V

September 30th, 1904

Herr Loewengard, the man whom I have had in theory at the Conservatory since I have been here, is going to Hamburg, so we shall have a new one. I don't know whether to go on with it or not; I sometimes thought the class wasn't worth much to me. The various branches of theory are very important to every musician, I think, and are worth thorough study — absolutely necessary for facility in composition. But in the Conservatory I don't think either the teacher or the pupils were so very much interested in it — and I really can't blame Herr Loewengard for not being especially interested in some of the ones in our class.

October 8th

Last week I was out . . . Wednesday evening at an opera, *Rigoletto*. In *Rigoletto* an Italian tenor, Enrico Caruso, sang, who created a furor last year in New York with the Metropolitan Company. He has the most gorgeous voice I ever heard in a man, or ever hope to hear.

October 24th

I finally decided to keep on with Fugue, as I may never have another chance to study it free. The new man seems to be very good.

It is something marvelous how Bernhardt keeps so young. If we hadn't actually known she was sixty-three, one should have said she was thirty-five at the most. Her smile and all such things were just like a young girl. Even her voice didn't show any traces of age as far as I could see. Of course her face was wonderfully made up, so that she looked the part perfectly — she was supposed to be a young singer. Sometimes I thought she exaggerated a bit in the harassing parts, but it made the shivers run down your back the way she did some things like taking a knife and stabbing one of the men. The table was laid for supper, and on it was a big dagger-like knife. And you could just see how, when the man's back was turned for a moment, it entered her mind suddenly to take that knife. And you shivered as she crept up and took it and concealed it for a moment as he turned, and finally stabbed him. It was like a snake. I shall never forget the way she did that whole last act.

November 6th

The German bouquets are the limit. Sometimes in one little bouquet they will have twelve or more different kinds of flowers of every color and description, and generally not more than one or two of each kind. It looks as if they had taken odds and ends of everything and put them all in together. Then they are always choked tightly and stiffly and generally fixed so that from one side you see everything and from every other side nothing except the back of the flowers. Instead of putting them around artistically, they will place all in a geometrically straight line through the middle of the dining-table, reminding one of a funeral. Then the water is never changed so that they wither in about two days; but in this withered and dirty state they are left on the dining-table at least a week longer. And that is what becomes of flowers in a German pension.

January 1st, 1905

[TO MISS BROUGHTON] — He [Wölcke] also has another project for my composition, and that is that I try to get with Humperdinck, the composer of *Hänsel und Gretel*. Humperdinck takes pupils only upon recommendation, but Herr Wölcke seems to think it might be accomplished, though I don't exactly see how myself. It would be simply dandy if I could, for of course in Germany he is almost like Richard Strauss and is regarded as one of the very best teachers.

January 29th

Since I have begun orchestration in my composition work I just have to begin to study up scores and especially to learn to play from score — for which Herr Wölcke furnishes the music and a good part of the incentive. He simply insists on it and brings over the music, so I want to practice it regularly, until I can do it fairly well. It is extremely hard at first, for of course one has to take in at a glance anywhere from twelve to twenty or more staves, some of them written in queer clefs where they have to be read higher or lower than written, and all such things. I know I shouldn't get half such a broad and general musical knowledge from the advantages here if it weren't for Konrad. He makes me do things I should never think of otherwise or, if I did think of them, shouldn't do them in the end. It is rather a fault of piano students and especially of Americans that they know nothing except the piano and its music. They practice it all the time and go principally to piano concerts and in the end never learn anything except just that. And of course a real musician has got to be a good deal more than a piano player.

Friday was the Kaiser's birthday — forty-sixth, I think. They say it is always sure to be fine weather then, and it certainly was this year. At 12 in the morning I went to a sort of celebration of the Royal Academy of Arts, of which Professor Rüfer is a member of the Senate. It was quite a gay affair, and I felt almost out of place with my common suit and no order hanging on it. The Senators and members — or at least I suppose they were members — sat on the platform. The Senators were very gorgeous in robes of wine-colored velvet, lined with the same color of satin, and with flowing satin sleeves, and finally velvet caps. Among them were Joachim, Humperdinck, Xaver Scharwenka, and several others whom everybody knows. First there was a chorus of Bach, performed by an orchestra and a chorus, which both sounded and looked amateurish. Joachim directed, which didn't help matters much as he is anything but an orchestral leader. Joachim was covered with orders and chains of all kinds. Professor Rüfer said he had so many that he had to wear some of them in back, but that morning he had them all packed on in front some way. After this first chorus there was a long — and tedious — speech by one of the Senators on the fate of an artist and closing with three hurrahs for the Kaiser. Then the chorus gave a thing of d'Albert's which he had written especially for the occasion and of no very great merit, so far as I could see. And with that it was over.

March 5th

Mr. Bertram's concert finally came off Friday night. . . . Konrad was disgusted with it all, and I am afraid after this it would be impossible to drag him to a concert given by an American, or an Anglo-Saxon.

Do you know exactly how it is with Miss Broughton? . . . If she can give me the money for next year without its being a sacrifice to her I should be willing to do it. I mean that I

As a student

shouldn't hesitate about the borrowing for another year as I could pay it all back in the end surely and would stand so much the better chance of doing so soon. . . . It is such a misfortune not to have any money when there are so many who could easily spare it.

March 14th

[TO MISS BROUGHTON] — My overture is almost finished in the sketch, and now soon I have to begin working out the instrumentation in detail. Professor Rüfer said the Conservatory orchestra will give it in the Beethoven-Saal at one of the June performances, but I am sure I don't know whether it will be feasible for such an amateurish and unpracticed orchestra. Herr Wölcke says it is really very interesting and not a bit Wagnerian — which is very pleasing, I think, as I hate orchestral compositions which sound only as if they were patterned after Wagner. However, I am no doubt not yet far enough along to know how to use the Wagnerian effects. Professor Rüfer said once it was at least " *ganz orchestral gedacht.*" From now on I shall have to spend hours on the mere copying part.

Do you really want me to stay another year? And I wouldn't want you to think of it if you would have to make the slightest sacrifice on my account.

June 11th

I almost forgot the principal thing, and that is that I am to play the first movement of my own *Sonata* [in F minor] in the Beethoven-Saal on the evening of Thursday the 22nd. It has been impossible to finish my overture by the first week of June, and it would have had to be ready by that time on account of copying out the voices, rehearsals, etc. So I shall play the *Sonata* instead. I have worked awfully hard on the overture and especially lately, but it seemed to be impossible. You see the other two new ones [pupils] have taken up the time, and then lately we have lost several lessons through holidays. I am disappointed in a way, and yet relieved, for with that poor Conservatory orchestra and its director I know I should never have recognized it as my own thing. And now the whole thing lies with me personally. Perhaps next year I can hear the overture. I shall finish it up in private lessons, but I must finish it before the vacation.

June 25th

I played in the Beethoven-Saal [June 22nd], as you probably know by this time. I suppose you want to know all about it. Well, I was not satisfied, nor was Konrad, nor was Galston, nor Professor Rüfer. But several to whom I spoke afterward didn't seem to have noticed anything, so I suppose I ought to be satisfied. I wasn't a particle nervous and didn't get mixed up or anything like that, but I simply didn't play as well as I might and ought to have, considering that it was my own thing. It was due to not having studied it enough, though I practiced it real industriously the last week or two beforehand. I was recalled twice, and Konrad at least insists that I was the only one who was received with applause when I first appeared. I was the fourth, and after that I went out and sat with Konrad, and we stayed for most of them. As you see they were all compositions of pupils. . . . Konrad is extremely fond of it, but I think myself he is rather prejudiced.

September 4th

We have finally decided that I might as well stay with Galston, so I shall do that, but with private lessons. Miss Broughton seems to think it better to be in the Conservatory, but I feel that I have had enough of the Conservatory. I think you get twice as much from private lessons, and you don't miss lessons all the time which you have paid for. . . . About composition, I don't know yet. For this last year I need someone more modern and who will give me more incentive. I think Konrad is of the same opinion, and Galston also told me that last June.

September 19th

He [Galston] seems real interested in my composition work, and his first question was what I was going to do in that this year.

October 23rd

My best news this week is that Humperdinck has practically promised to take me as a composition pupil. He lives out in Grunewald, and I was out there to see him twice last week, the second time, Saturday, finding him home. I was there about twenty-five minutes and played him parts of my different things — of course I had taken everything with me. He was extremely quiet and said almost nothing, made one or two remarks about the compositions, and then finally said he thought he could take me as it seemed to be worth the trouble. His price for private lessons is thirty marks an hour, which is of course fearful for me. I said right out that I didn't know whether I could pay so much, and that I hadn't until now been able to pay anything like so much for lessons. Then he said he was fearfully busy now but later in the winter might be able to give them to me cheaper. I hope, too, that he won't wait until much later before he does that. But of course he wants to find out a little how much I can do and whether I am worth it.

October 28th

[TO MISS BROUGHTON] — I have begun a letter home telling that Humperdinck has accepted me as a pupil, but I am afraid I shall not have time to finish it this week, so I can tell now what I haven't already written in the other. Saturday I was out to see him with my compositions, and after I had played parts of them to him he said he would take me but wanted to see my counterpoint and fugue exercises first. So with fear and trembling I took them out to him, but he hardly looked at them. In the beginning of the first book were two or three exercises that I had done with you those couple of weeks I studied a little counterpoint, and in one of them were parallel octaves. Well, of course, his eyes just struck this exercise and the octaves. I said I had done that in America when I didn't know much; then he laughed and said: " *Octaven sind wohl in Amerika erlaubt, ja?* " I have my first lesson Friday P.M. at 4. His specialty, or at least a very strong point, is the application of contrapuntal devices and all such things in compositions, so in order to find out how much I can do in such lines, he has given me some chorales to harmonize and put counterpoint to. Then I shall take something else with me, also. . . . To have been his pupil would help me a great deal, I should think, in practical ways, for he is one of the best known of the modern composers, and his recommendation ought to go far.

October 30th

As I wrote in Miss Broughton's letter I took my first lesson at Humperdinck's last Friday. He is very friendly and quiet and seems extremely nice personally. He said he had his pupils out sometimes in the evening and would like to have me come too, so he took down my address. I hope he won't forget it. It is going to be much more difficult with him, of course, than with Professor Rüfer, as he requires more and is stricter. Then of course I want to do more. In fact I wish just at present that every day were about twenty-four hours long instead of twelve.

I enclose one of the tickets to my first real appearance in Germany. I think my name looks real swell in print. I have mentioned this Herr [Hans] Kalinke several times, I think, as singing at Konrad's. And now he is going to give a concert, and I am to accompany and play also alone. I shall play four or five Chopin pieces. Yesterday we practiced all the P.M. at Konrad's until I was about dead. Herr Kalinke has a very good voice but is by no means a finished singer, and doesn't appear as such, so the concert is not to be advertised at all, and there will be no criticism in the paper. But he is in rather need of money, and wants to try and earn a little in this way and at the same time see if he can't win a few friends for his voice. The tickets are to be had only through him and acquaintances. He is a sort of protégé of a friend of Konrad's, and that is how we know him.

November 7th

I enjoy so much going out to Grunewald for my composition lessons. Everything is so fresh and lovely out there. Originally it must have been one big forest of fir trees, and the villas are mostly built in the midst with firs still standing all around in the yard. Then in the spaces in between there are still woods. It is beautiful, and it smells just like the woods.

November 13th

The concert Saturday night [November 11th] went very well, so far as I was concerned at least, and for the first time in my life after such an occasion I felt pretty satisfied with the way I had done. I wasn't a particle nervous and was just as much at home as if I had simply been playing for a couple of people at the Wölckes'. So the things went well musically and technically. As an encore I played *Si Mes Vers*, one of those two little French songs of mine which Mrs. Barron sang that time at my concert. I have played it a lot as a piano piece, and most people seem to like it very much, so I am afraid it will be doomed to stay a piano piece. The accompaniments also went splendidly, so that even Konrad was pretty well satisfied with most of them, and he always declares that I do not accompany especially well as a rule. He turned over the leaves for me. I think there must have been at least two hundred fifty or three hundred people there, as the little hall was quite packed. . . . I think Herr Kalinke must have taken in quite a little, and there were practically no big expenses as the hall was free and he had the grand piano from an acquaintance. After the concert Herr Kalinke gave me a Wagner score which I have been wanting for a long time — he had asked Konrad, of course, what he could give me.

At my last lesson with Humperdinck Friday I was disappointed to learn that he is going to America for two weeks, so will be away about four weeks in all. It was a very sudden decision, he said; he was to have gone this week some time, so he may be gone already. One of his operas is to be given in New York, and I suppose there are other things to attract him too. I imagine he has some kind of an offer or special invitation. Of course, he gave me some work to do while he is gone, but I hate to miss so many lessons when the time is so short.

November 27th

On the 17th of December I shall be assisting at a real concert probably. Fräulein W—— gives a concert in her home, Bielefeld, a town two or three hours from here. She is going to be assisted by a violinist here, Alfred Wittenberg, one of the best younger artists in Berlin, and it is practically settled that I am to accompany him (she has one from Bielefeld for herself). I get fifty marks from it, from which have to come my expenses of course. It isn't bad for my very first concert, according to German conditions, and especially when I have only to accompany a couple of pieces.

December 4th

Friday night I had a ticket given me for a concert by an American violinist of seventeen years. He had a splendid technique but played like a stick of wood. I went principally to hear the person who assisted him, for she played on the clavecin, the old French instrument. I sat just behind Isadora Duncan, an American dancer who has created a sensation here for several years back and made lots of money. She has a villa out in Grunewald and is sort of bringing up eight little girls who live with her, so far as I know, and learn dancing, physical culture, and all such things from her. She goes around in Greek costumes and does all such queer things. The eight little girls were also there with her and were also in Greek costumes. After this [Wanda] Landowska played the clavecin, they each received a little bouquet from Isadora, and then they all filed into the artist's room and gave them to her.

December 25th

I haven't told you yet anything about the Bielefeld trip. . . . We got there at 2:30, and the W——s called for Herr Wittenberg and me at our hotel to have a little rehearsal at the hall. Then I was tired and lay down until concert time. The concert went off well, and I think everybody was satisfied. I am sending you the criticisms and a translation of what relates to me. I have three or four copies and think it may help me in America. . . . Of my fifty marks I had nineteen left after I had taken out the fare and hotel bill. Konrad insisted on my buying with part of it the piano score of *Die Meistersinger* as a remembrance of my first concert money earned in Germany.

Chapter VI

January 6th, 1906

[TO A. MARGUERITE GRIFFES] — Yesterday afternoon right after dinner I took together what composition work I had been doing and went with fear and trembling out to Grunewald to see Humperdinck and find out when I could have a lesson. I had not only the good luck to find him at home, but to find him with nothing special on hand, so that he gave me a lesson on the spot. It was to be only a half hour as I hadn't brought any counterpoint work with me, but in the end I was there an hour. The "second half hour" I am to have Friday P.M. at 4. I tried to draw out of him just what an impression America made on him, but he said very little and that little was cautiously polite. Beside New York he was in Washington and Niagara Falls — Niagara Fall, as he called it — but he didn't mention any other places.

January 16th

Friday P.M. I was at Humperdinck's again. I told him again that I shouldn't be able to pay his price for the lessons, and he said I needn't let that disturb me, as the money didn't make any difference. I don't know whether he meant that I didn't need to pay anything at all, or not, but at any rate it would certainly be very little. And it seems to me more probable that he meant I could have the lessons for nothing, as I don't suppose a part of the price would be of any special value to such a man. At least for the present I shall not say anything about paying him.

January 21st

[TO MISS BROUGTON] — Don't you think it is fine that Humperdinck has been so interested and kind about the price of the lessons? I feel as if I ought to work all the time on composition, to show him that I appreciate it and that the time is not lost. You know in my lessons with him I have contrapuntal work and then free composition. I am still doing chorales, but each lesson they get harder. . . . Now I am doing them with text in each of the voices, so that they have to be singable. I brought him a Scherzo for string orchestra the first lesson after the vacation, and he wants me to go on and make a suite of it with four or five movements.

February 4th

I thought at first I would go to one of the galleries, but it was so dark that I finally gave it up and stayed home and played and worked some on a piece I am arranging for piano. It is a piece of Mozart's which Herr Galston let me take, and which is originally for a large sort of music box, called a musical clock. It has been arranged for orchestra and for two pianos, but Galston thought not yet for piano solo, so he said it might be good practice for me.

Before I go to bed I very often take an orchestral score or some piece of music and read it through in my head — sort of directing it, so to speak. Sometimes I do it to make me sleepy.

February 18th

It is also quite clear to me that whatever I do next year I want to and ought to come home for the summer. Whenever we talk about it Konrad insists always that I shall surely come back again next fall, but I personally am rather in doubt, as I don't see how he is going to bring it about, however much he might like to. Anyway I am not counting upon it.

Friday night I was at a concert of Vladimir de Pachmann, the Polish pianist, who is so well known in America as a Chopin player. Some of the things he played absolutely perfectly, according to my taste, and then others I didn't like a bit. . . . When he first came out and sat down, he talked first of all to the piano awhile and made all sorts of motions to the effect that the stool didn't suit him. Then he got up and went off, and some men came on and pretended to do something to the stool, and he finally began. It is too disgusting and inartistic for anything. But the audience is still more disgusting. They behave themselves as if in a circus, and the more ridiculous de Pachmann is, the more they like it.

February 25th

I forgot to write in my last letter that Herr Kalinke is to give another concert on Saturday, March 3rd, and that I am going to assist again—this time only with solos. . . . I play two groups again, six pieces in all. I had rather short notice, but hope they will go decently.

March 19th

I have been to the opera twice since my last letter, *Siegfried* and *Tannhäuser* (both Wagner). *Siegfried* was especially fine, as Richard Strauss directed. It is really a wonderful privilege which one has here of hearing him direct at the opera. I have heard him so often both this year and last. In America people paid so much to hear him direct one concert, while here he is at the opera (Royal Opera) two or three times a week during the principal season. I don't know what I shall do in America without all these things. The Opera is so fearfully expensive there and then only a few performances each year if one isn't in New York. And then they always give such a lot of things which I shouldn't care especially to hear. In some ways it is certainly a pity that I wasn't born to live in Germany instead of America, for I have become entirely converted to German ideas and ways of thinking in music. I know I shall have an awful disappointment and disillusion when I get back and find everything and everybody so different. I have become fearfully spoiled by my friends and my atmosphere here. (Especially Konrad studies with me and takes as much interest in all my things as I do myself, and of course all this will be lacking there.) I only hope that I stick to this present way of thinking and to these German ideas of art, even if no one else around me has similar ones. I am especially anxious to see what I think of the Metropolitan Opera and other things there.

April 3rd

You see Humperdinck has recommended me [in a testimonial letter for use in America] as an orchestral conductor. I don't know whether he did it because he thought I was looking for such a position, or whether he really meant that I would make a good one. It is very possible that he doesn't know or has forgotten that I am making a specialty of piano and want such a position, as I haven't spoken of it lately. But I thought of course he knew. In his recommendation as conductor, he shows his meager knowledge of American music conditions as of course there are no small orchestral positions there, and the big ones in New York and in other cities are filled by old and experienced conductors. One must either form his own orchestra or perhaps try some conservatory one, and of course that could be only side occupation.

A week ago Saturday night I accompanied Herr Kalinke again in two songs at a small concert of one of the boys' Gymnasiums here.

April 16th

Especially interesting [at the Aquarium] were the sea-horses, of which you of course have seen pictures. They are tiny things, stretched out at the most five or six inches long, with a head and neck just the shape of a horse's, a horny body, and a tail which is sometimes curled and sometimes straight. They swim by means of a lightning vibration of a tiny fin on each side of the head and a web-like one on the back, and instead of swimming in a horizontal position they are vertical in the water. . . . Then they have little black eyes like beads. I could have stood hours before the case where they were. . . .

May 1st

Friday was my last lesson with Humperdinck, which was a great disappointment. I had expected to have two or three more and had just begun a new piece; however, I shall go on alone. He is going to the country somewhere, I think, in order to be able to work undisturbed.

May 23rd

Of course I am sad to read what you say about coming back here for next year, but I can't deny that your reasons have weight and that they have already occurred to me also. I told Konrad in the very beginning that you might feel you would need me in America and that it would look queer and cowardly of me to outsiders. If there were no other reason except the latter I should let people think what they wanted to, and do what seemed best to me. . . . However, I know what you mean when you say that it seems as if everything were so uncertain and nothing is to be counted upon, for I have felt it so much myself. . . .

September 2nd

[ON HIS RETURN FROM AMERICA]—It seems now as if I had hardly been away at all, and Konrad says the same. I got here last Sunday morning about half past 12, and of course Konrad was there to meet me. . . . You may imagine that we had lots to talk over that day and those since.

Konrad's sister-in-law is going to have piano with me and has her first lesson tomorrow afternoon, and I have another pupil who is as good as sure, a nephew of Frau P——. His father was over at the pension to see me this noon about it, and I think he will begin right away. I am going to have six marks ($1.50) an hour, which is very good for a young teacher in Germany.

September 9th

We telephoned out to Humperdinck's and found that he would probably be here some time this week, so I have written him enclosing the program of my concert (on account of my own compositions), hoping that it may awaken enough interest so that he will let me come out to him again off and on. However, I am afraid he will feel he is too busy. Two of the Shakspere dramas are to be brought out soon with incidental music by him, so he will have a lot on his mind just now.

September 23rd

I have been home practically every night lately, finishing up composition work and copying it out. You see, I wanted as much as possible to take out to Humperdinck, but

I needn't have hurried so much in the end. I went out to see him Thursday, but he excused himself as being extremely busy and asked me to come about the 1st of October. I don't even know whether he meant by that he would have time for me once in a while or whether I could simply come out again and find out about it. At any rate I can't do anything except work on for myself and then go out later, and hope for the best.

November 7th

    I have another pupil now, a girl from Vienna — a regular Viennese. She has already studied the Leschetizky method with an assistant of his there in Vienna, and came here with a recommendation to Galston. He was too busy at present to take her, so he sent her to me until the spring when he has more time. . . . This would be my fifth pupil, if the one lady who began were still taking.

November 25th

    I don't think I have written you yet that I finally had an answer from Humperdinck that he was extremely busy now and didn't feel able to spare me the time for lessons. I really can't blame him, as I think he is writing a new opera at present and of course wants to keep his day as free as possible from outside disturbances. Any lesson is a disturbance when one is in the midst of such work, and then of course he was giving me his time for nothing. I haven't gone to anyone else yet and don't know exactly who would be best. Konrad thinks I might work for a while alone, and at present I am doing that of course. All the good teachers are so busy and also expensive.

January 4th, 1907

    I have begun now to accompany Frau B—— regularly . . . whom I know through Konrad and whose youngest daughter has lessons with me. She is a splendid singer, and I shall enjoy it. I get three marks an hour. I don't know yet how often it will be, but I hope twice a week.

January 13th

Frau Wölcke finally passed away last Tuesday evening. The doctor told them early that morning that there was no possibility of her getting better and that it was only a question of a few hours. It was a dark, dreary day, and it was still drearier sitting in Konrad's room waiting for the end to come. From noon on Konrad's brothers were there, and I also, as Konrad wanted me, and all the afternoon we sat and expected every minute the nurse to come and say that it was over. . . . For the first time in my life I was at a deathbed and saw someone dead whom I had known so well in real life. I thought so much that afternoon and evening of you and how it must have been a year ago November.

January 27th

I don't know whether I have written you yet that Herr T——, my first piano pupil, is also having harmony with me now. He has a half hour every week, and I get three marks for it the same as for piano. Konrad is also beginning harmony with me, and I think we will try to have regular piano lessons too.

February 10th

I will send you back the *Woodland Sketches* of MacDowell, which Katharine probably means. I very seldom play them here, and it is no trouble to send them. I am much obliged for the *Outlook* article as I never really had read much about MacDowell before. I personally am not very fond of his things, though I really don't know the bigger part of his compositions at all. . . . The Richard Strauss opera *Salome* was produced for the first time in Berlin the beginning of last December and had its very first performance anywhere about a year ago December in Dresden. About three years ago I saw the drama *Salome* of Oscar Wilde, the English writer, and at that time I may possibly have written you the description which you mention in your letter. The opera is almost a literal translation of the Oscar Wilde play, only a few passages being left out for the sake of conciseness. There were very absurd things about the work in the New York papers which I had from Uncle Charles. Also Conried made himself ridiculous in the eyes of art by giving a concert before his performance. The opera lasts only a little over an hour and a half, and Strauss, foreseeing that some directors might therefore be tempted to give a ballet or some other thing beforehand, forbade them giving anything else on the same evening. That has been carried out every place else, but of course in New York the fashionable subscribers would have kicked up a row at a performance that lasted only an hour and a half, saying they hadn't gotten their money's worth. Then they might say the same thing because the cast of *Salome* is small and offers opportunity for at the most three or four stars, so Conried came upon the idea of giving a concert beforehand with an extremely miscellaneous program in which all the stars could appear who didn't sing in *Salome*. So thus the audience would be appeased. It is too ridiculous, and one cannot wonder that musicians in a place like this make fun of the music in America.

March 8th

Last Monday Konrad and I were at the Royal Theatre and saw Schiller's *Wilhelm Tell*. I was very much disappointed in the performance, though there were two or three very good parts and splendid scenery. We were both especially interested in it as I have been thinking some of experimenting with my capabilities and trying to write some music to it. There would be several songs to compose, and then I would write "preludes" to the various acts and perhaps at one or two other places something. I don't know whether it will go any further than the idea.

Tuesday evening I was at the opera with the Norwegians and saw *Salome* for the fourth time.

March 18th

        Yesterday afternoon I accompanied at a little concert at a "Working-girls' Home" here. . . . I accompanied Frau B—— and another singer acquaintance of hers yesterday. I was supposed to be the only man there, but I brought Konrad along to turn over the music for me. The head of the affair asked him to "keep as much as possible in the background, so that the attention of the young ladies should not be too much diverted by the sight of a man's face." We roared at that. This very proper person evidently forgot that the "young ladies" were mostly in factories and such places where they saw men all day long.

April 28th

        I have now only two pupils. Frau P——'s nephew, who is a law student, has so much to do now that he had his last lesson yesterday. Then J—— B—— has also begun new schoolwork so that she has no time to practice at present — and I hardly think she will begin again before I leave. I still accompany Frau B—— regularly. Fräulein P——, my Vienna pupil, is with Galston himself now that he is back.

Two weeks ago today I was at a very interesting concert, made up entirely of compositions of the Norwegian composer Edvard Grieg, and under his direction. There were several orchestral numbers which he conducted, and then there were also a singer and his piano *Concerto* played by a Norwegian pianist, all of which he himself accompanied, partly with the orchestra and partly at the piano. I don't care so very much for his music, but it was interesting to hear them from him, and above all to see him. He is a tiny old man with long white hair. . . . I was with the Norwegian girls from the pension, who know him and his wife personally.

May 5th

Thursday I had an interesting afternoon. I had a lesson with Galston in the morning, and then he asked me to go with him to Busoni's in the afternoon. So I am finally introduced there. It was one of his "days," but there weren't more than twelve people there. We sat around the dining-room table and drank tea. It was all absolutely informal and easy, but rather tedious after a while as they were mostly ladies who chattered nothings like parrots. There was more French spoken than anything else, as there were three French ladies there most of the time. One of them was a very fixed-up and dressy old person who formerly had a well-known "salon" in Paris, as Galston afterward told me. I was pleased to find that I really understood a bit of the French; but I laughed to hear myself introduced as "*Monsieur Griffes, un élève de Monsieur Galston.*"

Frau Busoni, a native of Finland, is a charming woman, and they are both so friendly as one could wish, hoped I would be sure and come again the next time, which I shall probably do. There was no music, I am sorry to say, but Galston said that very often Busoni or someone played. They have about the most interesting house I have ever seen; it was not so frightfully elegant, but every chair and picture was a gem—lots of old things, and an immense collection of beautiful books. The

Busonis talk every language going, I guess; one moment they talked French, the next German, and the next English. I enjoy such people.

June 20th

I got all my baggage off yesterday P.M. and now have only my suitcase. I gave up my room yesterday also and am going to stay here with Konrad the rest of the time. I have so much to do and so many things to think of that it is hard for me to settle down to much of a letter. The last few days are of course burdened with good-by calls and all such things. Besides running around getting things done, copying some music of mine, and some practicing, I am not doing much else. In the evening I am always with Konrad.

Chapter VII

On his return to America in 1907 Griffes obtained a position through a teachers' agency as musical instructor at the Hackley School in Tarrytown, New York, about an hour's distance from New York City. Towards the end of July he made a brief tour of the place, wrote his mother about the charms of the Hudson locality, and arranged to return for work in September. Unfortunately, he was to remain there for the rest of his life. His first six or seven years, of which it is proposed to give only synoptic treatment in this and the succeeding chapter, constitute the period from his arrival in America to his emergence on the musical scene, and are of lesser biographical importance.

The Hackley School was founded by Mrs. Caleb Brewster Hackley, a wealthy widow who had long cherished the ambition of establishing a school for boys. In the fall of 1899 she converted her home in Tarrytown to that purpose and engaged a Unitarian minister, the Reverend Theodore C. Williams, to serve as headmaster. Thus the school, though nondenominational in character, developed within a loosely Unitarian framework from its inception. By 1900 additions to the original building had to be made to accommodate a student body that had increased from its original enrollment of seven. Mrs. Hackley next bought a near-by estate known as "Waldheim," a spacious and beautiful expanse about half a mile from her home. In 1902 the school was moved there amid a general construction of impressive new dormitories, school buildings, and chapel. The chapel, though completed three years later, was not opened till the installation of its organ in the year of Griffes's arrival. The same year witnessed the opening of the gymnasium, which included a sixty-by-twenty-foot swimming pool and a portable stage. By the time the headmaster's house had been erected in 1909, the school had further acquired a hospital for the isolation of contagious diseases, a cottage for the help, a laundry, a coal-pocket and boiler-house, and a water-tower. The reclamation of a swamp, resulting in a football field encircled by a cinder track, the laying out of tennis courts, and the development of another field, made provision for athletic activities. A board of trustees gradually took shape that included the Reverend Samuel A. Eliot as its president, and such members as Albert Shaw, editor of the *Review of Reviews*, and Ira A. Place, vice-president of the New York Central System.

Hackley was patronized chiefly by well-to-do families as a sort of cram school for recalcitrant young, emphasis being placed on preparation for entrance into one of the colleges known as the "big three"—Harvard, Princeton, and Yale. Or as the students discreetly expressed it in one of their annuals: "One idea, however, has never been altered. The school has always been essentially a college preparatory institution. In every course special attention is paid to preparation for examinations. . . ." The result of this concentration on preparing the offspring of the wealthy for admission to their parents' heart's desire was a general hiatus in the cultural and intellectual life of the school. The debating club, that lively staple of most sec-

ondary schools, proved an unwarranted whetstone at Hackley, where it died an early death. Notwithstanding the reduced
size of classes, courses of instruction were often limited
to material that would prove directly helpful in meeting examinations, for the instructors could not be unaware of the
obligation that lay on their shoulders. Where mathematics and
botany were strained to the most readily digestible purée for
jaded palates, music was sheerest superfluity. (The fine arts as
an integrated part of the preparatory school curriculum, one of
the things that MacDowell had plumped for in his dispute with
Columbia, was still widely considered an impractical ideal.) It
was entirely optional, so that Griffes's financial subsistence
waxed or waned according as this or that irascible adolescent
decided to commence, persist in, or discontinue tinkering with
piano. "I have only fifteen pupils this year compared to eighteen last year. That means economy, I suppose." Three days
later: "S—— told me tonight his mother didn't want him to
take music after all. Oh! it is so discouraging!" In all his years
at Hackley, Griffes was never to have one pupil in whom he
might take genuine pride, one truly outstanding pianist to tide
him over the dull ones. To the end his duties remained the
purely menial chores of a musical drudge. He could not afford not to keep after any negligent youngster who might
be lax about practicing. "He had a life which we boys never
glimpsed," wrote one of the more percipient Hackley students
years later, "yet the life which we *did* see was the life of an
amiable, intelligent, serviceable man, who performed uncom-
plainingly duties which were far below his powers."

Mrs. Hackley remained a more or less potent influence at the
school till her death in 1913. Her much bediamonded fingers
and dawdling at meals and pet mina became familiar trade-
marks. In the words of the boys again: "Hers was the inspiration, hers the generosity, hers the devotion that made Hackley

School possible. This was the chief of her many interests, and here she found her deepest enjoyment and satisfaction. In her last years it was her keenest pleasure to live with 'my boys' at Hackley, to watch its growth, to provide for its needs." So far as Griffes was concerned, all that this meant was the additional duty of playing court jester to the moods of Mrs. Hackley. Whenever the aged matriarch felt in need of music or musical companionship, to him fell the privilege of assuaging that want. However much he might bemoan the imposition in private, it was futile to complain.

Nor was Mrs. Hackley his sole adversary. There was also Mr. William Boutwell Gage, a short, imperious man with bristling mustache, who was fittingly dubbed the "King" by students and teachers at Hackley. Mr. Gage had joined the faculty of Hackley in 1900 and made himself increasingly valuable in the management of the school's finances. After the Reverend Mr. Williams resigned in 1904 and a Mr. Eels and a Dr. Callahan had each served his brief incumbency, Mr. Gage stepped into the headmastership, a position that he maintained throughout Griffes's stay. He was an uneasy speaker, unable to render convincingly the brief necessary speeches entailed by his duties. It was only with some exertion that he managed to stumble through the reading of chapel services. As a graduate of Harvard and a former member of its football squad, he was favorably disposed towards both these institutions. These loyalties sometimes intertwined with local results, as for example in the declaration of a school holiday at Hackley when a former student had won his football spurs at Harvard. Like Mrs. Hackley's birthday, the occasion was honored by adjournment of all classes. Mr. Gage had himself made a unique contribution to athletics at Harvard, and this was the subject of an amusing anecdote that he narrated to faculty members at Hackley. Despite apparent limitations in his musical background, Mr. Gage seems to have felt himself competent to criticize Griffes in the discharging of his duties at the school; the training of the choir waited on Mr. Gage's sanctification for the proof of its success. His cavalier disregard in the matter of taking professional services for granted almost matched that of Mrs. Hackley herself. "Gage thanked me today [two days later] for the accompaniments on Sunday night! Rather late, but he said I left too soon afterward. Nobody ever thinks of thanking the accompanist, and I told him so. They have no idea what it means." He also possessed a firm sense of order. One Saturday, Griffes, feeling unwell, had gone home and to the doctor's. Returning the next day at noon he "found Gage all excited because someone had told him that I had gone home sick, and he thought I wasn't going to be back for service." Mr. Gage influenced the purse-strings, and as late as five years after Griffes's arrival at Hackley there was still parsimonious quibbling about his salary guarantee. It was definitely agreed that he should return the following year, but his guarantee remained a matter of dispute. "He [Gage] does not want to increase it from $1300 to $1400." Griffes's unhappiness at Hackley became a constant refrain in his correspondence, and provides a keynote to the irrational moods of despair by which he was at times inundated. The tone of his daily life was stark tedium. "Today is an awful bore. All one can do is to sit around and wait for tomorrow to come. I have seven lessons to give and can't bear the thought of them. This afternoon we have a big Christmas tree in the gym for the help and any stray children which they possess. It is quite amusing. The mandolin club performs, and I always play a few Christmas carols to excite the Christmas spirit. Well, even that will pass by."

So autocratic a setup in the administration of a school both reflected and reacted upon the boys who composed its student body. They could not be oblivious of the social and financial distance that separated them from their pedagogical hirelings. They could dispense money on personal frivolities with a largesse that shocked their less affluent masters. Their costly excursions to New Haven, Princeton, or wherever, to see all the games, made their more prosaic studies almost a poor man's intrusion. Odd years the school chartered a boat to West Point. Other instructors besides Griffes considered that the boys were distinctly patronizing to them. They were made to feel their position. (Others besides Griffes liked beautiful things and rejoiced in the week-end invitations to luxuriously appointed homes.) What else might have been expected, however, under an administration where instructors were not represented on the alumni committee and where all complaints on this score were countered by the rejoinder that instructors who were also alumni were indeed eligible to the committee? There is nothing remarkable about the finality of the crack-up between faculty and administration that eventually took place: it is only wonderful that it did not come sooner.

Griffes was bound to Hackley by certain family obligations that he faithfully shouldered for the rest of his life. Before departing for Germany he had solemnly promised his father that in the event of the older man's death he would assume his share of family responsibility. In effect this meant that Griffes put aside monthly checks for the welfare of his family totaling at least $600 or $700 a year, a burden probably no greater than that sustained by many another composer with wife and children to support. Uncle Charles also helped.

His own playing, as he had discovered, was not exceptional enough for a career as concert pianist. Although he was almost perfect within a certain limited range, he was not capable of the greatest technical dexterity, and his performance in passages requiring such skill was apt to sound miniature. He planned rather to compose and to teach, and with this intention made several visits to prominent musicians, seeking their advice on how to become established in America. They could not help him. There were few openings for a younger man in any important musical institution. A depressing interview with Ernest Hutcheson made it clear that there was no place for him in the Peabody Conservatory and left him feeling almost fortunate with his Hackley position. His only concert appearances, except for participation in school musicales, were miscellaneous affairs, as at the residence of Mrs. Daniel S. Lamont on January 30th, 1909, and at the New York Northfield Club on April 26th, 1913.

His playing won him several appreciative listeners at the school. It was natural that on the faculty he should have made the friendship of Hugo Schmidt, "the Dutchman," with whom he conversed like a fellow German, and of Frank Ellis Bogues and Lawrence Whittier Newell, cultured men who were alive to literature and music. Among the students, Ira Farquhar, James Blaiklock, Hoxie Fairchild, Blaine Stevens, Willard Place, Arlo Garnsey, Sturtevant Steese, and others were attracted by his brilliant pianism and genuine personality. At the home of the Steeses he was a welcome guest, and Arlo Garnsey's father, a painter, also entertained him at their home, so that in time he became too the friend of an older son, Julian, who was interested in art and music. Nicholas Roosevelt, one of the Hackley students, after graduation presented Griffes with a tray of etching implements, which left him equipped henceforth to pursue this hobby.

On Sunday evenings after hymns a visiting artist performed for the boys, occasionally assisted by Griffes, whose task it often was to procure a guest musician at the modest fee set aside

Hackley School [photograph by Griffes]

by the school for that purpose. Then followed a private informal recital by Griffes in his own quarters. A faculty colleague later gave an impression of these Sunday evening interludes. "Almost every Sunday evening, at about eight o'clock, he would be in his studio, where a group of friends and pupils, or, perhaps, some who merely liked to listen to good music, would have the keen joy of hearing him play the piano. Two things especially impressed me. One was his seemingly endless knowledge of all music. One of his guests would ask for a special piece, and never have I known Charles to hesitate a moment. He would instantly swing around to his piano and we — listened! The other was that he had *absolute* mastery of the tool and of himself. It was so utterly amazing that I would often hold my breath in awe. It didn't seem possible that a human being could have such complete control. And in connection with that was a strange effect: he always left me completely cold. I was filled with utmost admiration for his utter *skill* but he never reached my heart. . . . He seemed to me always a man of intellect, living in an inner world of thought. Whether that was the real Charles or whether it was an outer covering, a protection, who shall say? Had that anything to do with the fact that I did not consider him a good accompanist? Yet it was *only in connection with his music* that I felt what seemed to me an intellectual coldness . . . he actually disliked the organ." As Griffes wrote: "I don't share or understand the Garnseys' enthusiasm for the organ."

A Hackley student later supplemented this account. "He lived at the school in a small but comfortable suite — living room, bedroom, bath. Unlike the other masters, he had no responsibility for the conduct of the boys outside of his teaching; he was not in charge of a corridor in the dormitories. There were no courses in 'history' or 'theory.' He gave private lessons to those boys whose parents wanted such luxuries, played hymns on the piano at morning assembly and on the organ at Sunday chapel, and trained the choir. The religious tradition of the school was such that the chapel music was necessarily thin and meager. Very rarely, when the school was on dress parade, he was asked to give a piano recital." One such recital was the "Chopin Evening" on January 25th, 1908. Griffes, who admired the Polish composer's mastery of the piano, frequently complied with Chopin when asked to perform, and already from Germany had written: "People who have heard me play much always say that Chopin suits me. At any rate I am extremely fond of him, and of course what one likes very much one plays well."

Griffes's physical appearance was later uniformly described by those who knew him — five feet, five and a half inches tall; thin brown hair; high forehead; straight nose; full mouth; medium-dark complexion; and very small hands and feet. His extraordinary sense of humor was his most striking personal characteristic. Lawrence Gilman, the music critic, who eventually came to a slight acquaintance with him, later wrote: "Charles Griffes had a delicate perception of mortal ironies, both humorous and tragical. He was a poet with a sense of comedy." The philosophy from which that comic awareness arose, the viewpoint that informed its irony, was something that Griffes retained all his life, refining a point or two here, discarding a few details there, but never substantially altering its trend. It was a view that he himself cheerfully, if oversimply, described as "atheism," that his friends referred to by more temporizing names, and that later critics have designated mysticism. A concept so basic in Griffes's life and art calls for some explanation.

From his earliest childhood Griffes gave signs of an unmistakably religious temperament. There had always existed a special bond between him and his devoted grandmother, Mrs.

Tomlinson. After long confidential sessions with the boy in the privacy of her bedroom, Mrs. Tomlinson was wont to tell her daughter: " Clara, you've got a fine piece of satin there." Later reading and thought, however, had bred a profound dissatisfaction with the Baptism of his youth, which, Griffes said, made too little provision for the realities of experience. By the time of his settlement at Hackley he was outspokenly opposed to institutional religion. When the Griffes family, moving from Elmira to New Jersey, obtained letters of presentation to the ministry of the new area, Griffes wanted none. He often pointed to the sharp disparity between church attendance and its effect upon the lives of churchgoers. The shipment of defenseless children to Sunday school once a week he plainly declared a crime. He studied higher criticism and above a text in his Bible one day inscribed: " *Si Pierre le premier pape de Rome était, il était aussi le premier unitaire*," following this with appropriate verse citations. In 1907 Griffes read in German translation a book that gave form to his confused and inchoate atheism. The book was *Niels Lyhne*, the autobiographical novel by the Danish writer Jens Peter Jacobsen; and even five years later when Griffes read the autobiography of August Strindberg, with whom he had a great deal more in common psychologically than with Jacobsen (for example, the Oedipus factor in Strindberg that he also diagnosed in himself), even then he recorded: "Strindberg's *Lebensgeschichte* seems to contain more of myself than any other book I ever read, with the possible exception of Jacobsen's *Niels Lyhne*." What is found in Strindberg's autobiography is, in fact, almost the same story as is found in Jacobsen's autobiographical novel, the story of a deeply religious temperament in the post-Darwinian era seeking to live fully and honestly without reliance upon a god or other supernatural concept. In both cases there is variance or betrayal of this ideal, but the pattern of effort is the same. In Jacobsen, Griffes found more than recognition of his own strivings — even an acceptable formulation of belief, a mythical standard of conduct on which to found his own life. The next year he acquired in German translation more of Jacobsen and before long had read all the Dane's works. It is dangerous to label a given work the starting point of a man's philosophical attitude, yet that is the conclusion almost forced by the prominence of Jacobsen and *Niels Lyhne* in the chronology of Griffes's orientation. As late as 1919, when a friend confronted him with the charge of professed atheist and practicing mystic, Griffes suggested that she read *Niels Lyhne* for her answer. Earlier he had termed the book a mirror of his own belief. His disquisitions on the nature of religion, shocking to his more conservative associates, were often verbatim accounts of the mystical atheism propounded in *Niels Lyhne*. His references to the " difficult death " and his interest in manner of death were not morbid preoccupations with a frightening subject, but rather the echo of Jacobsen's "difficult death" as an affirmation of life. Griffes must certainly have had this in mind when he spoke of those who accepted last-minute conversion as in a sense betrayers of life. His own death, in which he steadfastly refused religious consolation, is like one of Jacobsen's conceptions realized. Finally, a reading of *Niels Lyhne* convinces one that Griffes was right: it is a major key to the understanding of his character.

The writings of Jacobsen, unlike those of his countryman Søren Kierkegaard, have not yet penetrated American intellectual life. They are remembered chiefly for their tremendous influence on the work of Rainer Maria Rilke. " Now *Niels Lyhne* will open up before you," Rilke once wrote, " a book of glories and of the deeps; the oftener one reads it — there seems to be everything in it from life's very faintest perfume to the full big taste of its heaviest fruits. There is nothing that does not seem to have been understood, grasped, experienced, and fully known in the tremulous after-ring of memory. . . . You will experience the great joy of reading this book for the first time, and will go through its countless surprises as in a new dream. But I can tell you that later too one goes through these books again and again with the same astonishment and that they lose none of the wonderful power and surrender none of the fabulousness with which they overwhelm one reading them for the first time.

"One just comes to enjoy them always more, to be always more grateful, and somehow better and simpler in outlook, deeper in one's belief in life, and in living happier and bigger."

Jacobsen, a scientist who had translated Darwin's *Origin of Species* and *Descent of Man* into Danish, and who had earned a gold medal for an original monograph in botany, wrote *Niels Lyhne*, as he informed his friend Georg Brandes, in order to translate the predicament of a new generation of freethinkers who must live intelligently in the light of the new knowledge, without appeal to heaven. The doctrine of moral responsibility, of accepting the natural consequences of one's acts, was what Jacobsen asserted, as against reliance upon an outside supernatural agency that can intervene to remove these consequences. One must not indulge one's romantic imaginings, he therefore cautioned, "forgetting — what is so easily forgotten — that even the fairest dreams and the deepest longings do not add an inch to the stature of the human soul." Towards the end of the novel, Niels explains to his wife the doctrine of the new atheism. "He explained to her that all gods were the work of men and, like everything else made by men, could not endure eternally, but must pass away, generation after generation of gods — because humanity is everlastingly developing and growing beyond its own ideals. A god on which the noblest and greatest of men could not lavish the richest gifts of their spirit, a god that did not take his light from men, but had to give light by virtue of his own being, a god that was not developing but stiffened in the historic plaster of dogmas, was no longer a god, but an idol. Therefore Judaism was right against Baal and Astarte, and Christianity was right against Judaism, for an idol is nothing in the world. Humanity had gone on from god to god, and therefore Christ could say, on the one hand, looking toward the old God, that He had not come to destroy the law, but to fulfill it, while on the other hand He could point beyond Himself to a yet higher ideal with those mystical words about the sin that shall not be forgiven, the sin against the Holy Ghost.

"He went on to teach her how the belief in a personal God who guides everything for the best and who punishes and rewards beyond the grave is a running away from the harsh realities of life, an impotent attempt to take the sting from its arbitrariness. He showed her that it must blunt compassion and make people less ready to exert all their powers in relieving misery, since they could soothe themselves with the thought that suffering in this brief earthly life paved the way for the sufferer to an eternity of glory and joy.

"He laid stress on the strength and self-reliance mankind would gain when men had learned faith in themselves, and when the individual strove to bring his life into harmony with what seemed to him, in his best moments, the highest that dwelt in him, instead of seeking it outside of himself in a controlling deity. He made his faith as beautiful and blessed as he could, but he did not conceal from her how crushingly sad and comfortless the truth of atheism would seem in the hour of sorrow compared to the old fair, happy dream of a Heavenly Father who guides and rules."

Earlier in the book Niels had summed it up to Hjerrild, the scoffer, in one cryptic oracle: "There is no God, and man is his prophet." When Hjerrild protested that such a belief made greater demands on humanity than Christianity had done, and inquired where Niels would find all the strong individuals to make up his atheistic community, Niels replied: "Little by little; atheism itself must develop them. Neither this generation nor the next and not the next after that will be ripe for atheism, of that I am quite aware, but in every generation there will be a few who will honestly struggle to live and die in it and will win. These people will, in course of time, form a group of spiritual ancestors to whom their descendants will look back in pride, and from whom they will gain courage. It will be hardest in the beginning; many will fail, and those who win will have torn banners, because they will still be steeped in traditions to the marrow of their bones; it is not only the brain that has to be convinced, but the blood and nerves, hopes and longings, even dreams! But it does not matter; some time it will come, and the few will be the many." This was the task that Griffes took unto himself, the new atheism as Jacobsen conceived it: "What did it all mean, what was it all but tinsel names for the one simple thing: to bear life as it was! To bear life as it was and allow life to shape itself according to its own laws!" Nowhere in Griffes's life was there an appeal to God. Strindberg, a follower of science, even like Jacobsen interested in botany, had accepted the Kierkegaardian alternatives in early youth—all or nothing—but through an inordinately complex psychological nature had instead wavered incessantly between these extremes till his life guttered in a pietism that was neither.

Even the present loose discussion, based on literary works, does injustice to Griffes in its rigor. For systematic philosophy or formal metaphysics of any kind repelled him. "I remember," a friend once wrote him, "you always said that 'philosophic discourse' bored and tired you to death." He rejoiced in the potentiality of life without any need for a codification of his ideas.

Griffes accepted the findings of science, liked to read popular works in the subject, and, as he possessed no aptitude himself, later wrote a student: "Of course, having no talent for the sciences myself, I feel it a good thing for other people to know them thoroughly." At the same time he was moved by the power of simple experience itself. What were his extensive readings in comparative religion, in Oriental philosophy, in mystic poetry, in primitive anthropology — what were these but an effort to affirm his essential belief that "Judaism was right against Baal and Astarte, and Christianity was right against Judaism, for an idol is nothing in the world. Humanity had gone on from god to god . . ."? A close friend later wrote him: "All religions have the same truth — whether it be of Brahman or Tao or God. You who have felt the East so much — must have some sense of its great mysticism, its power of *meditation* and the Emanant God." In so far as he was comfortable at all in the terms of philosophic discourse Griffes would probably have agreed that this was a fair statement of his general experience. He only denied that about this experience there was anything supernatural — outside life itself — or rather that there was anything "unnatural" about the supernatural. Indeed, once he had consolidated himself in this view, he began to find that life was rather narrowly construed by his antagonists. He became interested in psychic research and later in life attended several meetings of societies devoted to investigation of psychic phenomena. The mediumistic intuition of a woman acquaintance of this later period also aroused a respectful interest in Griffes. On one occasion he himself appears to have undergone a kind of ecstasy that he ascribed to psychic origin. The atmosphere seeming to become suffused and heightened by color, Griffes dashed from the room, only to regret afterwards not having remained for what might have occurred next. His great fondness for the novels of Dostoevsky, and other writers in whom he found support for his view of life, persisted throughout his reading.

The result of a character formed by this personal atheism was the impression that Griffes made upon friends and associates. A faculty colleague was to write of him as "so utterly an individual that he feared neither man, God, nor the devil. He always said exactly what he felt like saying, and did, always, as he pleased. As a social being he was friendly (with those whom he liked); witty (always); quick to see the absurd; basically scornful of all that was mean or false, yet always kindly to the offender; abounding in energy — the sensitiveness and response of a finely bred animal." The same witness added: ". . . Although to many he seemed unreligious, I always felt that he was deeply spiritual."

To an observer of the present day, it becomes clear from all this that Griffes was but another representative of a peculiar modern sensibility that begins to make itself felt in American culture from the time of the Darwinian revolution. This is a strongly religious, nostalgic, poetic temperament seeking to ground the elements of religion in life itself and, by expunging the false and outgrown from the body of living belief, hoping to bring it into accord with the new knowledge. (Griffes in one place marked a statement that superstition is the parasite on religion.) He is a link in the chain that extends from a figure like Edward Rowland Sill in the nineteenth century to one like the early T. S. Eliot in the twentieth. Indeed, in the distinctively elegiac quality of much of his music, in his lonely desolation at the decay of contemporary values and integrity, Griffes already offered testimony of a kind that Eliot was to familiarize after him. (For it is to literature and not to music that one must next turn; Griffes's immediate successors were for the most part thick-skinned as well as unmusical.) Nevertheless one must beware pushing historical analysis too far. Griffes, lacking the rounded intellectual approach of these earlier and later figures, regarded himself more simply as one of the small "group of spiritual ancestors" with yeoman service to perform in his generation.

The effort not to forget this, not to be overcome by longings and dreams, is what characterized the whole of Griffes's psychological struggle and accords it dignity and meaning. It is a realistic striving towards self-knowledge. Fairly soon after discovering the nature of his impulses he appears to have assumed the full responsibility of his predicament. He studied the findings of psychology and history, read Wilde and Gide and Whitman, among others, and kept a long list of books dealing with homosexuality. He brought the same unsparing realism to his own experience, and his almost painfully honest notes give the record of a determined escape from illusion. He had a dread of injuring others who might not have equal knowledge, and a friend to whom he explained this attitude later emphasized "his fear of losing a friend who might have remorse. Charles had the *belief* that he was in every way natural."

Not the special sufferance of society, but a personal formula was what he pertinaciously sought after, and the personal formula that he did arrive at slowly through the years might be summarized: to expect little and to learn to find much where that little was offered. ". . . Our relation now cannot efface the charm of our former one. But they could not last." For a man of strong feeling it was perhaps a difficult final adjustment, but it was not impossible. He well appreciated the risks of such an adjustment, the dangers to the personality in reticent, uncomplaining, and undemanding resignation. "Sometimes the horrible thought comes to me that some people may think me the kind of person that Eugenio Bardelli is," he once wrote, referring to the character in Castelnuovo's *I Coniugi Varedo* who remains an episodic minor figure, always present, never jelling into anything determinate; Bardelli, the tender, self-sacrificing soul, blindly involved in the toils of others, the shadowy sympathizer who never achieves a totality of his own. (Griffes read a good deal of Italian trash, which was recommended to him for vocabulary by an Italian minister with whom he studied.)

It will not in general be necessary to inquire into this side of Griffes's life, but some mention must be made of a Hackley student with whom he became acquainted during this early period and who meant much to him in the years after. At Hackley, as at most preparatory schools in the country, there was a certain amount of adolescent homosexuality among the student body by virtue of the segregation imposed upon its members. The emotional constriction that is a concomitant of the superior educational advantages obtained by the preparatory school system is well known to educators, whose reforms have since curbed and cured this condition. Romances were flourishing when Griffes arrived. Early in his stay he recognized the danger of immersion in the lukewarm bath of immature emotion thus accessible, and resisted it with almost entire success. The exception was Robert Corby, a student whom he watched over with special affection and concern. At all times Griffes was aware that the emotion was one-sided, his own and not the other's, but the feeling persisted till he could only regard it with a dismay that presently found overtones in other aspects of his life. Everywhere over and beyond such repressed affections hovered Griffes himself, lamenting his awareness with a voice that is a blend of the shrill cackling of a disillusioned old man and the intense yearning of youth. " Man likes to be deceived and to deceive himself. . . . But the desire to feel a possession of a loved one is strong! "

Griffes remained in America henceforth, except for two visits to Germany, one in the summer of 1908, and the other in the summer of 1910. The first was to attend the wedding of Konrad Wölcke, who soon after his mother's death married and devoted himself to rearing young for the fatherland, though at the same time continuing his role of sponsor to promising musical young men. While in Germany Griffes also visited Galston, who played him some of Busoni's new compositions. The second trip to Berlin was to preside at the baptism of Konrad's son named in his honor. Griffes stood by while the newlyweds fussed over their baby. Galston, to whom he later played a number of his compositions, advised him to study in Paris for a year, but that was impossible.

Although he missed travel, in the diversity of New York he came to find an acceptable substitute. For him it was the city of eternal wonder. There was more than jest in the constant iteration of his letters to Babe Shoobert: "I repeat once more: 'Life isn't worth living anywhere else.'" He frequently composed on the train journeys to and fro between Tarrytown and New York and often found himself with something important to develop upon his arrival at one or the other of these destinations. He haunted Manhattan's secondhand bookshops and for very small sums began to accumulate a large and varied library. Concerning Griffes's tastes in reading it is almost impossible to frame any valid or approximate generalization, so diverse and almost crazily unrelated were they in scope. One fairly programmatic year, however, included Baudelaire, Poe, Verlaine, Goethe, Hawthorne — of whom he never tired — Hearn (especially the letters), Gordon Craig, Mirbeau, de Amicis, and d'Annunzio, outside of his reading on music. The safest generalization is his concern with literary treatment. "I gave up Shaw's *Man and Superman* as too boring. To be sure, single witty places are very amusing, and the whole idea is clever, but the execution bored me." He also built up a vast and representative music library on the foundation of the scores he had received in Germany. On few things in musical discipline was Griffes more adamant than the importance of knowing all that was being done by others and that had been done by others in the past — even to music " that is quaint for a while but appeals only to our sense of the curious and archaeological, not to our present-day emotions."

His own musical activity during and immediately after the years in Germany might be characterized, academically, as the transition from a propaedeutic period of German influence to a period of modern experimentation. On February 4th, 1909, he signed a contract at 10-per-cent royalty with G. Schirmer, Inc., for five German songs to texts by Lenau, Heine, Mosen, and Geibel: *Auf dem Teich, dem Regungslosen, Auf geheimem Waldespfade, Nacht liegt auf den fremden Wegen, Der träumende See,* and *Wohl lag ich einst in Gram und Schmerz.* Again on June 7th of the following year Schirmer's accepted another song to Geibel — *Zwei Könige sassen auf Orkadal.* Mrs. Herrick and Mr. McKnight sang them in Elmira, and one was performed by Mr. Robert Winthrop Seeley, a musical acquaintance, at a small concert. These songs earned him a total of $28 in royalties to July 31st, 1910, and then $5.10 more to July 31st of the succeeding year. They by no means exhaust the quantity of his Germanic output, which includes, besides an early choral effort, a huge sheaf of songs to other texts by Heine, Lenau, Geibel, Mosen, and Eichendorff. (*Auf ihrem Grab, Elfe,* and *Könnt' ich mit Dir dort oben geh'n,* to poems by Heine, Eichendorff, and Mosen, were published posthumously in 1941.)

Opinion varies as to the worth of these German songs, which have strangely held a certain popularity on the concert platform. William Treat Upton says: " It is the remarkable assimilation of the technique of these masters of song [Strauss,

Brahms] that makes these early songs so notable. Original perhaps they are not, at least in the sense of setting new patterns of beauty; but a rose-garden is perhaps no less beautiful than a garden filled with unfamiliar, exotic bloom, provided always, of course, that the roses be perfect of their kind." And in *Auf geheimem Waldespfade* "we begin to perceive the shadow of the future thrown across its very first measure, in the tonic chord colored by its sixth. . . . So early had he been attracted by the beginnings of a new idiom." Dane Rudhyar, in another criticism, finds that "Griffes's music has a peculiar nostalgia and inner sadness akin to the German *Sehnsucht*, and truly this lied of his, *By a Lonely Forest Pathway*, ranks with the most perfect of Brahms and Wolf." Griffes was sincerely revaluating his German education and German models. On reading of Richard Strauss as one "whom the cognoscenti call the greatest maestro that ever lived," he tartly commented: "If they do I never met any of them." Another time he took part in a discussion of "decadent art, literature, and music, including Strauss in the latter." Viewing a performance of Humperdinck's *Königskinder* with the original cast, Griffes confirmed an earlier impression. "I felt more than ever this time that the opera should end with the death of the two Königskinder; what follows is a superfluous anticlimax. Humperdinck must have felt this, for the music seems to come to a perfectly satisfying close here, and one could stop without changing a note. Is it an opera one can see often? The last act is certainly one of the best things since Wagner. The first act didn't interest me so much this time." An original two-piano version of Humperdinck's *Hänsel und Gretel* was rejected by publishers in 1912.

Following his German period Griffes employed only English texts in his songs. "Last summer I read various things by Wilde," he wrote Gottfried Galston on November 30th, 1911. "Some of his poems are not to my taste; others, however, I find wonderful. I tried composing to one or two, but was not very satisfied with the results." He eventually agreed with a critic in his reading who judged that Wilde would be remembered as a significant figure in the aesthetic movement rather than for his actual works. Nevertheless the value of a poem did not determine its suitability to musical setting, as Griffes often insisted, and among the songs of this early period are Wilde's *La Mer*, *La Fuite de la Lune*, and *In the Forest*, all composed on October 29th, 1912 (and later superseded by an opus called *Four Impressions* and consisting of *Le Jardin*, *Impression du Matin*, *La Mer*, and *Le Réveillon*). Also to words by Wilde was the *Symphony in Yellow* composed at about this time. *Pierrot*, to words by Sara Teasdale (Griffes was much interested in the new American poetry movement), was composed on May 6th, 1912, and completed nine days later with the comment: ". . . But don't know as it is of any value." An earlier American poet, Sidney Lanier, was the author of *Evening Song*, of which the revised version may be dated July 11th, 1912. A Rumanian *Song of the Dagger* belongs to some previous year but was revised on October 25th, 1912. John Tabb furnished the texts of *Phantoms*, *Cleopatra and the Asp* (of which one version may be dated April 16th, 1912), and *The First Snowfall*. The last mentioned was part of a group of four English songs, including also *Evening Song*, *The Water-lily* (1911), and *The Half-ring Moon* (1912), that were learned by Miss Gertrude Flint Frisbie, an early Griffes admirer, who sang *Evening Song* and *Water-lily* at her native Lowell, Massachusetts, in May 1912. (*Evening Song*, *The First Snowfall*, and *The Half-ring Moon* of the hitherto unpublished English songs were brought out posthumously in 1941.)

Some of Griffes's best liked piano pieces belong to this early period: *The Lake at Evening* (1910), *The Night Winds* (1911), *The Vale of Dreams* (1912), the *Barcarolle* (1912), and the *Scherzo* (1913). (The *Notturno,* usually associated with this group, was composed in 1915.) Of these *The Night Winds* was first conceived as a song and the dedication offered to Noble Kreider, a Midwestern composer friend, who refused it, preferring some more typical work. Many of the piano pieces were composed without title or explanatory verses, and only after completion prefixed with a bit of Yeats or Poe, or whoever, and assigned a title. Several were in a free sonata form.

The foregoing loose collation of songs and piano pieces — published and unpublished — of the German and succeeding period is incomplete but may serve to acquaint the reader with the complicated Griffes bibliographical problem.

In a country that lacked an indigenous musical tradition at the level of thought and of feeling at which he intended to compose, Griffes seems early to have decided upon a course of personal salvation. As he later concisely stated: ". . . It is only logical that when I began to write I wrote in the vein of Debussy and Stravinsky; those particular wide-intervaled dissonances are the natural medium of the composer who writes today's music." (To the two names he mentioned might also be added the name of Busoni, with whose music Griffes was most familiar and whose notions of concinnity are certainly honored in the early piano compositions.) Mr. Upton dissents with regard to the songs. "He seems least influenced by Debussy and his school. Whatever may be true of his other forms of composition, we find no single song showing any marked trace of that influence. . . . It is to the later French and Russian schools that he turns."

Griffes's first encounters with the French school were anything but enthusiastic. Of a pianist in Berlin whose program included five modern French compositions by Bizet, Debussy, Fauré, Saint-Saëns, and Chabrier, he had written: " I think she completely wasted her energy in all those little French pieces, for while they were perhaps pretty, they were certainly nothing more, and I should think them hardly worthy of being on a Berlin program when it is to be her only one this season." As early as the year of his return to America he was heard practicing Debussy so that he was familiar with the new idiom even at a time when he continued to compose in accordance with his German training. Indeed, what is most outstanding about the whole course of Griffes's musical development is the manner in which he scrupulously and patiently assimilated only those things that were personal to him. His English critic, Norman Peterkin, in the *Chesterian*, mentioning Griffes's French and Russian influences, justly asserts: "Unlike some of his younger American *confrères*, however, he was never enslaved by these influences, but was able to extract from them precisely those elements he needed to set free, and to express his own personality." This is the fact that must strike anyone who makes a careful historical study of his music. What Griffes called "logical," however, others found less so, and these included not only the people who could not understand or who were opposed to the new schools of music, but also the people of whom Griffes wrote in 1912: "They like the modern French music but are still at the stage where they think that all music showing its influence at all or even having unusual harmonies is a mere imitation of it." As late as 1940, when the lack of a serious native musical tradition was no less acute than in Griffes's time, Oscar Levant, in a book of shallow journalism, placed Griffes among the "pseudo-American" or "ideologically hyphenated."

The dangers of the new influences Griffes had comprehended from the beginning, as his early strictures on some of Debussy show: "In a way, the picture painting here is a bit too obvious" or ". . . A thin texture of mood painting with little thematic material of any kind at all." Also for Griffes, to whom music was a part of life, there was bound to be regret at the consequent estrangement from "the layman who doesn't like deep problems or psychological strivings in any branch of art" but who heartily approbated those theatrical intermissions in New York where "a vile orchestra played Thomas's *Simple Aveu* and other trash." Griffes's own compositions, both the piano pieces and the songs, were regularly and unfailingly rejected after the period of his first German music. And as often as they were resubmitted with the hope of attracting a different manuscript reader they were rejected again, till at length he nearly lost hope of attaining second publication.

The public taste against which Griffes pitted his own musical standards is not a separate phenomenon from that general decline in Western culture whose nature and causes are the present concern of all sociology. Music was not exempt from the ravages of the prevalent cheapening process, and the widespread commercialization of music produced the same disastrous results in creating a debased and sentimental public taste. On February 5th, 1900, after the première of Charpentier's *Louise*, Claude Debussy wrote a friend: "But then people don't like things that are beautiful. . . . With many more works like *Louise* any attempt to drag them out of the mud will completely fail." By 1912 Griffes was writing about "the worn-out plea of the lack of melody in Strauss and Debussy. People are so narrow."

Yet the conditions with which an American had to contend were more extreme than elsewhere, and of these something must be said before proceeding further.

Chapter VIII

THE ADVICE that had been tendered Stephen Foster by his publishers in 1849 "to compose only such pieces as are likely both in the sentiment and melody to take the publick taste" had been gratefully accepted by a long succession of popular composers after the Suwannee minstrel. Most of their output was of the sort characterized by Céline, in his *Voyage au Bout de la Nuit,* when he refers to Americans and " their attempt at music, whereby they too try to ease themselves of accustomed burdens and the crushing sadness of having always to do the same thing every day; it helps them to shuffle around with a world that has no meaning, while it's playing." Yet like some of Foster's own, some of their compositions, particularly in the later style known as jazz, achieved an immediate celebration of mood and a subtlety of line that compel genuine admiration. In the summer of 1910 Griffes heard a band " play various American ragtimes with such a swing that they really sound quite fine." A whole nation was to repeat the discovery, and when a new emphasis on manner of performance later produced a renaissance in jazz it was this very " swing " that was to give the movement its name.

Griffes knew, however, that the popular was not his medium. Not that he held it in any contempt or even deprecated its success. He honestly respected Scott Joplin's well-known *Maple Leaf Rag*, which he sometimes tore off in private conclave for the delectation of a choice few students whose secrecy could be trusted. A girl who once called upon his family's neighbors in Passaic Griffes declared to be an excellent pianist because she could play that number so well. He liked to amuse the Hackley boys with skillful demonstrations of how all their popular favorites might be reduced to bits from the classical repertoire with change of time and stress. Any current number of which they could carry the tune he could promptly bang out on the piano for them. But he knew where his own true inspiration drove him. It was there, whatever the obstacles, that he intended to make his mark. "Of course," he wrote Babe Shoobert in 1909 when his first German songs had been published, "I don't expect to very soon become a millionaire either from these or any subsequent things that come out. But nobody nowadays becomes rich from composition except Richard Strausses or people who write such things as *Love Me and the World Is Mine*. By the way I was seriously advised by an experienced person the other day to write something like that and get rich in a week — that is, of course, if it should take." Even so realistic an appraisal of his prospects, however, could scarcely have prepared him for the shocking reality.

The publication of music in America had early in its development concentrated into the hands of a comparatively few. Whereas American literature had compelled its own outlets throughout the different sections of the country, each with its own clamant problems and needs, whereas even American painting had benefited from the regional and specific, music by its very nature precluded any such widespread demand for local sources of distribution. In newspapers, magazines, and books of many kinds the American writer might find his pub-

lic. The painters might exhibit independently. The composer
was in a less fortunate position.

American music publishers had started under the enormous
business handicap of an already established and flourishing
German music industry in Europe. They could not hope to
compete on a correspondingly world-wide scale and therefore
dared not overlook any of the more grisly possibilities of the
home market. Certainly they could not afford to indulge in idle
gestures of " prestige " or to build up " good will " in the German manner. Unlike their competitors in other countries, they
had not even a serious nationalist market to fall back upon.
American music publishers, apart from their pedagogical output, were interested mainly in the publication of the accepted
classics and the works of contemporary European composers.
It was not alone love of the classics and respect for distinguished European reputations that dictated these preferences
in a field where the dead claimed no royalties and almost non-
existent international copyright laws so inadequately protected
the living. Well known in American musical circles was the
legend of Xaver Scharwenka in America. Old Gustav Schirmer
had escorted the musician about his publishing house. When
the tour was completed, Scharwenka had quipped sardoni-
cally: "You've shown me your *Druckerei* [printery]; now
let's see your *Nachdruckerei* [reprintery]." Book publishers
might pirateer all they wished, but ultimately they had to meet
a demand for literature dealing specifically with American
life. In music a demand of this kind could not be.

The creation of stronger international copyright laws
brought no substantial improvement in the lot of the American
composer. For the same cliques, by now in firm control, monopolized his outlets. He must compose to the publishers' taste
or suffer neglect. The more prominent publishers, moreover,
were usually related to one another, either by family connec-

tion or by the transfer of manuscript readers from one firm to the other. They were few in number and appreciated the advantage of working together. The story of the sale of Ethelbert Nevin's *Rosary*, perhaps the best known song by any American composer, is worth telling in this connection. *The Rosary* had been sung in concert performance with great success and music stores had already received many orders for it before the song was submitted for publication. Mrs. Nevin, dissatisfied with the 10-per-cent royalties her husband had been getting from the Boston Music Company, had it accepted on a 15-per-cent royalty basis by Rudolph Schirmer acting for the firm of G. Schirmer. Soon afterwards she received a letter from Rudolph backtracking from his agreement, followed by another to her husband from Gustave Schirmer asking for the song on behalf of the Boston Music Company and appealing to Nevin's sense of loyalty. Mrs. Nevin was no fool, and her reply came to the point: "It is not a question of sentiment at all, but purely a question of living. . . ." She got her 15 per cent, and *The Rosary* embarked on its epoch-making course of yearly sales.

But where Ethelbert Nevin, with his conventional style and wide popular following, might survive this refined beating-down process and even insist on his price, the serious American composer was vanquished at the outset. He was made to feel (and indeed the objective situation soon came to justify the feeling) singularly blessed when any work of his was accepted for publication. Publication, instead of providing the natural medium through which composers reached out to their prospective audience, became a supreme accolade of musical achievement. They therefore knuckled under to their master's requirements. They permitted their music to be dictated to them as well as corrected when they had done. Those who managed to accumulate a personal following were treated to a degree of independence in evolving their own style, but almost none attained final exemption from the adulteration process. Publishers of verse were not likely to tamper with a poet's meters or substitute for his rhymes. But it was nothing for a serious composer to have his work "improved" upon for him. As late as 1918 Oscar G. Sonneck, of Schirmer's accepting Griffes's song *The Rose of the Night*, subjoined a note that the postlude ought to be shortened. "There are two good ways of doing it which Schindler [a consultant] can indicate to you." Griffes knew better than to refute these suggestions. In a pointless bit of self-gratulation, Mr. Sonneck smugly informed the composer's sister after Griffes's death: "You may not know that the last section (or movement) of the *Sonata* was changed by him under the influence of criticism of mine. He was very sensitive about the criticism and would not commit himself, but he changed the movement nevertheless and improved it." This appalling boast can better be appreciated when it is recalled with what eagerness and with what gratitude Griffes welcomed suggestions that he considered of value. He was not unduly sensitive about accepting criticism, whether favorable or unfavorable, that seemed artistically valid. Farwell, Galston, Busoni, Ganz, Betti, Mason, Tuthill, Barrère — as will be seen — were only some of many whose opinions he thankfully embodied in the texture of his work. He remained the same Griffes who had written in 1915 of the early sonata: "Galston tore the poor sonata to pieces until there was not one note left on another, but he said some very true and good things about it, and I was very glad."

The little cliques that reigned over American music publishing have a terrible share of the responsibility for the history of American music. Their members, however splendid may have been their accomplishments in musical scholarship, exerted a blighting and enervating influence on American music itself. They remained impervious to the American landscape and infected the surrounding air with their tepid ideals. Their own compositions, those elegant stuffed owls that they set upon the shelf for posterity, show only too plainly what standards they had in mind. Innocuousness and cleverness were the values they prized most. What Bernard Shaw termed the "professorial school" in England had its counterpart in America, but the American school was in a position to do a great deal more damage. Like Shaw's target, they esteemed "the workmanship shown in the score, its fine feeling, its scrupulous moderation, its entire freedom from any base element of art or character, and so on through a whole epitaph of pleasant and perfectly true irrelevancies." As with the English group, their musical prestige was wholly self-generated. "If you doubt that *Eden* is a masterpiece," said Shaw, "ask Dr. Parry and Dr. Mackenzie, and they will applaud it to the skies. Surely Dr. Mackenzie's opinion is conclusive; for is he not the composer of *Veni Creator*, guaranteed as excellent music by Professor Stanford and Dr. Parry? You want to know who Dr. Parry is? Why, the composer of *Blest Pair of Sirens*, as to the merits of which you have only to consult Dr. Mackenzie and Professor Stanford."

Although they were not malevolent so much as musically stupid, they were not above the personal viciousness that is the corollary of petty hegemony. W. S. B. Matthews, editor of the *Music Magazine*, delineated the prototype neatly in 1902: ". . . the supposedly competent and judicious musician to whom manuscripts are referred for acceptance or rejection. Now this sort of job naturally appeals to a well-instructed and well-read musician, of temperament compatible with spending day after day over disagreeable and generally imperfectly written manuscripts. It is a purgatory position, anyway, but not necessarily Hades; there the little devils come back at the reader; here he has it all his own way. Now music is a particularly difficult kind of product to place at the behest of this kind of person, because the more a thing appears original the more it strains him, and the less likely it appears to him to result well commercially. The more the author vaunts his originality and his high ideals the less the historical imagination of the reader rises to him. It often happens that a reader has a grudge against an author for some fancied slight in some previous contract. I have myself been assured that a certain extremely successful manuscript of mine was rejected by two readers of the foremost publishing house in America for a reason of this kind — at least this was the information given me by the publisher himself many years later, with the acknowledgment of his mistake."

Griffes's unfortunate relations with his publishers, therefore, were not an isolated phenomenon. Side by side with his publishing tribulations should be placed the spectacle of Charles Ives in New England printing his own works. The merits or demerits of American music, the question of whether the American composer "has it in him" or not, are not relevant here. The point is the near impossibility of any dignified musical inspiration making itself felt in an atmosphere where the composer's own artistic conscience was not his guide, but where, like some dependent schoolboy, he must await the teacher's corrections and grading as his final standard.

There were ephemeral sparks of revolt, like Arthur Farwell's Wa-Wan Press founded in 1901 in Newton Center, Massachusetts. Farwell, himself a composer, whose special interest was American Indian and folk music, surveying the plight of his colleagues and finding that "just in proportion as they were at all 'advanced' they were correspondingly discouraged, as the publishers would take only their more casual and conventional works," and having been a printer as a boy, had decided to start a press of his own. In a manifesto issued in 1903 he avowed his desire to offer "encouragement and incentive to young composers who may under existing conditions feel that the highest possible development of their talents is not desired, and who would be deterred from devotion to their highest ideals did they not have a positive demand for their most sincere efforts." Despite the canard that has persisted to discredit the enterprise, its sole objective was not the exploitation of native Indian material in American music. That was admittedly one of its aims, but in the countless essays that introduced his publications Farwell, who was something of a metaphysician at heart, delved deep to the roots of the universe, emerging with the at least respectable hypothesis that the distinctive quality of American music might prove to be in its variety and vigor. Farwell seldom pulled his punches in assailing the entrenched musical oligarchy: "A man whose word is law in several of the continents of the musical world of Boston and who sets the gauge of thought for the population of his dependencies, told me recently that the only two things of artistic importance in American musical life are the Boston Symphony Orchestra and Schirmer's publishing house. The sublimity of this remark entitles it to consideration. . . .

"The remark in question is approximately true if we accept the standpoint of its author. Translated into other terms it means — There is no worthy musical activity native to America; the Boston Symphony Orchestra and Schirmer's publishing house represent European musical art; they are the two oases in the desert of American musical life. Lo, must we not respect one so powerful that he shall reduce musical America to zero at the wave of the hand. . . ."

It was inevitable that to such a man Griffes should have turned when, following the line of his natural development from a period of German influence to a period of modern, he had encountered a barrier in Schirmer's seeming unwillingness to countenance the change. But by then the Wa-Wan was no more. After the brief span of a decade Farwell's interests had carried him elsewhere, and he turned over his stock and catalogue to G. Schirmer, Inc. As W. S. B. Matthews has correctly predicted, the project had remained "outside the channels of trade" because its subscription basis and its policy of selling pieces only in groups of three rendered it commercially inconvenient beside the organized companies. Nevertheless Farwell remained an amicable influence. He recognized Griffes's daemon at once and never had any doubts about its eventual triumph. He encouraged the younger man and with sympathetic insight apprehended his true character, the "nervous, active, eager personality, with that keenly awakened and mobile inner life that often goes with genius," as Farwell later phrased it. "He was almost pathetically anxious to get ahead and make progress with his compositions. . . ." It was Farwell who tried to facilitate that progress, both by searching criticism and by attempts to smooth over the temporarily deadlocked relations between the composer and his publishers.

In 1912 he brought Griffes to Schirmer's and personally introduced him about before they left some of his piano pieces. These were rejected a few days later. Griffes, inquiring why, was informed that they were "not so deep as my German songs." "Saw Farwell afterward, who was much surprised about the Schirmer affair." Galston's visit to the United States in the same year precipitated new unpleasantness. Griffes "went to see Mr. W—— at Schirmer's about their publishing a translation of the *Studienbuch*. He thinks there would be no call for such a book, but will consider the matter before saying 'no.'" Soon after Griffes "learned that Schirmer's are thinking seriously of publishing a translation of Galston's *Studienbuch*. Saw M. H. Hanson [Galston's manager] afterward, and he wrote an urgent letter to Schirmer's recommending me as Galston's personal choice for the translation. If I can get it!" In the end he was simply eased out. "Hanson says the *Studienbuch* affair is still undecided, but W—— at Schirmer's told me the other day that they would probably give the translation to their regular man, Dr. B——. Cheaper!" He submitted four English songs, which were soon rejected. "I don't believe there is any use in sending them anything more at present. I am done with them." As though to punctuate this caesura in their dealings his royalty statement on the German songs revealed no sales at all that year. "Strange!"

On a sincere and questioning artist like Griffes the general publishing situation had one good effect. Disenchanted with the reliability of outside judgment, he was thrown squarely back upon himself for his criteria. Sonneck had said that music was a business and that publication must be divided between "commercial" and "prestige." Yet why were the two indistinguishable in practice? In 1912 Griffes could still write that he was "in a bad humor all day because Schirmer's write that they don't want my three piano pieces. I don't know what to think of it. Is it Schirmer's mercenary spirit, or was Farwell mistaken in thinking so highly of the pieces? It takes away one's confidence. Am I on the right track or not?" But by 1918 he knew. "Keep *your* conscience," was the advice he wrote a fellow composer, "Keep *your* conscience even if the publishers have none — in fact just because they have none. Somebody must have one, you know." It was both a logical and artistically valuable process that led him from the question to its answer.

In all fairness it must be admitted that Griffes's intense confidence in his own creative gift would have proved a strain even in a more congenial aesthetic milieu. For example, to a young lady at Salem College to whom he was mentioning the *Barcarolle* he wrote in 1916: "If Schirmer's were hustlers for advertising their new publications they would have sent you people at the College copies when they first came out in September." He should also perhaps have rested content with the ugly outdated wrappers in which most music was then published, expecting no special dispensation of modernity in his own case. Instead, he could not help sketching possible covers and lecturing on design. And how should any business firm have guessed the desperate urgency to be financially able to compose that underlay an autocratic message like this in 1917: " A friend of mine wrote me that he had inquired at Schirmer's for my Chinese songs, but could get no information about them. That looks bad. Wouldn't it be a good idea to request all the clerks at the vocal department to tell people who ask for them that they are expected from the press any day? Then they will at least call again and not go away thinking some other house has them "?

It would be crude oversimplification, moreover, to pretend that music publishers were responsible for the infamous state of American musical life. They were a part as much as a cause of the general condition. Griffes, reading von Bülow's 1875–6 letters from America, gaped at a prophecy that there would be a growth in artistic matters that it seemed to him had hardly taken place. Music in America followed chiefly in the orbit of an obstreperous group of concert luminaries and their sycophants. Their motives were commerce and vanity. Their power was relentless and not often disputed. The musical press was a forerunner of those movie fan magazines that would make an appearance with the advent of the cinema. Replete with little snapshots of the stars at play and the most trifling personal interviews, they catered to the sentimental interests of their readers. Snobbery and avarice alone enabled them to disregard for so long the significant contributions of the Negro jazz musician and to relegate to obscurity sincere performers who could not afford to buy space in their columns. The newspaper critics were little better. They fawned upon one another and unashamedly exacted return from native composers for their praise and attention. Griffes was on many occasions thus approached by critics high in the newspaper roster. Unfortunately he had insufficient means and sufficient self-respect to make fruitless these sallies on both. Accordingly, recognition was delayed and its advance slackened.

Where the personality of the musical interpreter came to the fore the importance of the musical experience itself diminished. Consequently the choice of musical fare customarily set before the public was calculated to exhibit the virtuosity of the stars rather than the intrinsic worth of the music itself. There was a deadly homogeneity about their programs. Griffes, advised to hear everything possible in order to " find himself," asked: "But how shall I? " " If European artists were to boycott America," wrote Busoni in 1911, on his next to last visit before leaving the country in disgust, "America would be like a great hall in which the electric light had suddenly gone out; they would have to find their way with matches and burn their fingers." Even European artists were made to conform, however, if they wished to survive. When Gustav Mahler died in the same year that Busoni made the reflection quoted above, Alma Mahler told the press something of the conditions her husband had been working under in New York. "In Vienna my husband was all-powerful. Even the Emperor did not dictate to him. But in New York, to his amazement, he had ten women ordering him about like a puppet." Above all, the unruffled calm of the American audience must never be disturbed. Gottfried Galston, planning an American debut, was advised by his concert management that his programs were too heavy for an American audience, and Griffes privately concurred. Galston finally submitted and wrote his former pupil that "the only pleasing thing about his trip is that he will play the Steinway piano."

American composers could not help but be affected by such a state of affairs, not only in the creation of their music but in the unwitting transformation of their lives. They needed to live in two worlds at once. As early as 1894 Ethelbert Nevin, the American professional par excellence, was writing his wife: ". . . I don't want you to lead the life I do when I am at my concert work. It isn't that one does anything that is radically wrong, but it seems to me I'm a 'Mr. Hyde' when I am battling with this worldly life, and I want to be true and honest in my life with you and the children." Before that he had advised one of his pupils, young Daniel Gregory Mason, that "without a good strong constitution you can never stand the strain of a music life." Griffes himself never escaped the wearisome necessity of playing "Mr. Hyde." He became a master of the long tasteless letter and the short insipid note, innumerable missives dispatched to performers and celebrities whom he scarcely knew, in the hope of interesting them in his work. He paid as many embarrassing visits with the same purpose. Victor Herbert, who deplored the lack of a musical patronage in America, had come to the parting of the ways with his friend James Huneker when he told him: "You can keep to your ideals, Jim. I want to make money." Afterwards, when Herbert had made money and dissipated even his footling talent, he magnified this honest preference into a factitious altruism. "That time has passed when intelligent persons are content with any work, music or literature, of which they are forced to remark: 'Yes, it is very beautiful, indeed, although I do not understand all of it.'

"Personally I hold that that which is not 'popular' is not of much benefit to the world."

American composers, unlike American poets and novelists,

could not afford the luxury of dedicating their efforts to friends and beloved. They dedicated them to prominent musicians in the hope of thereby securing performance. These same numbers then turned up pleasantly enough on their respective stars' programs with the legend beside them: "Dedicated to Mr. —" or "Miss —."

Nor did the local symphonies and choral groups scattered throughout the country provide a more convenient outlet to the composer. Their statistical rise and geographical spread, enthusiastically chronicled by publicists of American culture, are unimportant beside the fact that they functioned as so much deadwood in the American scene and contributed little to the musical taste of the country. The simple presence of orchestral societies is not the musical vitality of a nation except when the musical life of that nation is in a languid state.

Composers need performance. It is true that composers of meager talent or weak resolve have used the condition of music in America as an excuse for the mediocrity of their work or the prostitution of their gift. A certain romantic type of mind also persists in believing that if there were some improvement in the material circumstances of the American composer a great American music would at once gush forth like torrential waters through a smashed dike. Both these views slight the driving force of inspiration itself as the mainspring of artistic effort in favor of external factors. Nevertheless they do serve to point an inescapable predicament. Composers require performance in a way that authors do not require publication and painters do not require exhibition. For the composer, performance is a primary need. The author whose work is not printed, like the painter whose canvases are not shown, may still persevere in self-development. The one may study his own writing, as the other may examine his own painting. The composer who is not performed, however, is wounded at the very heart of the creative process. His music remains nothing more than a series of complicated hieroglyphic markings set down on paper. The mere accumulation of stacks of paper covered with markings in this way can never come to represent artistic growth. For such growth springs in large part from sureness in the manipulation of the experience for which those markings are only a symbolic shorthand. He cannot compose without opportunities of hearing his music and of learning for himself what there is for him to learn about the physical being of that music. (The deaf Beethoven of the later works presupposes the audient Beethoven of the earlier.) His need for performance is thus overwhelming. It is more than the desire to communicate and the desire to subsist, which are common to all artists, but is for the composer a part of the desire to create.

The music of American composers amply reflected the hodgepodge of academicism required by publishers and surface brilliance demanded by performers. When Louis M. Eilshemius, the American painter, eccentric, and composer of sorts, decoyed space in the *Musical Advance* in 1914 to excoriate " The Crazy-Quilt School," composers who indited their work from " stray patches of cloth, silk, and laces " from the classics, he was formulating a truth that better balanced judgments than his could not have phrased so well. Rupert Hughes in his *Contemporary American Composers*, published in 1900, had already decried " the surprising abundance of purest namby-pamby " in the American song. " There has been a persistent craze among native song writers for little flower-dramas and bird-tragedies, which, aiming at exquisiteness, fall far short of that dangerous goal and land in fragrant silliness."

Academicism and cleverness also took their proper toll in quaintness. Thence proceeded all those Persian market places, Oriental bazaars, Hindu rituals, Chinese pagodas, Indian war dances, Japanese rickshas, and other picturesque bric-a-brac that cluttered up the musical landscape and publishers' catalogues for years. Exoticism by virtue of its onomatopoeia was a short cut to effectiveness.

Griffes, it is true, pursuing the line of his own artistic evolution, may seem to have run almost parallel at times to this antiquarian trend. But, as he later said of *Kubla Khan*, ". . . If I have written into my score Oriental sounds and Slavic themes it is only because those tonal combinations and melodies have said and expressed the thing I wanted to say." For Griffes's Orient was something apart, a fount of his deepest spiritual as well as musical inspiration, and in his style too he was attempting something of another order. He was there seeking an independent rediscovery in his own terms of those musical innovations that the European modernists were reporting from abroad. As will be seen, Griffes himself fully appreciated this difference, and it was in point of style that he later explicitly distinguished himself from the school of "American exoticism." It is also true that this Eastern inspiration represents but one aspect of his work. "I don't want the reputation of an Orientalist and nothing more," he later wrote.

Nor did he participate in the self-consciously American movements that resorted to Indian, Negro, mountaineer, and cowboy music for their "Americanism." The visiting Antonín Dvořák, writing in *Harper's* of February 1895, had merely recommended an old nostrum for a chronic ailment when he offered Negro folk music as a tonic for the musical inanition of America. That had already been tried. After Dvořák, as before, the would-be nationalists continued to worry their folk material in vain. More often than not the sinewy, original stuff on which they relied far surpassed their harmonically inflated apotheosis of it. Five years after Dvořák's article, Mr. Hughes, in his book on American composers, elaborated the real weakness of the whole nationalist school: "Centuries of differentiated environment (in all the senses of the word environment) are needed to produce a new language or a new art; and it was inevitable that American music should for long be only a more or less successful employment of European methods . . . we are in a large sense of English lineage. As the co-heirs, with those who remain in the British Isles, of the magnificent prose and poetry of England, it was possible for us to produce early in our own history a Hawthorne and a Poe and an Emerson and a Whitman. But we have had more hindrance than help from our heritage of English music. . . ." Nevertheless Mr. Hughes considered that a new day was at hand and proceeded to fill the more than four hundred pages of his survey with uncritical encomium and lavish description of the nonentities who made up American music.

It is significant that Griffes's only essays in American folk music should have been the direct melodic transcription of the children's pieces, *Six Familiar Songs*, arranged in the treble clef by "Arthur Tomlinson" (*My Old Kentucky Home*, *Old Folks at Home*, *America*, *Yankee Doodle*, *Maryland, My Maryland*, and the *Old Oaken Bucket*), and the *Six Patriotic Songs*, also by "Arthur Tomlinson." His string music made only such highly individual use of Indian thematic material as might have been made of any novel and apposite material that had come to hand.

In so far as Griffes had a musical program, it was to follow his own natural bent. In so far as he developed a credo, its gravamen is contained in the article — by a fellow composer, John Alden Carpenter — that he clipped from a newspaper and kept among his manuscripts. " It has become the fashion with many of our musical observers and musical critics during the past half dozen years to wring their hands and demand, for the future at least, if it is impossible for the present, a more unmistakably ' American ' quality in American music.

"Such a demand must inevitably result in the impression that we have a greater concern for affixing the national label than for the contents of the package — it must inevitably result, for the composer who allows himself to be influenced by it, in a self-consciousness which is death to the real creative impulse. That impulse, if it is to be real, has nothing whatever to do with volition. You may lead your creative impulse to our very best American folk-music material, but you can't make it drink . . . [the American composer] must be writing what he feels like writing, not what he thinks it would be good policy to write, and certainly not what some friendly critic or critical friend may urge upon him. The real creative impulse, it is worth while to repeat, cannot and will not respond to this kind of suggestion. Whether we like it or not, that impulse will always reach out and choose its own inspiration from whatever source is the most natural and, therefore, the most impelling." Mr. Carpenter summed up: ". . . The American composer is going to be 'American' enough to suit our most fastidious patriots, because in the final analysis he can't, thank God, be anything else."

Chapter IX

1914, the turbulent year of Sarajevo, was ushered in at Hackley by such dire and fluctuating weather as almost matched the vagaries of statecraft abroad. In the second week of January there was a cold wave accompanied by a violent wind. The thermometer dropped continuously. As winter set in, to a constant barrage of wind and rain, the rain froze, coating the branches of the trees with ice. Sometimes in the evening a dry flurry would descend, and Griffes returning from choir practice would note how it sparkled and glistened over everything like a crystalline artificial snow. Soon followed a warm spell, with snow melting to slush, and then a blizzard. A trolley with about thirty-five passengers stalled near the school, and the cozily sheltered academics took supper and blankets to the marooned. Sunday services were held in one of the school buildings on account of the storm. Griffes did not miss the organ. And as the blizzard rampaged, with barometers everywhere hitting record lows, trolley service was discontinued, and trains into New York on the Pennsylvania Railroad stopped running. All transportation became undependable and irregular. Mail arrived only in the late afternoon. On his way to give lessons at the Lower School, Griffes could walk upon the snow in some places; in others, he sank in above his knees. At last the frost gave way to warmth and slush and water. A few robins made their appearance. Then it was cold again, everything frozen beneath a new snowfall. And then it was warm again. So the weather oscillated, back and forth, till even the most confident despaired of predicting aright.

It was not a year of overwhelming creative activity on Griffes's part. The specter of his manuscripts collecting unwanted in piles scarcely galvanized him to new frenzies of composition. Clearly, neither publishers nor public had yet caught up with him. Prospects were gloomy. When his mother forwarded a letter from Uncle Charles praising him as a success in life, Griffes moodily reflected: "I wish I could feel that way about it." There had been no sales of his German songs for the last two years, and there were to be none that year.

But his music was heard occasionally. Leslie Hodgson, the young Canadian whom he had known in Germany, was proving an appreciative friend, willing to propagandize his music not for personal glory but because he sincerely esteemed it. Hodgson was a former pupil of Teresa Carreño, the Venezuelan pianist, whose concerts Griffes had enthusiastically followed in Berlin. Later Hodgson had settled in New York, where his poetic, almost lapidary style of playing, unevenly balanced by a controlling nervous tension, began to attract a loyal and intelligent audience. He it was who encouraged the disconsolate Griffes with both heartfelt words of admiration and the concrete tribute of performance. He was a friend whose influence carried. On April 4th Griffes attended a recital by Hodgson at Chamber Music Hall that included *The Lake at Evening*. His regard for the pianist was shared by the audience. When they recovered from the musician's spell, however, many later requested information about the composer.

During the first two weeks of July, Griffes also copied off

his *Barcarolle* for Hodgson, who began practicing it for recitals and eventually performed it at Chamber Music Hall on December 11th. Six days before, he played it to Griffes for approval. To his surprise, the composer burst out laughing when he had done. Griffes had not yet learned the difficult lesson of relinquishing his own precise conceptions of his music to the differences in another's interpretation. Hodgson asked him to sit down and play it. He complied, and there was less volume on the climactic passages, more restraint in the execution. Yet he generously consented that Hodgson play it according to his own lights.

Others besides Hodgson helped out. Miss Frisbie continued her support. On November 3rd, Griffes assisted her in a program at Lowell, where he gave the *Barcarolle* its initial performance. The local paper commented on "the vigorous and effective climax that suggested that this particular aquatic adventure was no canoe trip on the Concord River." Miss Ethel Whalen, a singer whom he had assisted the year before and to whom he brought his manuscripts, made good suggestions from a practical background of vocal experience. She would try to use them when possible.

By and large it was a year of lying fallow. The ardor of his inspiration could not be quelled, but it was considerably dampened by the indifference to which it was subjected. Deprived of any tangible recognition, it exhibited itself only in desultory spurts. He read Robert Louis Stevenson's *Letters* as "incentive to work." Balked in his musical advancement, he was driven in more upon himself and his personal problems. The school environment made increasing inroads upon his life as well as his time.

There was the eternal cycle of hockey, basketball, baseball, tennis, and football, with the accompanying celebration or grief when Hackley was victorious or defeated, and the innumerable "snacks," "eats," and "spreads" endemic to prep school life. Lecturers who came to the school were often long-winded and dull. The clubs chose their members down in the gym. Mr. Gage tried letting the boys select their own hymns on Sunday evening. It sounded like an auction in which Griffes obliged the noisiest and most persistent bidders. Mrs. Hackley's will was finally probated, and more than a million dollars went to the school. Her demise the year before had gone off blamelessly so far as Griffes's end was concerned. "Last Sunday," he had written on October 31st, 1913, "we had a memorial service to Mrs. Hackley. Mr. Eliot, the head of the Unitarian Association of America, and Mr. Baker, one of the trustees, each gave a short talk on Mrs. Hackley, the choir sang, and the service was very successful in every way. We have gotten so used to having hitches with electric lights or some such thing at our public functions here that we heave a sigh of relief when one passes off successfully."

Playing cards offered some diversion. So did tennis. Several fuses blew out during a service, and the organ was incapacitated for one Sunday. Griffes did not miss it. Three boys ran away from school and took the *Wolverine* home. The seniors and the juniors promised each other not to smoke. Two boys were caught in the basement under the faculty room listening to a faculty meeting the day after another had got himself in trouble for trespassing rules. Griffes began earning a little extra money by teaching German conversation to those who needed special tutoring in the language. Christmas made no ripple in the calendar. "It has never seemed so little like Christmas at the school." The choir became progressively worse, and the task of training them correspondingly impossible. "The choir disgusts me now. The sopranos seem more rotten all the time." Later: "Thank goodness that I am through with them for this year." It improved only slightly with the infusion of new voices in September. "It is dreary to have to begin again." His general situation improved not at all.

Griffes's school duties without his constant efforts at composition would have been manageable. There were twenty boys taking piano, and trips to the Lower School during the week. With composition, this proved a heavy schedule. More and more of his free time in the morning and in the afternoon was occupied in snatching naps. Sometimes listening to an enthusiastic pupil discussing the choice of a vocation Griffes became "so sleepy that I could hardly follow what he said." Yet on a Sunday after choir practice, chapel services, evening hymns, management of the weekly concert, and playing for guests in his room, he was restless in the night and could not sleep. It was not always easy to compose even when there was leisure. There would be interruptions, and he would put aside his work. When he worked too long at copying out his manuscripts his right eye became overtaxed by the minute focusing and pained him. The eccentric weather did not help. Inevitably he came down with tonsilitis, headache, and disordered stomach. Up again, he was unable to elude their aftereffects. His letters to his mother minimized the sickness and exhaustion. "It has been the kind of a cold which used up handkerchiefs mercilessly, but had no other disagreeable feature." Or: "I should write more but I must finish it this evening, and I feel as limp as a rag."

Photography, in which he had recovered an intense interest the year before, lightened much of his time. He had confined himself at first to landscapes that were not characteristic of any locality. Now he tried portraits and detailed studies. Perspective and developing and printing, and all the intricate ritual of the darkroom, engrossed his attention. He painstakingly examined each print for defects. Not that he aspired to anything more than amateur status. But he was convinced of photography as a medium for conveying beauty and liked to excel in anything to which he put his hand.

Wednesdays and Saturdays were Griffes's free days, and when the weather did not forbid he seized them for trips to New York. Babe Shoobert was in town all year till the middle of November on a visit to her sister Ethel, the wife of Dr. Frederic Bancroft. Together he and Babe would wander about Chinatown, often on obscure errands, more often just for the atmosphere. Griffes could never get enough of Chinatown. He would go alone in search of lanterns or incense, indolently traversing the byways of Mott and Pell Streets in the quest. "*Dîner à la chinoise*" became an infallible source of delight. After Chinese dinners together he and Babe would be escorted to the kitchen, which they at once pronounced immaculate and appetizing. His private zeal carried him even further: to Balkan, Japanese, Turkish, German, and Italian restaurants — wherever the food was exotic and also inexpensive.

Babe and Mrs. Bancroft sometimes tried to inveigle their recluse friend into dancing. He declined, but not long after started on private dancing lessons, in which he proved most adept. The more conventional steps were quickly superseded in his repertoire by the maxixe, the tango, and the hesitation. Babe taught him the castle-house tango. In dull interims at the school he and the boys would practice new steps together. His proficiency emboldened him to public appearance, and he not only gaily obliged Babe and her sister but danced at occasional school affairs.

Babe and he became ardent movie fans as well as dance addicts, for this was the year they saw *Captain Alvarez*. It was "the first film that ever satisfied me." Faithfully thereafter Griffes tried to keep up with the moving pictures, and his tastes were very catholic. Of *A Million Dollar Bid* he recorded: "There was a wonderful thrill when the pictures of the sink-

Think I shall make today a day off for writing several much-needed letters. There is so much to do that I am going to take it just as easy as I can until Commencement is over. I only practice enough to keep things up. I guess it is a long time since I wrote you, so I don't know just where to start in. I can't say just when I shall leave here but it will not be Commencement Day anyway. Mrs. Steere has asked me over to their home at Ma—

Sample of handwriting

ing yacht came. The cabins were shown gradually filling with water. I don't see where the photographer sat. The film was kept on till the woman's head was practically under water — an almost terribly thrilling scene." Mr. William Brady, the theatrical magnate, whose son attended Hackley, sometimes sent films to the school. Griffes never missed.

He renewed his enthusiasm for the circus, where, on the alert always for novel sounds, he noticed an effect in the spectacle "caused by the continual striking with hammers of innumerable metal pieces which gave the tones C and G, the whole accompanied by drums. It was an awful din but very weird." The same interest brought him to the rooms of the Greek help at Hackley to hear their phonograph records. "A Cretan cradle-song was great."

He attended the 101 Ranch Wild West Show at Madison Square Garden, once alone and once in the company of Hodgson and some friends. There were good concerts that year, too. He saw Pavlova for a second time. Of a Paderewski recital he wrote: "About half the program was abominably played, I thought. The Chopin was poor except for two mazurkas, which were bewitching. He played eight encores. Liszt *Rhapsodies* Nos. 2 and 13 were astounding and fascinating. He doctors them up a lot. The capricious gypsy element was marvelous, rubato inimitable. From the standpoint of the Slav temperament with its fire, melancholy, and capriciousness, Paderewski is certainly at the very top. He pounds at times frightfully." The Metropolitan's all-star revival of Weber's *Euryanthe* was illuminating. "It was a beautiful performance of a beautiful work. Here are Wagner's ideas of the music drama anticipated many years before him. I think it was written about twenty years before *Tannhäuser*, but *Tannhäuser*, *Lohengrin*, are so astoundingly anticipated dramatically and musically that it is almost amusing to put your finger on the exact spot in *Euryanthe* where some of his most famous and striking passages in those two operas came from. Wagner himself admitted his indebtedness to the earlier opera, but I don't think he realized or admitted how enormous this indebtedness was. Many things seem like direct cribs." One day " I spent the first part of the P.M. at the Philharmonic concert at Carnegie where they played Rimsky-Korsakov's *Scheherazade* and *Till Eulenspiegel* and by rushing down to Aeolian Hall heard the Symphony Society play Debussy's *Ibéria*. The first and last were my first hearing of them. *Ibéria* rather disappointed me. The middle movement is in Debussy's most fascinating style, I think, the first and last movement seem a bit tawdry and superficial in spite of some clever effects and dance rhythms. I like the first better than the last movement. I want to arrange the *Perfumes of the Night* for piano if possible."

Debussy and in fact all the French moderns were an increasing disappointment. For Griffes wrote Babe Shoobert after she had left for her home in Sausalito: " I wish there were some new modern French things that seemed as interesting as the earlier ones. Somehow I can't help feeling that Debussy's latest things are a step backward instead of forward; they seem to lack the freshness and spontaneity of his earlier pieces." He became more and more interested in Russian music, read books on Russian opera, and brought to school the scores of *Boris Godunov* and *Prince Igor*. There were tantalizing rumors that the Metropolitan might produce the latter. All year Griffes played through sheafs of music, highly critical and appreciative. " Tchaikovsky's *Casse-noisette* is extremely *salonmässig* and cheap on the whole. Only the *Danse Arabe* is at all good on the piano. Chabrier's *España* seems too long and monotonous on the piano. The orchestral color is necessary." Although he disliked the music of César Franck, he was swept off balance by the *Prélude, Fugue, et Variations* and swiftly proceeded to learn it. One Sunday night a Hackley boy brought in a cousin who had studied with Schönberg. With wry good humor Griffes observed: "He found Schönberg perfectly natural the first time he heard him. I played him No. 2 from Op. 11. Debussy and Strauss do not seem to go with the Schönbergites. On the other hand Busoni pleases. I played the latter's *Berceuse*."

His own efforts in composition numbered a few scattered piano pieces and settings of Fiona Macleod, Oscar Wilde, and some rondels. The rondels were taken from an anthology titled *Ballades and Rondeaux* that he had purchased in November of the year before and now worked on whenever he felt in the mood. The first two stanzas of Henley's *We'll to the Woods and Gather May*, for example, he sketched on the afternoon of May 15th while seated on the banks of the Sawmill near East View. He let himself go in a spontaneous burst of song that is entirely apart from the main body of his work. It is, as Mr. Upton has said, "carefree, utterly oblivious of all responsibility, even of all thought, and that too, written in the simplest, most unsophisticated style imaginable; a song of mocking humor and heedless of all restraint! We may well take note of it, for never again shall we find this mood in his songs."

The last statement is accurate description. For from this time forth Griffes's music would reflect in greater and greater degree his relentless struggle to achieve honesty and balance in his emotional life. It was in this year that the problem first presented itself in all its ramifications. Because he would not simulate what he did not feel nor cheapen a valuable association by protracting it under false pretenses he had nearly sacrificed a companionship of long standing. The man involved was a science teacher in a Brooklyn high school. He was also an art instructor at a Y.M.C.A., a student of ecclesiastical architecture, and author of several magazine articles on the subject. A married man and the father of two children, he had too late discovered the mistake in his life, and eagerly sought Griffes's fellowship. They met whenever possible and attended theaters and concerts together. Under his friend's tutelage Griffes investigated church edifices, to which he had always been impressionable. He often visited St. Thomas's in New York: "The blue windows above the altar were exquisite in the sunlight. The effect is still beautified by the shadow which an adjacent building throws on the lower part of the glass." After prolonged introspection, however, Griffes could not honestly tolerate a continuance and had to insist upon some adjustment.

He was still in Robert Corby's company, though hampered by a tormenting restraint that bitter experience had taught him to adopt. Together they took long hikes along the Sawmill. They would go in wading, lie on the little sand island in the middle of the brook, and pedal their feet in the air to dry them. When Bob invited him on a visit home Griffes told himself that it was the boy's earnest fondness that prompted the invitation. ". . . Bob seemed more attentive and interested in my visit than last year. I think we are much better *friends* than a year ago." Yet he was at the same time contending with the truth — that he was not free of his special interest in the boy, that it was a source of both joy and anguish to him, and that the most poignant episodes of his life at the school centered around Bob's presence.

There is no doubt that his fortunes in these and kindred affairs gnawed him at times with despair. From this source arose the occasional *moralischer Katzenjammers* — as he called them in the slang of Berlin — that menaced his efficient energy. Much of his time, though, was filled with the clear, untroubled solace of his natural surroundings. It was a fine year for rare and stunning birds, which he eagerly identified wherever seen, and for flowers, which he gathered in great bunches on his long solitary strolls. His reading became more stimulating and varied all the time — Dostoevsky, Turgenev, Ibáñez, Chinese poetry, Hawthorne, Poe, Lafcadio Hearn, Fiona Macleod, Reinach, Galdo, Hoffmann, de Gourmont, Barrès, Descaves, Hueffer, Stoddard, Bülow, Balzac, Soulié, Claude Farrère, Charles Pettit, Fogazzaro, Maeterlinck, d'Annunzio, Villiers de l'Isle-Adam, de Maupassant. He read in all and took what he wanted from each. He began to study El Greco and Velásquez, whose paintings now intrigued him. Any day that yielded no return in nature, friendships, or art he counted a loss, "a most unsatisfactory day. Nothing accomplished in any way."

Griffes was expanding the range of his social and artistic acquaintance. Harold Henry, whom he had known in Berlin, came into town from Chicago occasionally to give recitals. Griffes also met the Mallet-Prevosts, musical people at whose home he passed some pleasant hours. The Steeses and the Garnseys were as cordial as ever. Sometimes he was asked to the Harvard Club. Julian Garnsey examined his etchings and advised him that he was fully prepared for classes in New York; but the cost of ten dollars a month was prohibitive for a hobby. Burnet ("Bones") Tuthill, salesman and amateur clarinetist, whom he had met at the Garnseys', asked him to quartet evenings and concert parties. At one of the latter, in December, he first met Percy Grainger, the Australian composer-pianist who was staying in the United States with his mother. Through Tuthill, Griffes was invited to the summer home of Mr. and Mrs. Charles Larned Robinson in Intervale, New Hampshire, for a refreshing visit in August. The climax of the trip was a breathtaking ascent up Mt. Kearsarge.

It was at one of Tuthill's concert parties that the brewing international situation first impinged upon Griffes's personal life. On April 25th while he was in Tuthill's box at the Oratorio Society at Carnegie Hall, Andrew Carnegie appeared during the intermission and announced the intervention of the

South American republics in the Mexican affair. As the year wore on he read disquieting things in the papers. "The papers report that many German musicians of note are reduced to playing in cafés for a living. The art treasures in Paris are all buried or in vaults to protect them from bombs. London dealers are also offering to keep temporarily the works of art in Antwerp which the Germans are reported about to besiege. An American architect declares Reims Cathedral beyond restoration. A movement has been started in Belgium to replace the library at Louvain." From Konrad he heard nothing for a long time. Then he learned that Konrad had been drilling recruits near Berlin in early October, while expecting to be called to the front at any moment. Griffes's German background enabled him to plow through the rising tides of patriotic confusion a little more surely than his bewildered countrymen. With Hugo Schmidt he attended a lecture on "*Deutschland und der Krieg*" delivered by Professor Eugen Kühnemann of Breslau. "He changed my views of the war in some ways. New to me was his statement that everybody in Germany was backing up the Kaiser and the war heart and soul. He says they are confident of winning. The German audience applauded this and other statements violently." On another occasion he and Schmidt "almost had a very heated discussion of the war. Fortunately we both stopped in time." In November he received a batch of pamphlets in defense of Germany mailed from Amsterdam. Since his address was given complete and correct, he merely wondered whether they had come from Konrad directly or through the government. They were followed by an even greater bundle, this time entirely in German, including several newspapers, and mailed from Italy.

The dark clouds that overhung his year were pierced by a ray of hope towards the end of November when Schirmer's accepted five songs for publication. Early in May, Griffes had taken them a selection but had been told that nothing would be accepted till Mr. Schirmer's return from Europe in the fall. On the succeeding 21st of October, therefore, he tried again. Having stayed up till twelve o'clock the night before, recopying the Clinton Scollard rondel, he marched into the publishers' office next day with *La Fuite de la Lune* (Oscar Wilde), *Symphony in Yellow* (Oscar Wilde), *We'll to the Woods and Gather May* (W. E. Henley), *This Book of Hours* (Walter Crane), and *Come, Love, across the Sunlit Land* (Clinton Scollard). He saw one of the readers and Mr. Schirmer. "The latter claimed to be very busy so all I could do was to leave the five manuscripts with him upon his assurance that they would have his personal attention. That means nothing, I suppose, and I expect to get them back soon." Several weeks later he received a letter from Mr. Schirmer and then one from the composition department accepting his songs for publication. He was to get a 10-per-cent royalty on them.

At long last the years of unbroken waiting were over! Griffes could not help being heartened. Yet he was still far from optimistic. For, as he wrote Babe Shoobert after receiving the news, it was always easier to get new songs before the public. "There are so few pianists here who are willing to play new American things." As to some piano music of his that she had admired, he was going to submit that too. Not with any hopes, however. "It is too unconventional, I am afraid."

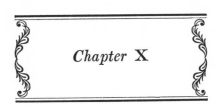

Chapter **X**

GRIFFES spent the brief Christmas vacation as usual at a sister's in New Jersey. He relaxed and went in to New York to occasional concerts. "Kreisler played very beautifully; the war doesn't seem to have affected his technique at all." Then came the perennial anticlimax of returning to school for the new semester. "It is very dull and stupid to be back." But January is a time of beginnings, and he had just been spurred on by the acceptance of five songs. So, despite a handicap of unexpectedly warm and enervating weather, Griffes began 1915 in a splurge of creative activity. On the 15th he started the piano arrangement of *Les Parfums de la Nuit*, from Debussy's *Ibéria*, that he had contemplated a month before. The next night he took advantage of a school dance to remain in his room and work on it, and the day after finished it. On the 20th he played through the *Scherzo*, simplifying it in places, and two days later recopied it when he copied the new *Ibéria* arrangement. On the 24th he began his *Notturno*, which was completed in three days. Before the end of the month had elapsed he brought his *Barcarolle, Scherzo, Notturno*, and *Lake at Evening* into Schirmer's. Kurt Schindler, to whom he played them, pointed out that they could have little popular success. Griffes was writing too subjectively. Moreover Schirmer himself was away then, so in the meantime why not try taking them to Busoni, who was now in America? Griffes thanked him and left with the manuscripts under his arm.

January held other ups and downs as well. He heard from Konrad and his wife at last. He acquired reading glasses on the optometrist's advice. He attended the first of Leo Ornstein's famous winter of 1915 piano recitals at the Bandbox Theater. For Griffes, who, unlike many of his contemporaries, no longer found anything revolutionary or unfamiliar in Debussy, Ravel, and Schönberg, it was not a program of startling novelty. Indeed, his companion at the concert declared that Ornstein played Schönberg too impressionistically compared to the way Griffes played him. Griffes himself thought that Ornstein "took liberties with everything. His own *Wild Men's Dance* was a most terrific acrobatic feat on the piano, as music brutally ugly." Once earlier he had played through Ornstein's *Three Preludes* and *Impressions of Notre Dame*. "There is about a page of each of the last two where I seem to get a ray of meaning." Directly after the concert he ran over Schönberg's Op. 19 for some friends — "strange nothings, very easy to play."

The same month brought an ominous letter from Miss Broughton. "She wants a note for her $1800, which I guess is right. She always said that I needn't worry as the debt would be canceled in case of her death. Probably that was only on account of uncertainties." Now that he had a regular position perhaps things seemed different. "Or is it the war which has changed things? At any rate 5 per cent seems to me too much. The whole thing worries me. I must begin to pay back."

His hunch was correct. "Or is it the war which has changed things?" Elmira knew. Miss Broughton had been at Grenoble when war was declared, and her patriotic concern had mounted in a steadily accelerating crescendo of hysteria ever since. There were those among her associates who honestly feared for her sanity, since her behavior was nearly demented at times. The lonely evening vigils in the chapel playing Chopin's *Marche Funèbre* increased in frequency and length. The particular image of British soldiers in Belgian prisons became an obsession with her as the image of one young Britisher confined in a sanatorium had been for so long. She scarcely permitted herself a lump of sugar or a smile for the duration of the war. She knitted straight through the long nights and cooked in her room to save money on food. Famous about Elmira was her invitation to come up at teatime for "half a roll." She chafed at America's qualms and hesitation and later solidly applauded the decision to fight. When a women's parade to stimulate the sale of Liberty Loans was promoted in Elmira, Miss Broughton participated. Each woman carried one of the Allied flags, and Miss Broughton stumped by hoisting aloft the American flag — a spectacle that straightway convinced many the war would not have been in vain.

All the while that she was abstemiously garnering every penny that she could for the Allies, Miss Broughton had other cares. Discouraged by the advent of the gramophone and the improved pianola, she saw little future in musical pedagogy and gradually changed over to a professorship in modern languages. Even her name underwent a change when, upon discovering the correct spelling of her mother's, she became henceforth Mary Selina Broughton. She brooded a little upon the responsibility of eventually returning a certain inherited sum to the New Zealand relatives through whose kind co-operation it had come to her. And if yet another straw were needed to unhinge the distraught woman it was provided with the death in 1915 of Dr. A. Cameron MacKenzie, president of Elmira College and her friendly benefactor for years. His going was a profound grief to her, and her antipathetic relations with his successor a constant aggravation of the original loss.

Griffes sent Miss Broughton a note for $1800 in March. But by then things were looking up again for him. Schirmer's had accepted six of his piano pieces for publication. True, they had been taken on a mere 5-per-cent royalty basis (to become 10 per cent after seven hundred fifty copies had been sold), but none other than Busoni himself had interceded on his behalf. Early in February, Griffes had written Busoni asking for an interview in which to play his manuscripts. Awaiting the outset, he relearned his *Night Winds*, in which he had made some simplifications, and gave his choir a rest during one of Mr. Gage's temporary absences. Later in the month he saw Busoni's concert manager, Hanson, for whom he had once compiled Galston's program notes, and gave him four manuscripts to show the Italian. They were departing for Boston that day, and the manager promised to show them to Busoni on the train. Two days later Griffes received a letter telling him that the artist had reacted very favorably and had said: " This man has a talent." He was advised to come back to the dressing room after Busoni's recital in New York on March 6th. It was not like Griffes to obtrude upon anyone, and he went to the manager four days before the recital to be reassured. " He says Busoni is really interested in the manuscripts and for me by all means to go back after the concert on Saturday. I don't like that, but it is the only way probably." When the time came, though there were crowds about the performer's door, Griffes was ushered through, " and Busoni was very nice about my coming up. I made an appointment for Thursday. He remembered all about me." On Thursday, March 11th, Griffes went up to see Busoni. " I was there three-quarters of an hour and found both him and Mrs. Busoni very cordial. Strangely enough I felt very much at home with both of them. Mrs. Busoni said at once that she remembered my face, wanted to know where she had met me before. It rather surprised me as I haven't seen her since I was at their house in Berlin in 1906 or '07. Busoni asked me to play my manuscripts. To my own surprise I didn't feel at all nervous but played them fairly well. . . . He asked me what I had done for orchestra and said he would recommend me to Stock in Chicago. Then he sat down and wrote a letter to Schirmer recommending my pieces very highly. Busoni did not look especially attractive; he had on a peculiar and rather soiled collar and no tie. His hands did not look so large to me at close range. I thought Mrs. Busoni seemed much stouter." The high recommendations from Busoni had telling effect, and the piano pieces were promptly accepted.

Soon Griffes was informing Leslie Hodgson that he had decided to retain the latter's ending to *The Lake at Evening* in preference to his own. Hodgson said nothing but examined the manuscript in privacy to discover what the difference might be. There it was. He had always read and played an unresolved sixth in the last two measures. That was not how it was written, but the composer had seen an improvement in his error.

New sparks of hope generated from the numbers of people Griffes was meeting all the time. He acquired guest-memberships in the Century and Harvard Clubs through the kind offices of Julian Garnsey. Hodgson took him up to the offices of *Musical America*, the national weekly, and he met Herbert Peyser, first critic on the staff, who subsequently invited him to concerts by Ernest Hutcheson and Josef Hofmann. In the former Griffes carefully noted " excellent technique and very serious, but dry tone and conception," and in the latter " most stunning brilliancy and verve." Peyser also lent him books and music, the *Pathos of Distance* by Huneker, which he read with interest, and the dances from *Prince Igor*, which he learned by heart. Through Burnet Tuthill he met Louis Koemmenich, a

German-born musician and composer, and Cecil Forsyth, an English composer staying in America. He also became acquainted with the American composer Harvey Worthington Loomis, some of whose Indian pieces he had learned for an Indian musicale that his sister's club was having in New Jersey. "He insisted on my staying to lunch — an extremely frugal one — and I enjoyed his conversation. Afterward I played some of my things which interested him very much. He looks upon his own composition as a thing of the past (what he must have gone through!) but is a keen appreciator of others and especially modern things."

Miss Frisbie encouraged his song composing as always. She liked the Rumanian thing he had been working on, and Wilde's *Le Réveillon,* but thought the words of *Les Ballons* impossible. That song, however, was Griffes's challenge. "I can't give *Les Ballons* up, somehow." Its soaring colors were not lightly put by.

At the same time that he was striving in a professional direction his life at the school must be conducted on schedule. The choir was as hopeless as ever. "The choir sang again. I wish we had a few good voices which would make it more worth while." Mr. Gage continued to expect miracles. "Walter jumped on the choir badly today, says they have no ginger and that I ought to put it into them." Mrs. Hackley's will, after some litigation, was finally decided in favor of the school. Evening table arrangements were monotonously changed, so that Griffes did not ever long remain surrounded by his friends among the student body. The organ went out of order once, and he got through the hymns with a few noises. Mr. Gage finally raised his guarantee to $1500 for the next year. The days became bright and balmy, and he would lie outdoors sketching out themes for his music. Mr. Brady distributed passes to Grace George's latest plays. There were visiting lecturers like

Thomas Mott Osborne, warden of Sing Sing. "One felt the charm of a very genial and kind personality. There were quite a good many of the outsiders up. I was glad to get out of the hymns." Later on in the year Hamlin Garland gave a dull lecture on the Indians.

Griffes struck up a new friendship at the school, with Frank H. Towsley, the science instructor, whose keen mind and trenchant insight into social affairs won Griffes's admiration. Sometimes he would accompany Towsley's botany classes on their field trips. Other times the two would tramp out into the woods together. It was Towsley who persuaded him to read Peck's *Twenty Years of the Republic*, an unlikely independent choice, and they enthusiastically discussed the work. Towsley also owned a rifle and interested him in target practice. Griffes would break a bottle at twenty-five yards or shoot through the center of a tin can or hit a tiny target four times in succession, then exult over his marksmanship. His partner's great aim in life was to demolish one of the many crows that infested neighboring fields. They had to be careful, however, that they were not observed by the Hackley boys, who might carelessly imitate their interest in rifling with disastrous results. Sometimes the two would skip out after dinner to White Plains, where they saw a vaudeville and movie and then a rathskeller cabaret. They went downtown together for war news such as the sinking of the *Lusitania*. " Some prophesy war," Griffes noted on that occasion. On the whole, Towsley's lively intellifence and spirit of good fun made life at the school more bearable.

Mrs. Tomlinson died, and Griffes wrote a word of consolation to his mother.

He read a good deal of Gautier this year, particularly *L'Espagne*, of which he was very fond. Baudelaire and Flaubert, as always, impressed him deeply. Of the latter's *Hérodias* he wrote: "I had the feeling that one ought to read it several times to get hold of all the wonderful things Flaubert has crammed into this short tale." He also read de Maupassant's *Une Vie*, Huysmans's *La Cathédrale*, and much in Dostoevsky. As his music took up more and more of his free time, however, there was less time for reading.

His *Ibéria* arrangement came to nothing, for the French publishers controlled the copyright, and it could not be brought out in the United States. He was kept busy through May correcting the proofs of his songs and marking the fingering and pedaling on his six piano pieces. On May 20th the first three pieces, to be published as *Three Tone-Pictures*, Op. 5, were marked and ready. Griffes went in to New York to look up suitable poems for them at the library. Then they were delivered to Schirmer's. Six days later he and Hodgson spent an hour at the library looking up a poem for the *Barcarolle* — which was dedicated to Galston — of the other three *Fantasy Pieces*, Op. 6. They "finally found a combination from Fiona Macleod. The *Notturno* has verses from Paul Verlaine and the *Scherzo* a couple of prose sentences of my own. After that I took the mss. over to Schirmer's to their editor." The prose sentences Griffes wrote for the *Scherzo* were: "From the Palace of Enchantment there issued into the night sounds of unearthly revelry. Troops of genii and other fantastic spirits danced grotesquely to a music now weird and mysterious, now wild and joyous."

It is worth while re-emphasizing this procedure, for critics have sometimes made much of Griffes's reliance on poetic texts in his piano works. Although he occasionally had a text in mind while composing a piece, he most often simply designated the composition by its key till completion. Then he would seek an appropriate bit of verse with which to introduce it. This was true also of his titles. It was not till June 7th that he could think of a title for No. 2 of the *Tone-Pictures* — *The Vale of Dreams* — which title he sent on to his waiting publishers.

The White Peacock, which he began on May 30th after baccalaureate services, was one of the pieces that worked the other way. The theme had formed itself, he later told a friend, when he was idly watching a sunset on the train between Tarrytown and New York. But it must have early associated itself with the peacock image, for he kept Fiona Macleod's poem, *The White Peacock*, on his piano all the while he composed on that theme. Since his first glimpse of the bird in Germany Griffes seems to have been stirred by some symbolic dimension in it: ". . . as the breath, as the soul of this beauty, / Moves the White Peacock." He clipped pictures of white peacocks from wherever discovered, and there is one large awkward photograph that he may have taken himself. By June 8th he had practically finished up the piece, and on June 16th started copying it out, a task that he completed next day. At first he considered including it with the *Tone-Pictures*, then later decided to hold it for a collection of Macleod compositions.

"Fiona Macleod" was the pseudonym under which William Sharp, the mystical Scoto-Celtic writer, gave voice to the "half a woman" that he sensed in himself, and under which he successfully perpetrated the hoax of a dual literary personality till his death in 1905. He was not a new influence in American music. Edward MacDowell had written to "My dear Madam" in 1902 that "your words have been a most powerful incentive to me in my music," and three years later Lawrence Gilman, American music critic, wrote "Miss Macleod": "You would be surprised, I think, to know how the Celtic impulse is seizing the imaginations of some of the younger and more warmly tempered of American composers." For Griffes, Sharp was an inevitable affinity. It was not only that the poet's duality in some ways paralleled his own, and that the mystic temperament always awakened a strong answering response in Griffes,

Photography by Griffes

but "Fiona Macleod's" dictum "To live in beauty — which is to put into four words all the dream and spiritual effort of the soul of man" summed up the very credo by which, after his own fashion, he tried to live.

Griffes resolved to spend the summer in New York practicing and working on his music. He was inquiring about studios and rooms, even deliberating quarters in the Metropolitan Studios, when a better offer came. William Earl Brown, a singing teacher with whom he had become acquainted, offered to rent half of his apartment at 12 West 46th Street for $35. It had a large Steinway grand. Griffes accepted and moved in the last week in June. Brown had studied with the celebrated Italian singing master, Giovanni Battista Lamperti, at one time acting as his assistant. In America he was now expounding the vocal philosophy of his revered teacher to his own circle of pupils. It was by no means solely confined to the narrow athletics of voice control that such teaching usually connotes. "Broaden your knowledge of literature, painting, etc. — the 'beaux arts.' This increases your 'desire' for beauty, from which springs the instinct to sing," wrote Brown many years later in a book on Lamperti. And: "Failure to sing well comes from four sources: loose breathing, mouthing words, spreading voice, and disjointed muscular effort." He was able to offer Griffes many pointers on the vocal line in song composition. By discussing in detail such questions as breath control, vibration, and resonance, he conveyed something of the singer's point of view towards a song. Griffes's own view was inclined to disdain for the priggish misgivings of performers who attempted his songs. Singers must learn too.

Brown nevertheless keenly appreciated Griffes's music, complimenting him that he never repeated himself, and the summer passed very pleasantly. Griffes in a lighthearted mood went to see the *Follies of 1915*. He and Brown would wander about Bleecker Street, or visit Coney Island, where they admired the beautiful dancing of a Tunisian girl. He practiced diligently, not only his own compositions and recent enthusiasms like the Ravel *Sonatine*, but old chestnuts from Liszt as well. He learned the Chopin *Sonata in B-flat minor* and Franck's *Prélude, Chorale, et Fugue* by heart. There was a series of Russian symphony concerts at Madison Square, and he was usually invited to these by the Garnseys or others. He read Cable's *Creole Days*, George Moore, and Loti.

The summer in New York also saw an unexpected stabilization in his emotional life through his friendship with the policeman Dan C. Martin. Hitherto every hope of a satisfactory and continuing association he had been forced to recognize in the end as chimerical and deluded. It was therefore with the old sensation of impermanence that he embarked on his friendship with Dan C. Martin, a mutual fondness that was to last and to become the major affection of his life. In the little book of addresses and pharmaceutical remedies (significant conjunction) that he always carried with him he entered: "*J'ai connu Dan C. M. le 28 avril 1915*," marking an important date and one that he and Dan celebrated faithfully each year thereafter. Yet though he had first met Dan in April of 1915 it was not till the summer of that year that their contact developed into any intimacy. It was not unlike his acquaintanceship with numerous other policemen, conductors, and men in uniform. Then Griffes became aware of a qualitative difference about this affair. After one appointment he dazedly reflected: "The whole evening was a very happy one. I should like to remember everything we said. We have started calling each other by our first names already. All these little things come so naturally and unforcedly to us that I am sometimes astonished at the feeling he has for it. Can this really be a policeman and have we only known each other so short a time? I should have believed it almost impossible. . . . I'd like to have this evening over again." Sometimes he had his old doubts about the affair. "I am certainly a fool, but I can't pull myself away from him." As often, however, he subconsciously elevated that which he esteemed to his own level of taste and intelligence. Watching a fireman's parade in Tarrytown a few years back he had gasped: "How can those men be such idiots?" Now under Dan's spell he attended police carnivals and parades as occasions of dignified and splendid interest. For the rest of his life he would stoutly maintain that Dan was a very superior person. The man was, in fact, a burly policeman with a slightly better educational background than most and more definite aspirations towards advancement and a comfortable life. He studied law in his spare time. He was married, about seven years older than Griffes, and the father of two children. Whether he was flattered by the young composer's attentions or genuinely reciprocated the emotion, or, as is most probable, a combination of the two, is uncertain. Yet there is no doubt of his naïve sincerity and lasting devotion throughout the years of their life together. When he told Griffes that he had been thinking of him all day, or that he loved him more than any brother, or that he missed him all week, these trifles went straight to the heart and came as some compensation for the loneliness he endured. This differs, however, from Griffes's own blind estimate of the matter. For he respected the man beyond all objective justification of his merits. After Dan had told various incidents of his Broadway days Griffes came to the rapid conclusion: "He is one of the best and truest men I know." When he later introduced Dan to certain of his musical friends, he so expatiated on the policeman's sterling qualities that they felt their eyes to have deceived them.

In one respect, indeed, Dan was competent to advise the younger man. Having had some legal training and deeming

Griffes's recent 5-per-cent royalty on his piano pieces too meager, he determined to keep an eye on the composer's future business dealings. In this he was to have his good influence, through Griffes's admiration for his financial acumen.

The summer of 1915, with Griffes's presence in New York, clinched the new friendship. "It is wonderful that we can now be together so often. He too seems to be very happy that I am so close to him, spoke of it specially." They saw each other every day, and after Brown had departed for Maine on August 2nd, leaving Griffes the entire apartment, he was able to invite Dan up for suppers in the evening. Their little feasts of sausage, pumpernickel, Limburger, and beer were the highlight of the summer. Griffes in turn was sometimes invited to Dan's house, where the proud homeowner displayed every compartment from attic to cellar and introduced him to his wife and daughters. For one of the latter Griffes conceived a special fondness, visiting her at the hospital where she was ill some time later, with a gift of his music.

There were no visits to Bob or any other of the Hackley boys that summer. He could not afford it. Besides the cost of staying in New York, the year's expenses had been comparatively high. His music was not yet out, and there were no revenues from that source. The process of music publication was a slow one. In early August he was still correcting second proofs and sketching possible cover designs for his piano pieces. Two weeks later he was viewing the cover proofs and bewailing the fact that they were nothing like his suggestions.

Miss Broughton, in New York on a summer visit, gave unexpected encouragement. "She liked the *Barcarolle* very much —rather to my surprise." Where her favorite pupil was concerned Miss Broughton was gladly willing to set aside her nineteenth-century musical predispositions.

But however satisfactory his artistic progress, where was he getting professionally? He must make himself heard. And the months following upon his return to Hackley in the fall were crammed with activity to that end. Every free day that could be extricated from his school week he scampered into New York with manuscripts, trying to enlist the sympathies of any singer, pianist, conductor, or other performer who would give him time. It was at once a wearying and a futile round. Whoever had advice or promises he gratefully thanked. There was no concrete assistance forthcoming, however. A prospective recital at Stamford, for example, was called off.

Miss Marie Kieckhoefer, a musical agent, wanted to boost his pieces. "Her idea is for me to give a recital of them at the Princess Theater ($100) or at a smaller hall ($50) and get an audience of pianists and musicians to hear them. I am not sure about it all yet." It came to nothing because of the cost. He attended dinners and teas without number where wealthy and influential people heard him perform, expressed their admiration, and nothing further developed. Another friend suggested that he play his things to several big managers. An introduction to Maud Allan was promised by someone else. Miss Kieckhoefer thought that the best strategy might be to have his things danced out and played on as many occasions as possible. She wrote him introductions to various musicians and composers, including Leo Ornstein, whom he visited twice. The result was some interesting discussions on music. "He says any two notes have a connection, if you think of the notes in between. He agreed with me that the Chopin A-flat *Polonaise* is an unsatisfactory concert piece as a rule. I have never heard it yet when I liked it."

A typical day was October 7th, which ran something as follows. He took the 8:32 train to New York, then went up to see the pianist Alexander Lambert. "He told me at once that he did not understand or like modern music. I played him some of

mine, and he admitted that they were well made and far above
the *niveau* of some other Americans he mentioned. Ornstein
he had refused to meet. He called my *Lake* charming. He also
said: 'Do you know, you are an excellent pianist. You have a
very beautiful touch. Where did you study?'" Griffes then
called on Paolo Martucci, "who said he played little modern
music and then only of his father." Next, after lunch, he played
several new compositions for one of Schirmer's consultants.
Then over to two friends, who had shown an interest in his
work, and he played for them. After dinner, to a musician's
studio, where he played for an audience of ten people. "Took
the 12:35 train back and had to walk up the hill in the pouring
rain. It wasn't worth while."

It may not have been worth while, but it was grim necessity
if he was to make himself known as a composer. Occasionally
there were more hopeful portents. He called on the pianist
Charles Cooper and "found him unsympathetic toward 'impressions' and vague music, including all modern French, on
the other hand very interested in Schönberg, whom he admires
for simplicity of *Klaviersatz* and getting away from rhythm.
He is well worth knowing. He said he would like to learn the
Lake." In early December he called on Miss Winifred Christie
with *The White Peacock*, which she thought she might use on
a future program. Miss Christine Miller, contralto, was singing
one of his songs all through the West. His usual fare, however,
consisted of projects that did not turn out and of playing to
musicians who did not understand or who refused to commit
themselves.

He proceeded with his composing. There was not much of
interest in the work of his fellow Americans. With Farwell's
music he had never had any natural sympathy; still less now.
The MacDowellians with their Peterboro sketchbooks were
too unoriginal to his taste: ". . . All too much MacDowell to

suit me." There were occasional moments that autumn, as when the Kneisel Quartet played Ravel's *Quartet.* "It excited me and stirred me greatly." So did Moussorgsky. His reaction to Loeffler's *Mort de Tintagiles* was revelatory of a phase in his own evolving aesthetic: ". . . much too long, I think, in spite of much beautiful work in it. I can't listen to a Beethoven symphony through any more without getting bored." Brevity had become one of the canons of his art.

Conditions were more conducive to work at the school. Though he retained living quarters in the dormitory, his studio had been moved to a basement suite beneath the chapel. The resultant privacy from general earshot, and freedom in which to entertain his friends, proved a real boon. Before long he brought over " S. B.'s " old library desk from Elmira and in his usual orderly fashion fitted out an attractive and tidy studio. It became the students' delight to repair there on Sunday nights for the weekly impromptu recitals.

In his new sequestered abode he sketched out piano compositions, vocal settings to more Macleod and Wilde (whose *Impression du Matin,* begun the day before, he completed on November 5th), and several string quartet movements. These last he took to Burnet Tuthill for criticism and suggestions. Another project occupied him at this time. Griffes had interested Georges Barrère, the eminent French flutist, in his music, and the latter had suggested that he arrange some of his pieces for the Barrère Ensemble of wind instruments. Griffes seized the opportunity. On the 10th of November he spent the whole morning on an arrangement of *The Lake at Evening.* Two weeks later he called on Barrère, who agreed to use the *Lake* and asked for arrangements of the other *Tone-Pictures* as well. A new consideration turned up at the beginning of December, after Griffes had visited the composer Daniel Gregory Mason on one of the regular jaunts to interest people in his music.

"He doesn't care for impressionistic or colored music; melodic line alone interests him, so he was not very enthusiastic. He liked the *Tone-Pictures* and of those the *Lake* best. He suggested a harp for the Barrère arrangements." The idea seemed a good one. Four days later Griffes wrote Barrère about a harp part in the *Tone-Pictures* and was notified that he might use one if he wished. He decided to make two arrangements, one without harp for use on tours. He asked some advice of Burnet Tuthill about the clarinets in the Ensemble, which consisted of nine wind instruments — one flute, two oboes, two clarinets, two horns, and two bassoons. On December 13th Griffes began his arrangement of *The Vale of Dreams*, completing it the next day and beginning his arrangement of *The Night Winds*. The day after that he finished *The Night Winds* and added a harp part to the *Lake*. December 30th he worked copying out the *Tone-Pictures*, and on the last day of the year delivered the *Lake* to Barrère.

People were at last beginning to hear about him. In May, Leslie Hodgson had introduced him to A. Walter Kramer, who reviewed for *Musical America*, and they all had lunch together. Early in November, Kramer came to Brown's studio, "and I played him all my things. He is going to review them for *Musical America*. He is very enthusiastic about them. He stayed almost two hours." A week later Hodgson instructed him to send his picture to *Musical America*, and on December 4th the review appeared, a long article on Griffes and his work entitled "A New Note in Our Piano Music."

After a lofty proem on the state of American and international piano composition in general, the essay began by welcoming a newcomer into the ranks of American composers for the piano. It would have been laughable had it not been tragic after the weary rounds of attention-seeking when Kramer pointed out that the composer "has hidden himself carefully from the light of publicity." In a more factual vein he explained that Leslie Hodgson had believed in this man's talent, playing his music at recitals for the last few years, ". . . and his belief was corroborated when no less an authority than Ferruccio Busoni waxed enthusiastic over Mr. Griffes's compositions. Mr. Busoni saw their merit and aided the composer in bringing them to the attention of one of this country's large music publishers, with the result that they are now to be had through the house of G. Schirmer, New York." The review contained glowing praise of Griffes. " First let me warn those persons for whom music ended with Beethoven that this composer is a modern — a full-fledged one! He has no desire to write fluent, pretty pieces; he is interested in vital modern music. And I know few native creative musicians who can compare with him for proficiency in doing so." The pieces were enthusiastically described: " *The Lake at Evening*, with its reiterated rhythmic figure, the effect of which is gripping in spite of the repressed character of the composition; his *Vale of Dreams*, with its swaying thirds, component parts of a very engaging secondary harmonic scheme . . ." "Mr. Griffes need never fear being charged with writing a barcarolle that sounds like somebody's else essay in this form. His is the only one I know that is not related by blood to some other composer's! . . . It is one of the most inspiring pieces I know. The climax lifts one up, while the careful development of the theme, its subtle harmonization, its treatment in canon and a host of other ways makes one confident that its composer knows well what he is about." There was also a generous sampling of the amateur anthropology that was a by-line in the musical criticism of the period. "Percy Grainger finds this music very American. There is considerable discussion as to what is American in music and what is not. I am sure I do not know. But there is a quality in this *Barcarolle* — I should like to call it 'punch' —

that suggests the live character of our country, and it must be that that has made Mr. Grainger find it typical of this land, which he has studied carefully in the time he has been here." The article concluded that the pieces "are a notable addition to our piano literature, for in them Mr. Griffes has combined the gift of having something to say with the ability to write it splendidly for the piano."

Griffes welcomed this long-delayed public reaction to his work. All the more since, as he wrote Babe Shoobert, it "is *not paid* but a 'spontaneous outburst' of the N. Y. critic who wrote it." That the venality of the musical press was by now thoroughly familiar to him is indicated by his italics.

The five songs had been published as *Tone-Images*, Op. 3, and *Two Rondels*, Op. 4, and an equally favorable review by Kramer appeared one week later. "Mr. Griffes has a melody, a peculiarly subtle one, and he works it out very clearly for the person who is willing to examine it in relation to the entire harmonic plan."

Still other forces were at work on his behalf. For during this period a remarkable woman whom he had met in New York during the summer assumed her rightful importance in his life and took part control of the situation.

Chapter XI

MRS. LAURA MOORE ELLIOT was one of those women who are unfairly remembered by history for the celebrities with whom they were associated rather than for themselves. All her life she was to be connected with great names — in music, literature, the theater, and social action — many belonging to persons of much less stature than Laura Elliot. Ohio born, she had begun the study of piano and voice at an early age, pursuing it at home and in Germany and France, with teachers like James Gibbons Huneker, Rubin Goldmark, and Jean de Reszke. Finally, abandoning her ambition to become a singer, and having cultivated an intense and original interest in the physiology of the human voice, she devoted herself to training others, and before long undertook clinical work on vocal cords at the Metropolitan Opera, where she benefited such famous artists as Melba. With her own method of training voices for the concert hall and theater, she also embarked on a private career as voice consultant — to the advantage of a group of pupils that eventually came to include such actresses as Katharine Cornell and Bette Davis.

A bitter experience with marriage had elapsed as no more than an interlude in an idealistic and activity-crowded existence. For Mrs. Elliot was interested in the new social equality movements, in current labor problems, and in socialism. It was nothing unusual for her to have to hustle in quick change from a fluffy chiffon necessitated by her theatrical work into a drab muslin more suitable for haranguing a mob of angry strikers. She was active in the Women's Trade Union League and participated aggressively in the woman-suffrage movement. She brought her knowledge of the theater to her social interests when she volunteered as director of music to the Labor Forum of the Labor Center Association, then under the direction of the novelist Ernest Poole. She was also head of the Voice Department at the Music School Settlement at 55 East 3rd Street.

Mrs. Elliot first became associated with the Henry Street Settlement as director of chorus for the festival and pageant that commemorated the twentieth anniversary of the Settlement in 1910. When the Neighborhood Playhouse, under the philanthropic and aesthetic auspices of Alice and Irene Lewisohn, was opened at Grand Street some five years later in conjunction with the Henry Street Settlement, Mrs. Elliot directed the choruses of its first presentation. The Playhouse was intended as a medium for insurgent dramatic activity, which included dance, music, pantomime, and the realization of all fresh talent. It was as much a concert hall for the new music as a theater for the new schools of Russian dramatic theory, "festivals" being the term applied by the Lewisohns to the experiments they tried in the combination of these forms. On their jaunts to Europe they continually replenished it with new ideas. To Mrs. Elliot the Neighborhood Playhouse became a natural object of interest.

Mrs. Elliot first met Griffes in the summer of 1915, when in her apartment at 12 West 46th Street she had listened to the strange practicing of the new tenant and, reached by some personal quality in his music, had asked her neighbor, William

Earl Brown, about the newcomer's identity. An introduction to Griffes followed.

Their friendship — rapidly developing through the fall and winter — became a great and beautiful thing in Griffes's life. Mrs. Elliot believed in his musical genius and dedicated herself to the task of freeing it from care and making it known. She insisted that her friend take occasional "loaf days" for the sake of his health. She listened appreciatively to his things and from time to time offered helpful suggestions, as when Griffes, composing a song to Fiona Macleod's *Dim Face of Beauty* and starting felicitously with a melodic idea suggested by the words, presently stumbled and tripped over difficulties whose cause, eluding successive modification, remained maddeningly obscure, so that the effort hobbled along with travail and ill success. Mrs. Elliot pointed out that the real trouble lay in the words, which were not suited to musical setting, and Griffes, usually alert in sizing up the song potentialities of a poem, finally agreed and attempted a piano piece on his original idea rather than burke so fundamental a criticism. He often brought her small bouquets of azalea that he had gathered in the woods. Sometimes, repressing his natural skepticism, he even escorted her to Christian Science meetings, where she, an ardent Scientist, sought to convert him.

Mrs. Elliot soon launched into practical activity on his behalf. "She had talked with Farwell about me and had lots to say. She thinks I must get into pageantry or some bigger thing. Farwell said there was no chance any more in the concert field. He told Mrs. E. that he had never before met anyone so sure of what he wanted and so successful in getting it as I, also that my stuff was filled with originality and virility."

She introduced him among her friends — Helen Marot, Mary Dreier, Rose Pastor Stokes, Rose Schneiderman, Ida Rauh, and others interested in social problems. His first meeting with

Arturo Giovannitti, the syndicalist poet, was memorable. "Giovannitti was in the Lawrence strikes a couple of years ago and is a leader of the I.W.W.'s. He writes poetry and plays now. Evidently very brilliant mind. He said that music had lost its thrills for him, and then I played the *Scherzo* and *The White Peacock*. He was very much excited and said he found something entirely new here. He knows Debussy well and said I was to him greater than Debussy, that there were ideas enough for several pieces in the *Peacock*, and that he had never yet heard such freedom from fixed tonality. In short, he was very much stirred and expressed himself volubly."

The stimulation provided by Mrs. Elliot's class-conscious friends caused Griffes to inquire more deeply into his social views. He had inherited a number of ludicrous "class" ideas in his legacy from Miss Broughton and had glibly echoed her talk of the "better classes" and the "lower classes" all during his youth, while his own habit of fraternizing with whomever he admired belied his words. It had not taken long at Hackley, however, for such empty prejudice to be knocked away by an awareness of the reality back of his aristocratic rodomontades. For it became transparently clear that if there were an alignment of "better classes" and "lower classes," he was irrevocably assigned to a place among the latter, whether he wished or not. However much he might confuse the issue by mental distinctions, the schism in his America was one of money alone. He had begun to read in social subjects at Towsley's suggestion the year before, and he now began a more purposeful study. He joined with his new friends in their discussions of socialism and labor action, made trips to the offices of the *Masses*, attended political meetings and parades, and startled a few of his conservative friends by distributing pamphlets on birth control among them. For Mrs. Elliot he also harmonized labor songs and accompanied at the piano during strikers' rallies, im-

Photography by Griffes

provising huge, militant, cannon-like figures in the bass. When the garment workers struck in 1916 it was to original music by Charles T. Griffes, who had joined them direct from union headquarters for a " Meeting at two o'clock down in Manhattan Hall on East Grant Street. Several hundred men packed in a hot noisy room. Mrs. E. managed them and got them to singing. . . ." The next day he was with them again at Webster Hall.

Once Griffes perceived that the socialism towards which his friends were striving was also an embodiment of certain values and ideals in which he believed, and that it was an intended corrective for the needless human suffering to which he too had always been sensitive, he could not help recognizing a partial community of aim. He was with them. Yet the Elmira acquaintance whom he encountered during this period and to whom he chatted of the need for social reform and the possibilities of a better world order was wrong when she returned to Elmira with tales of the wild-eyed radical their composer had become. In the first place, Griffes was simply not a political animal; he had little aptitude for systems of thought; and his response was sympathetic and co-operative rather than intellectual. He himself intimated as much in a letter to Babe Shoobert, on January 10th, 1916, at the beginning of his socialist activities. " I have been around with some people interesting politically lately — imagine me who am so utterly 'unpolitical.' But these are I.W.W.'s and such things." In the next place he could not agree with the more utopian of his cohorts that social revolution might ever achieve something more than a good social order. Fundamental human problems would remain. His labor song, projecting an ideal world commonwealth, was to contain the reservation: " Tho' pain and passion may not die." In their frequent lunches at the Peg Woffington, when Mrs. Elliot and he thrashed out the social problems of the day, Griffes often expressed agreement with ends — woman suffrage, economic security, and so forth — but could never be brought to a theoretical interest in means. That was outside his sphere.

Through Mrs. Elliot, Griffes soon became acquainted with Alice and Irene Lewisohn and was invited to gatherings at their home, where he met a number of congenial musicians, like Henry Gideon, who discoursed on Hebrew music, and Sacha Votitchenko, a Russian artist who owned and played the "tympanon," a curious small music box, prototype of the clavecin from the court of Louis XIV. Tolstoy was supposed to have heard the tympanon a few months before his death and to have compared it to the far-away echo of the voices of the Old Bards. Votitchenko became one of Griffes's most lavish admirers. "I played him my *Scherzo*, which impressed him. '*Magnifique*,' '*Génie*,' and the like, were his words."

The Lewisohns also invited him to the Neighborhood Playhouse and presently made room for him in their schedule. They were planning an original production of Stravinsky's *Petrouchka* — which had not as yet been presented in America — the score to be carried in a two-piano arrangement. Towards the end of December 1915, Griffes had called for the score at their home and then gone on to tea at Percy Grainger's, where he and Grainger played parts of it together. Griffes found it delightful and at once began practicing, despite the handicap of a slight ear infection that had already interfered with his appreciation of *Prince Igor* in its American première. "As an opera it is far below *Boris*. The ballet is the most interesting part. I didn't hear very well, which made me nervous." During the first week and a half of January 1916, while his ear was still infected, he copied more on the wind arrangement of *The Vale of Dreams* but did little else. Miss Broughton wrote about George Clifford Vieh, professor of music at Smith College, who had played some of Griffes's things at Elmira on the 11th and who was to play them again three days later at Cornell in Ithaca. Noble Kreider was in New York, and Griffes visited him briefly. He also read *Madame Bovary*, "which is wonderful," and Baudelaire. Then on the 16th, after his ear was in shape, he made some revisions in the four Wilde songs and started copying, and the next day revised the wind arrangement of *The Night Winds*.

He and Mrs. Elliot and Giovannitti followed the Diaghilev Ballet, alternately disappointed and enraptured. They saw *L'Après-midi d'un Faune* before the police censored Massine's closing movements, and *L'Oiseau de Feu*, which Griffes found "most gorgeous and wonderful music." On the 25th he started a setting of a Rumanian *Song of the Dagger*, using partly his older setting of the same poem. The next day, with a friend who sang, he performed his four Wilde songs for Gustave White at Schirmer's. "The latter was enthusiastic and said he knew the house would publish them." (They were returned in early March.) On the 27th he almost finished up the *Song of the Dagger*.

During the first half of February he tried to interest the dancers Maud Allan and Albertina Rasch in his music. To Miss Caroline Robinson, the daughter of his hosts at Intervale, who had written to him about his music, Griffes answered: "I am glad you are not afraid to play new things anyway. So many people think a piece must have the stamp of many years' approval to make it worth playing." He attended a special labor performance of *The Weavers* at which Helen Marot spoke, and conferred with the Lewisohns about handling the music for *Petrouchka*. "I think they will pay my price." They did. Miss Lily Hyland of the Neighborhood staff was to assist at the other piano. On the 23rd Winifred Christie gave *The White Peacock* its first public performance in a recital at the Punch and Judy Theater. "She played mostly modern things.

The *Peacock* lacked color. Mrs. E. said she played according to melodic phrases rather than harmonically, which is quite true." At Miss Christie's recital he renewed acquaintance with an old friend, Marion Logan — now Marion Clark, wife of a successful lawyer — who had come especially to hear his piece. Griffes often dined at the Clarks' thereafter.

He attended a party at the Lewisohns' and met Marie Tempest, the actress. "Sacha Votitchenko played his tympanon. It sounded better with celesta than with piano, and his best number was an old French minuet. I had to leave at 11:15 as the others were beginning to enjoy themselves."

There were practice hours with Miss Hyland and rehearsals at the Playhouse during the remainder of February and the early part of March. Even so he got the school choir into shape, and Mr. Gage complimented him on it three times. He made copies of his music and sent out the usual letters and made the usual trips in hope of attracting performance. Leslie Hodgson played something of his on the 3rd. On March 5th Griffes sketched out two songs to poems by William Blake and — after the dress rehearsals of *Petrouchka* during the next few days — copied out one of them, *In a Myrtle Shade*, for Mrs. Elliot on the 10th. On the 10th also he sketched out music for a poem by Giovannitti, whose poetry he had been reading the day before. On March 11th at 8.30 in the evening *Petrouchka* opened at the Neighborhood Playhouse. All went smoothly. The following day Griffes finished up *Phantoms*, his Giovannitti song, and took the train for New York, where " the performance went musically much better than Saturday night. . . . Everybody is extremely enthusiastic about the music and thinks we have reproduced a whole orchestra on the piano." During the ballet's run many New York notables, like David Belasco, showed up in the audience.

With his incessant commutation between Hackley and New

York, and now with the regular week-end performances at the Playhouse, it was no wonder that Griffes should have felt by the middle of the month: "I have seldom been so absolutely tired of school." Two days later he was nearly tardy to *Petrouchka*.

He visited Ernest Hutcheson, after having tried in vain earlier for an appointment, and this time found him more pleasant than at their interview years before. "Stayed an hour, playing my things to him and discussing modern music. He thought the *Peacock* showed the surest touch. He called my attention to the fact that *The Vale of Dreams* didn't have a single concord until the last note." Almost the whole spring vacation was thus spent in playing his things to people. This continued well into April. He met Ananda Coomaraswamy and Ratan Devi, who gave recitals of classic folk songs of India. "Dr. Coomaraswamy, her husband, told about the music first. She interpreted and sang the weird music remarkably and accompanied herself on a strange long-necked instrument. It had four strings loosely strung, with overlapping overtones, and no frets. . . ." He and Mrs. Elliot saw Charlie Chaplin's burlesque of *Carmen*, "the best thing I ever saw him do," which from a devout Chaplin fan was high praise indeed. Even Nijinsky, whom they watched immediately afterward, did not score so brilliantly. "I like Massine just as well."

On April 12th Tom Dobson, a self-accompanying singer with whom Griffes had placed his music, performed *A Symphony in Yellow* at the Punch and Judy. Two days later Griffes heard from Irene Lewisohn, who enclosed a check for $150 covering the first eight performances of *Petrouchka*. The school dramatic club presented its annual offering — "Rather long and tiresome" — and he also went to the circus with Hodgson — "It was rather poor." On April 23rd he composed music to Rupert Brooke's *Wai Kiki*, from the collected edition of

Brooke's poetry that Babe Shoobert had sent him at Christmas with a note saying: "Put more music 'around' those words." Griffes had studied the long front-page article giving Henry James's views on Brooke in the literary supplement of the *New York Times*, then torn it out and kept it with the poems. "I don't read much poetry," he wrote Babe, "but I do like work of this sort." The resulting inspiration, a song possibly closer, in its psychological intricacy, to Henry James than to Rupert Brooke, is one of the most baffling productions in the whole modern literature of song. Mr. Upton, who finds it "in some respects the most remarkable of all his songs" and who calls two passages "scarcely surpassed in all his writing," comments as follows: "When we like a song, we like it; when we dislike a song, we at least know where we stand with regard to it; but when we are frankly unable to determine whether we like a song or not, then there is unrest of spirit and continual irritation of mind! And so it is with *Wai Kiki*. One may well admire the clever suggestion of the native Hawaiian music and the skill with which the piano idiom is maintained throughout the piano part (here is no reduction of any orchestral score), and yet scarcely fail to be conscious of its exceedingly unvocal melodic line, and of the uncouth character of much of its harmonization, so that the song almost instinctively repels. Still, all this may well be a part of the composer's plan in expressing the psychology of the text."

On April 24th he sketched out a setting to Richard Middleton's *Nocturne*, and the following day revised *Phantoms*, his Giovannitti song. Two days later George Clifford Vieh played some of his things in Elmira again. At Schirmer's Griffes was informed that they had already received many calls for the unpublished *White Peacock*.

In early May he was busy corresponding with Yvette Guilbert and Rudolph Ganz about his music. His eyes were occasionally inflamed, so that he practiced with eyes closed. He wrote to Arthur Shepherd, a Boston musician and composer, who acknowledged the receipt of his compositions and told of his own work. On May 13th he called on Ganz "and had a splendid time. Played him all my stuff. He thought I was between Scriabin and the later Ravel and said some very flattering things." Then he proceeded to the Knickerbocker to see Yvette Guilbert. "Played my stuff to her and her husband, Dr. Schiller. He proposed a scheme of American concerts for next year. Something may come of it. Yvette is going to send me a poem to set to music for her. I found her winding threads on spools when I arrived." Nothing did come of it. He learned, however, that Julia Culp, a Flemish mezzo-soprano, had taken his songs to Holland with her.

He wrote to Ernest Schelling, George Copeland, and Ossip Gabrilowitsch and sent them his pieces. On May 24th he started a piano composition to Sharp's *Clouds* and, after two more days' work on it, finished it on the 26th, commenting: "It is very highly colored." The following day, the 27th, he "had some extra time alone at Mrs. Elliot's place and started another Sharp piece to the *Fountains*." Like the *Peacock*, both *Clouds* and *The Fountain of the Acqua Paola* were built up around poems by Sharp rather than independently evolved and later prefaced by quotation. On the other hand, *Nightfall*, another recent Sharp composition, had already developed a considerable way before acquiring its verses. He completed the *Fountain* on June 6th, by which time he had also finished copying out *Clouds*, *Wai Kiki*, and *De Profundis*, a piano composition that he had begun in November of the year before, and that he jocularly referred to as his tribute to Wagner.

Two weeks later the Lewisohns, increasingly receptive to his talent, called Griffes in to discuss their next year's plans with him. "They are thinking of a fine old druid legend for which

I may do the music. . . ." The legend was to be adapted from one of Édouard Schuré's *Les Grandes Légendes de France*,[1] and Griffes was to compose an exact musical counterpart to the ballet that they proposed, each gesture and attitude in their choreography finding its complementary moment in Griffes's score, and the whole comprising an effective amalgam of music and pantomime. After they had drawn up a carefully clocked libretto of the movement he was to compose to measure. By July he had set to work.

Musical America for July 1st carried an interview with Rudolph Ganz that mentioned him. "I was looking over some compositions the other day which a young composer, Charles Griffes by name, had brought me. I found them both interesting and beautiful. He goes his own way, though in style and workmanship his pieces are somewhat along the lines of Schönberg and Ravel. I showed them to Paderewski, who was much pleased with them." In early July, Griffes also followed with interest the bus strikes taking place in New York and donated his services at two strikers' benefits held at the Neighborhood Playhouse. Mrs. Elliot soon left for Glen Cove, and Griffes moved into her apartment, where it was agreed he should henceforth make his summer headquarters in her absence. Here at " 12 West 46, second floor front," as Griffes abbreviated it, he could practice and compose in solitude, close to his musical activities, and here he and Dan might share one another's companionship for longer than the brief, hurried interims they managed during the rest of the year.

On July 13th he finished a clarinet piece and played it several times with Burnet Tuthill the same evening. "He said it was very successful from the clarinet standpoint, which is encouraging." The next day he started a clarinet and piano *Prelude*. On the 16th he worked out some ideas for a third

[1] See Appendix I.

clarinet piece, and the day after finished up the *Prelude,* adding a few touches on the 20th, when he played it with Tuthill in the evening.

He had a long session with the Lewisohns about the pantomime, and again on the 25th: "The Lewisohns up this P.M. for a conference. They thought what I had done was too open and transparent and gave me then carte blanche to be modern and anything else I chose. So I shall cast these beginnings aside." On the same day he left to visit students in New England for a rest, and after a stopover in Boston — "It was a tedious day, and I detested Boston" — returned to New York refreshed at the beginning of August. On the 3rd he worked a good deal on the legend up to the "invocation." The next day he played what he had done to Mrs. Elliot, who dropped by, and when she found it too short Griffes agreed.

An American disaster of the period is strangely memorialized in the legend music, for after this talk Griffes proceeded to lunch "and then went over to the Rialto where they had three or four minutes of the weirdest stuff I ever experienced. The pictures were of the munitions pier explosions, and the director had arranged as accompaniment a combination of full orchestra, organ, whistles, etc., which was so strangely thrilling that it made my hair stand on end. I had to hold on to the seat in front of me. It gave me some ideas for the close of the priestesses' dance, which I came home and worked out." There was another sensation that month, noteworthy to a person of such eager sensibility, when Griffes was able to record: "I tasted alligator pears for the first time in my life." On August 11th Griffes answered Irene Lewisohn, who had written to confirm their business agreement. "Your letter of August 1st should have been aswered earlier, except that a friend of mine [Noble Kreider] from the West has been staying in town for a few days and taken most of my time.

"I think the financial arrangement you speak of will work out all right — $300 in a definite payment and 10-per-cent royalty from the receipts of each performance. You say you would schedule at least ten performances and probably more if it is successful, with prospects of later performances in other years." He had not as yet heard from two women who were supposed to provide him with Celtic airs for possible use. "In the meantime I am going ahead and making tentative sketches of various parts in order to get the whole thing blocked out. Today I was working on the scene immediately following the big ceremonial dance of the priestesses and the appearance of the boat. It offers unlimited possibilities."

Two days later he worked out the ending of Scene 1, and the day after sketched out completely the dance of the priestesses. On August 15th he arranged for horn and piano an old orchestral *Notturno* of his, and the following day a friend played it and gave him many pointers on the instrument. Early the next week he played the four Sharp pieces — collected under Sharp's title, *Roman Sketches* — to White at Schirmer's. "He was very enthusiastic and called them the last word in piano music. He seems to think they will go through all right and even wants to get them out this season." On the 24th Griffes started a new setting to one of the four Wilde songs, *La Mer*, and the following day worked a good deal on the *Stimmführung* and filling out of voices in the pantomime, and finished *La Mer*. Towards the end of the month the Lewisohns were up to hear what he had done and expressed great enthusiasm. On September 4th he worked over the sword scene in the pantomime and revised the Wilde songs again. Two days later the Lewisohns and Mrs. Elliot dropped in for a few hours. "Various disagreements about my music and psychology of some spots. It is agreed that I will work over the sword scene once more entirely." That was also his last day at 12 West 46th for the summer.

He worked at the Lewisohns', read Chekhov, and visited a few friends like Ida Rauh — "Very interesting, especially in ability to crystallize into words our feelings about people and things." On the 14th of September he started copying out the pantomime in a piano arrangement for rehearsals and "Got a new idea for the entrance of the high priestess and worked and enlarged very much the invocation and fire-lighting scene preceding the chant." He received a special delivery from the Lewisohns asking him to spend a day at Chappaqua with them on the 16th. "Auto was there to meet me. The girls are staying at a smaller house on the estate of their sister. We walked up to the big house through a magnificent apple and peach orchard, ate our fill of peaches and first went around through the beautiful landscape gardens which are full of all sorts of surprises. The big music room is full of old Italian Renaissance furniture and tapestries, with nothing modern but the Steinway grand. The atmosphere was that of an old-world château — an ideal place to work. We went through what I have done of the pantomime several times. . . . I brought back with me the worked-over scenario of the second scene." On the 18th he worked through the second scene to the warrior's arrival and the following day through to the crag music, so that it was then blocked out up to the point where the priestess goes into the cavern.

He and Mrs. Elliot called on Katherine Ruth Heyman, a talented pianist whom Mrs. Elliot had interested in his music. "She played me Scriabin's *Sonata No. 8* and other smaller pieces and also gave us interesting information about exotic scales." There were more rehearsals at the Lewisohns'. He kept hard at the pantomime on the 25th, and the following day

"worked through till the return of the eight priestesses and revised several other places." An article in *Musical America*, that
week, dealt with "futurist piano music" and singled him out.
"A real American futurist composer is Charles T. Griffes. One
musician, describing his compositions, said they partake somewhat of the manner of Schönberg and Debussy, and yet possess
a particular original quality."

Early in October he attended a play by his friend Giovannitti at the People's Theater. "The performance was very
Latin and awful in many ways, but theater was crowded and
audience crazy. They called Arturo out many times and threw
wreaths over him." Griffes had also obtained permission to
watch rehearsals of the Ballet Russe in New York, and at one
of these became acquainted with Pierre Monteux, the French
conductor, who invited him to the stage rehearsals of *Till
Eulenspiegel*. He made a further acquaintance — Adolph
Bolm, the ballet star — only after Mrs. Elliot had urged him to
overcome his natural reluctance and speak to the dancer. Mrs.
Bolm later recollected: "When appearing with the Diaghilev
Russian Ballet in 1916 for the first time in America at the Metropolitan Opera House in New York, he [Bolm] noticed several times in the wings after performances a young shy man,
who one evening, after one of the tumultuous ovations at the
end of a performance, approached Mr. Bolm in the wings expressing his emotion in a few modest but sincere expressions,
introducing himself. Mr. Bolm had to change for the next ballet and asked Griffes to see him at his hotel, the Claridge, where
most of the principals of the Ballet stayed. Griffes came one
afternoon, and this was the beginning of a long and faithful
friendship."

During the second week of October there was bad news at
the school. "We are quarantined on the hill on account of ex-

posure to paralysis, Walter announced at dinner, so no more New York for a while!" Towards the end of October he was permitted out again, and friends were once more laughing at the familiar sight of Griffes's rubbers under the piano when he had miscalculated the deceptive Manhattan climate from Tarrytown's. On November 7th he composed and copied out a setting to *The Old Temple among the Mountains*, a Chinese poem, on the five-tone scale.

He copied out sections of the pantomime, rehearsed with Miss Hyland the piano arrangement, practiced Scriabin Op. 63, and called on Edgar Varèse, the French composer, for "a most interesting time. He showed me an extraordinary score. His views are most radical. . . . We spoke German entirely. He seems well acquainted with Schönberg, Ravel, Debussy, Stravinsky, and everybody else. He was interested in my stuff and wants to hear the pantomime." *Musical America* for November 16th announced that "Charles Griffes, whose piano compositions have come into considerable vogue of late, has almost completed a pantomime-ballet for the Neighborhood Playhouse." On the 20th he copied further on Scene 2, making a few changes, and next day had copied up to the three mystic circles. During rehearsals in the following weeks he visited the studio of Herbert Crowley, the artist who was designing the set for the pantomime. Later they met again at the Lewisohns'. "Crowley there, and we had an interesting discussion about the music. He thinks movement will spoil it, and at least that it should be done behind gauzes." Charles Cooper in a concert on the 25th played something by Griffes, who attended with Hodgson. "He 'dissects' everything, but plays so seriously and earnestly that I like to hear him." Calling for Varèse at the Brevoort, Griffes once tried with another musician "to play a duet arrangement of Varèse's score but couldn't make anything out of it." Afterwards at Mrs. Elliot's, where Griffes played the pantomime to a large audience, Varèse turned pages for him, much interested. Scene 2 was voted the favorite.

On the first day of December, Griffes started the orchestration of Scene 2 and continued during the early part of the month, at the same time copying and practicing the finished piano arrangement. By the 12th he had nearly finished orchestrating it. There were a few outside chores and distractions. Maud Allan told him of having played *The White Peacock* to friends in London, and on December 19th the Barrère Ensemble performed at the Cort Theater the special arrangements of *The Vale of Dreams* and *The Lake at Evening* that he had made for them. But for the most part he worked intently all month — "Am spending all my spare moments in orchestrating," "Stayed home all day and orchestrated" — and on the 26th completed Scene 2 at the studio of Walter Henry Rothwell, a conductor with whom he had lately become acquainted. Two days later before going to bed he orchestrated the introduction to Scene 1.

Early in the month he had signed a contract with Schirmer's for the four *Roman Sketches* at 10-per-cent royalty, which became the standard royalty on all his future compositions. On the 30th he called on Winifred Christie, with whom he had left some new pieces a few days before, and to whom he had offered the dedication of one of the *Sketches*. "She has selected *Nightfall* for her piece, so Ganz will get the *Peacock*." Otherwise it was the pantomime every moment, for he was on the eve of his first major presentation.

Chapter XII

GRIFFES was determined to leave Hackley. His royalties from August 1st, 1915, to July 31st, 1916, had been $62.49, which, though not much, was the highest they were ever to be in his lifetime. The accumulation of a few adult pupils in New York, the engagements at the Neighborhood Playhouse, and an increase in the popularity of his music offered other encouragement. To set up independently as composer and teacher had long been Griffes's ambition, but it had always collapsed under family obligation. Though he might have been willing to take the risk himself, he would not subject those who depended upon him to so precarious an existence. Now it was clear, however, that he must make a blow for freedom or perhaps lose out altogether. The second semester at Hackley was on its way; his Uncle Charles died in January 1917; his brother was to be married shortly. Griffes felt his own personal responsibility more keenly than ever, and there was his debt to Miss Broughton. If these circumstances are borne in mind, the confused and unfortunate train of events involved in the rehearsals and production of *The Kairn of Koridwen* are more readily understood.

Griffes had first asked Barrère's assistance in organizing a small orchestra to play his work at the Neighborhood Play-house. Barrère in turn had recommended the services of Mr. Fred van Amburgh, long associated as clarinetist with the Bar-rère Ensemble and with the Barrère Little Symphony, of which van Amburgh was also orchestral and tour manager.

Griffes and van Amburgh met for lunch at an Italian res-taurant in the Forties. There the composer explained his poor finances, his unhappy teaching position at Hackley, and his fears that the Lewisohns might not produce his ballet if the mu-sicians should cost too much. He pleaded that all expenses be kept as low as possible.

In no time matters were under way. The price agreed upon for the musicians was the flat union rate of $8 per man for each performance and $4 per man for each two-and-a-half-hour re-hearsal. Van Amburgh as contractor was to be paid double. On January 7th Griffes wrote Irene Lewisohn to inform her of final arrangements. Because the musicians had other contracts February 10th would have to be the date of first performance for the *Kairn*. "I have fixed the first rehearsal for Wednesday morning the 17th at 9:30 o'clock. I'll leave the harp matter to you, but if you will send word to Mason & Hamlin about the piano, I will stop in next week and speak about the pitch. I find it doesn't mean much higher, hardly more than Interna-tional Pitch." With an eye to the future he added a post-script exhorting her to persist in a contemplated revival of *Petrouchka*.

There were many rehearsals. Then the first difficulty arose. Griffes's idea had been to do the ballet as an ensemble without conductor. Practiced at first without dancers, it had gone very well. When an attempt was made to weld music and panto-mime, however, the task was found almost impossible without a conductor. Griffes insisted that he would not do it except as an ensemble. Miss Lewisohn wished it done as an ensemble. Van

Amburgh declared that it could not be done without a conductor. Nikolai Sokoloff, the West Coast conductor, attended a rehearsal one morning when Griffes, van Amburgh, and Miss Lewisohn were in heated argument. During a lull in the altercations van Amburgh asked Sokoloff to step down into the pit and conduct. The latter complied and held things together so that the performance ran more smoothly than before. Griffes nevertheless maintained that the work could be done as an ensemble. In the ensuing rehearsals without conductor the ballet would not take shape, and Griffes became exceedingly nervous, insisting that the musicians were inattentive and rotten. Van Amburgh told him to find others. A compromise was finally reached, Sokoloff conducting after van Amburgh had convinced Miss Lewisohn that the performance could not go otherwise. Griffes did not like it. Nor, understandably enough, was Miss Lewisohn pleased at the cost of the many extra rehearsals necessitated by her composer's stubbornness.

The Kairn of Koridwen opened as scheduled on February 10th, 1917, and ran twelve performances all together. The cast included ten members of the Festival Dancers, headed by Blanche Talmud and Irene Lewisohn. Sokoloff conducted an eight-piece orchestra consisting of six members of the Barrère Ensemble, Lily Hyland at the celesta, and Griffes at the piano.

None of the performances was good. Griffes as composer continually took the tempo out of Sokoloff's hands, and the bewildered musicians did not know whether to follow their conductor or the composer-pianist. There were frequent arguments. Griffes became increasingly nervous.

Then came the blowup. The musicians had been hired for consecutive week ends. After several of these week ends had elapsed Griffes informed the contractor that one would be out, to be made up on the following week. Although this would make the number of performances the same, van Amburgh could not consent. His men had been taken for consecutive week ends and would lose out on other engagements if this arrangement was not observed. In the subsequent dispute all the stored-up venom and bitterness of the past few weeks burst forth. Miss Helen Arthur, business manager of the Playhouse, was called in, and she and Griffes and van Amburgh and Miss Lewisohn were soon embroiled. Griffes informed Miss Lewisohn that the men had not been hired for consecutive week ends. Miss Arthur, referring to their contract, discovered that they had.

No sooner was this conflagration doused than another flared up. The musicians had to be paid for the one week-end layoff and also for the week end extended. Miss Lewisohn refused. There was more bitterness, in which van Amburgh finally threw up the engagement. But it was of course impossible to change musicians at this late date. Van Amburgh was irate with Griffes and would have nothing to do with him. So Miss Lewisohn, Miss Arthur, and van Amburgh's wife met together, and the latter persuaded her husband to finish the engagement.

It was not like Griffes not to acknowledge frankly and honestly any shortcomings that were his. After the *Kairn* episode was over he apologized to van Amburgh for his erraticism. He had been tired and overwrought. He could never have afforded to pay for his mistakes. He had been fearful of losing the Lewisohns' patronage. These things were only too obviously true. The two men parted good friends. And to Babe Shoobert, Griffes later wrote of the *Kairn:* "They had an orchestra of the best players available in New York, and Nikolai Sokoloff did splendid work as conductor."

Whatever the shortcomings of its initial production, the musical worth of the *Kairn* was not obscured, and there is little doubt that certain of its passages rank with the best of its composer. Griffes's own valuation of the book was not high.

". . . The plot was criticized as being undramatic," he wrote Babe, "and the performance was inadequate in various ways. I think myself that the book was poor, but I had nothing to do with that. The Playhouse gave me the scenario to compose for them. As a story it reads very finely, I think, but projected on the stage, it seemed thin. But there were some nice chances for descriptive music in it." That he had taken full advantage of such chances there was little doubt in the minds of his audience, which applauded him vociferously after the first presentation. "It was really an enormous success for me." Besides the $300 for the score he received $100.35 in royalties on performance.

That was not all. "It brought me enthusiastic recognition from musicians." Griffes looked upon *The Kairn of Koridwen* as a sustained composition independent of its ballet complement, and in a letter to Rudolph Schirmer referred to it as "a continuous symphonic music in two movements or scenes, and scored for flute, two clarinets, two horns, harp, celesta, and piano." In another letter to a friend the following year he mentioned it again as "concert music."

It had not been easy to interest critics in attending Griffes's ballet-pantomime. Miss Arthur, urgently convinced of something vital and important in this new music, had set about the task with a will, but had faced genial discouragement on every hand. Richard Aldrich explained in gentlemanly fashion and sent an assistant. Someone else apologized that the Metropolitan was giving *Cavalleria Rusticana* and *Pagliacci* on the same evening. Henry T. Finck jollied her out of it: one did not ask a music critic to hear music if one were his friend. No critic could be had from the *New Republic*. The *Nation* sent Henrietta Straus. Paul Rosenfeld, tipped off by Nikolai Sokoloff, attended the dress rehearsal. All but one or two of the others frankly oozed boredom.

The *Evening World* reported the event on February 12th.

"The cozy little house seats only four hundred eleven persons, and it was crowded. It kept fashionable hours, too. The curtain rose at a quarter to nine, and many people arrived in limousines and taxis. . . . Mr. Griffes's music is as weird as the story. He uses his instruments in unusual fashion. In the first of the two scenes there is little of melody and not a remote approach to a tune, but his music has an exasperating insistence, and at least it is original. Mr. Griffes will bear watching."

The musical press was more or less in agreement. "Mr. Griffes has written a tone poem in the ultra-modern idiom, one of the first works by a native American in this daring style to have public performance, and whether the general public approves of it musically or not, one must confess that it has the quality of compelling attention and of stimulating the imagination." A. Walter Kramer, in *Musical America* for February 17th, pointed out that "Mr. Griffes has exhibited good judgment in writing his score in this manner, for had he followed the conventional he could not have given a really complete hearing of his music, considering the instrumentation ordinarily used in small theaters." He also commended the music, but for some reason considered modern harmony disqualified a priori from any full expression of human experience. "Neither the love idea in the second scene nor the grief of the druidesses at finding Carmelis dead is pictured in tone with anything like the intensity that a composer can sound in harmonies less modern."

One review made a noteworthy observation. It was the long and enthusiastic critique by Paul Rosenfeld that appeared in the April *Seven Arts*, which also contained the historic supplement on "American Independence and the War." Griffes sent copies to his publisher and to several friends, and when the *Seven Arts* later suspended because of its pacificist advocacy he visited the editorial offices to procure additional copies of the April number.

Rosenfeld's review was explicit recognition of a change that had taken place in Griffes's music, a new independent direction already struck out in the latest but not then published songs. Though it is long and belongs to an impressionistic kind of music criticism that, especially with the passage of time, seems to tell less of the music under consideration than of the mood of the appreciator, it is worth quoting in full because of this historical interest.[1]

Even at Tarrytown, Griffes's latest accomplishment did not go unheeded. The *Hackley*, school monthly, devoted a brief editorial to the subject, reaching a favorable verdict. "A large delegation of fellows who went in to see the performance pronounced it perfect and complimented the music most highly." There was someone at Hackley who did not approve, however. To one of Griffes's colleagues the administration dropped a polite hint that the music instructor seemed unduly occupied with outside activities. And when the implication was relayed to Griffes he was both worried and annoyed. He would leave eventually but dared not as yet.

Certain events at home and the darkening national scene made it out of the question to gamble security now. He would have to wait. But he was not an unknown any longer.

That he had in fact arrived seemed incontestable when the following month, on March 25th, Mr. Eugene Heffley delivered a formal lecture at the MacDowell Club on "Modern and Ultra-Modern Music," in which among the many modern composers discussed only Griffes and MacDowell illustrated American tendencies.

Heffley, a well-known musical pedagogue, was interested in

[1] See Appendix II.

all the new music. At his studio in Carnegie Hall one heard the works of men like Scriabin, Schönberg, Szymanowski, Ravel, Florent Schmitt, Erik Satie, Griffes, and many more. It was through Heffley that Griffes met a young lady who was to become a future dear friend. Miss Marion Bauer, a long-time disciple of Heffley's, had listened to one of his pupils playing something by Griffes and, struck by its novelty, excitedly inquired about the composer. Heffley relayed the compliment to Griffes, who, after further intercession on the part of Walter Rothwell, left a pair of tickets to *The Kairn of Koridwen* for his admirer. It was the beginning of a pleasant friendship. Miss Bauer was a newcomer to the American musical scene and the sister of Emilie Frances Bauer, the New York representative of the Chicago *Musical Leader*. What touched Griffes was her spirit of fresh cheer, so much in contrast to his own tiredness and intermittent pessimism. She had hardly tried her wings yet, and her feeling of hope was almost contagious. She and her sister were also good fun. Once learning of Griffes's penchant for chocolate cake they baked one for dinner, only to learn that they had committed the unforgivable error of mixing a white interior when what he really favored was "chocolate all through." There was always welcome frivolity at the Bauers'.

Shortly before the Heffley lecture Griffes had sold Schirmer's his unison chorus *These Things Shall Be* to words of John Addington Symonds—a composition that was to have a curious history. It had been composed at the dual instigation of Mrs. Elliot and Harry Barnhart. Griffes had first met Barnhart in early April of 1912, when they were introduced by Arthur Farwell. He had been quite impressed, finding Barnhart "an interesting talker who has thought a good deal about life and art and has some sane views about things, as well as a healthy, attractive, and robust personality. I envy such people. Farwell says he has knocked around a good deal." Operating on the sim-

Herbert Crowley design for *The Kairn of Koridwen*

ple discovery that people like to sing, Barnhart had gone into choral work, achieving spectacular results in the field of mass organization. When the founders of the New York Community Chorus wanted a leader in the spring of 1916 they called Barnhart to the job. In early August of that year Griffes accompanied Farwell to a Community Chorus rehearsal, where Barnhart put them on the platform and introduced them as young composers. Afterwards the three conferred in private, and Barnhart tried to interest Griffes in composing for the Chorus. "Barnhart thinks I can apply my particular talents to Community Music." It was an interesting hunch, and Barnhart did not leave off suggesting. He and Mrs. Elliot were acquaintances, so that often Griffes would play for them at Mrs. Elliot's apartment and listen to the man's strange involved thread of discourse, "part of it interesting and part of it hard to follow."

For a long while Mrs. Elliot, too, had been after Griffes to compose a labor song that could be used by workers at their rallies, strikes, and other militant occasions. She was always on the lookout for good English songs because the working population included large numbers of foreign born, and the repertoire of usable working songs had consisted mainly of European tunes with appropriate new words, or such ambiguously English productions as *The Red Flag*, with its familiar counterpart in *Der Tannenbaum*.

So it was as the fruit of these twin promptings from Barnhart and Mrs. Elliot that *These Things Shall Be* first saw the light. The words were a close approximation to Griffes's social philosophy. It sold at six cents and pleased all concerned. Mrs. Elliot considered it the finest labor song ever composed by an American, and Barnhart found it eminently successful with the Community Chorus. Griffes wrote Babe about his "short unison chorus song to wonderful words of J. Addington Symonds." "It was written in three-quarters of an hour, and I am not very much stuck on it myself, but it has been used a good deal in the Community Chorus work here in N. Y., and they like it." Actually he was far from displeased by the popularity of the work.

On April 6th President Wilson signed the resolution declaring a state of war. It brought no immediate alterations in Griffes's life. The next day he was having lunch with Adolph Bolm, who, back from a second American transcontinental tour with the Ballet, had decided to remain in the United States and organize his own company of dancers. He told Griffes of the trials of the Ballet Russe both before and during their tours. He himself had been operated upon only three days before dancing in New York. In the afternoon they went to see three plays of Negro life by Ridgely Torrence, and Griffes met Arthur B. Davies and Robert Edmond Jones, the artists. Afterwards they visited a Russian shop, and in the evening he induced Bolm to accompany him to the circus, where Bolm was much amused by the clowns. Griffes greatly admired the dancer both as an artist and as a person. "I have been going around quite a little lately with Adolph Bolm, the real star of the Russian Ballet, and a far more interesting dancer than Nijinsky. He is a most simple and agreeable man to be around with, speaks very broken English, and is extremely intelligent and well educated."

The next evening there was a party at Paul Rosenfeld's, where Ernest Bloch, the Sokoloffs, and Leo Ornstein, among others, were present. Ornstein played the d'Indy *Sonata* and some manuscripts of his own, including a sonatina and *Poems of 1917.*

Griffes began rehearsing for an eight-performance revival of *Petrouchka* at the Playhouse.

On the 18th he and Mrs. Elliot visited the home of a Chinese

Methodist minister in Chinatown. Mrs. Annie Wang, a Chinese singer, was also present, and Griffes took down from her dictation a song that she accompanied upon a Chinese harp. Its tone was that of a clavichord, and it was played with bamboo hammers. Both he and Mrs. Elliot sat spellbound.

Five days later the revival of *Petrouchka* opened, and Griffes was occupied with that for a while. There were some good times at the Lewisohns', where the party hilariously burlesqued everything from the ouija board to *The Kairn of Koridwen*. Griffes visited Herbert Crowley and "found how little his original design for *Koridwen* agreed with the final results." Sometimes he would play Russian dances for Adolph Bolm at the Claridge, and they discussed possible tableaux to *Islamey*. On the 26th Griffes, digesting last week's new material, started settings to two Chinese poems, *So-Fei* and *Impressions of a Traveller*. The next day the war came to Hackley. It was the first military drill day, with between sixty and seventy boys participating. Griffes finished up *So-Fei*. Two days later the war brushed by again when having dinner at the Garnseys' he learned that Julian was accepted for officers' training camp and that very soon Arlo was to take an exam. At a party at Arthur Whiting's he had an interesting discussion with Ananda Çoomaraswamy and Ratan Devi and met Richard Aldrich, the music critic. Albert Spalding and some others played trios.

On May 1st Griffes finished up the *Impressions of a Traveller* and copied out the first two Chinese songs. The next day he went to a rehearsal of some Jewish music by Ernest Bloch, where he sat with Paul Rosenfeld. Richard Aldrich, who was seated before them, opined that the pieces were too monotonous for a whole program. Thence Griffes called on Bolm, with whom he went to meet Mr. and Mrs. Ridgely Torrence. Bolm was considering a baseball ballet and demonstrated possible attitudes and movements. In the evening Griffes visited the Bauers', where Katherine Ruth Heyman and Robert de Bruce, young composer-pianist, played for him. The day after there was a special performance of *Petrouchka* for settlement interests.

On May 5th Miss Cadance Meakle, one of Heffley's pupils, gave a recital that included three of Griffes's things. Heffley devoted a brief talk to the composer as introduction. The next night was the final performance of *Petrouchka* at the Playhouse.

Griffes now found leisure to read W. D. Howells's *A Chance Acquaintance* and Flaubert's *Salammbô*, to go on brisk strolls with Schmidt, and to have an occasional dinner at the Steeses', in the days that followed. He visited one of Torrence's Negro musicians, who, with an orchestra of five men, played him some West Indian Negro music. Griffes detected a Spanish and French influence. On the 15th he copied out the fifth of his Chinese songs, and the next day played all five to Mrs. Elliot. Farwell sent word through Katherine Ruth Heyman that his Symonds song was having great success at the Community Chorus. He and Mrs. Elliot examined a choralcelo together. "The tone is so perfect as to be cloying to me; also there is too much organ tone in it."

The five Chinese songs were now complete and copied, but Griffes had been busy with other things as well, with piano motifs and various orchestral sketches. In particular he had been readying for performance the work by which, for better or for worse, he would eventually become best known.

Griffes first began composition on *The Pleasure-Dome of Kubla Khan* as a piano piece sometime early in 1912. Precisely when is uncertain, but as early as March 11th of that year he was working on it and wrote: "I can't decide on the form." Since he referred to the piece by its name always, there can be little doubt that it was originally inspired by Coleridge's poem and that the text was not later adjoined as an afterthought. In this connection the statement Griffes finally submitted to the annotator of the Boston Symphony program book may be quoted. "I have taken as a basis for my work those lines of Coleridge's poem describing the 'stately pleasure-dome,' the 'sunny pleasure-dome with caves of ice,' the 'miracle of rare device.' Therefore I call the work *The Pleasure-Dome of Kubla Khan* rather than *Kubla Khan*. These lines include 1 to 11 and lines 32 to 38. It might be well to quote in the program book some of the lines — at least the last six.

> "In Xanadu did Kubla Khan
>   A stately pleasure-dome decree:
>   Where Alph, the sacred river, ran
>   Through caverns measureless to man
>   Down to a sunless sea.
>   So twice five miles of fertile ground
>   With walls and towers were girdled round:
>   And here were gardens bright with sinuous rills
>   Where blossomed many an incense-bearing tree;
>   And here were forests ancient as the hills,
>   Enfolding sunny spots of greenery. . . .
>
>   The shadow of the dome of pleasure
>   Floated midway on the waves;
>   Where was heard the mingled measure
>   From the fountain and the caves.
>   It was a miracle of rare device,
>   A sunny pleasure-dome with caves of ice! . . .

"As to argument, I have given my imagination free rein in the description of this strange palace as well as of purely imaginary revelry which might take place there. The vague, foggy beginning suggests the sacred river, running 'through caverns measureless to man down to a sunless sea.' The gardens with fountains and 'sunny spots of greenery' are next suggested. From inside come sounds of dancing and revelry which increase to a wild climax and then suddenly break off. There is a return to the original mood suggesting the sacred river and the ' caves of ice.' "

Yet the genesis of this unique composition was more tortuous and complex than Griffes's few paragraphs in the program book would indicate.

On March 20th of 1912 he worked most of the day on *Kubla* "and sketched it way through to the end. It is much shorter than my original idea and illustrates only the beautiful side of the pleasure-palace." On the 4th of April he was already practicing it. But *Kubla* somehow would not resolve itself as a piano composition. Six days later he worked at it all morning and reflected: " It is getting along so far that I think I shall play it to Farwell soon. It is difficult to work out the details of the *Klaviersatz*. I am curious to see what Farwell says to the piece." The last day of the month he did a little work on *Kubla* again, " changing it once more." On May 4th he practiced on it, and on the 13th he was making some more changes, which required fresh work the next day. The day after that, the 15th, was a Wednesday, and Griffes was in New York. After lunch he "went to the library and looked through all their works on Arabian music, in order to find something appropriate for use in *Kubla Khan*." He " copied out one rather good air." On the 28th Griffes got the piece " into a playable shape" with the thought of trying it on Hodgson the next day. But Hodgson could not come, and it was not till July 17th that Griffes secured outside opinion on *Kubla*. On that day he played it to Arthur Farwell at his rooms on 50th Street. " *Kubla Khan* he thought stronger and more interesting in every way [than something else played to him] but impossibly *unklaviermässig*. He is right! " It was becoming more and more apparent that Griffes's original doubts about *Kubla* as a piano composition were justified. Two days after the Farwell hearing he "made some changes in the *Klaviersatz* of *Kubla Khan*, but don't feel sure that it can ever become really pianistic." On the 24th of July he worked about two hours on *Kubla*, and again five days later, when he reported: " It is becoming more *klaviermässig*." The day after that, July 30th, he was at it again and "worked out the chords in the return of the first subject, and sketched out a B minor dance episode which I may use in it." Throughout the remainder of the summer of 1912 Griffes worked at the composition off and on, sometimes devoting a whole day to its progress, sometimes a morning, sometimes only half an hour.

His labors continued spasmodically into the fall. No wonder that on September 23rd he wrote: "Today I commenced the half-final ink copy of *Kubla Khan*; never before have I changed and changed a piece so much as this. Even yesterday I changed a place again." What he did not know was that the long pilgrimage of changes and revision had only begun. Three days later he had about finished the copy. Huneker's later prognostication was correct when he said: " Think of it, up the State was a modest teacher of piano and all the while he marked despairing fingering for hopeless pupils, his brain cells made darkly magnificent pictures of the sacred Alph, and of the English poet's ' dome of pleasure — a miracle of rare device, a sunny pleasure-dome with caves of ice'!'" What he could not have guessed was that even this pleasure-dome was at times occluded to its maker, the times when he "practiced this morning on *Kubla Khan*, but without much interest as I felt miserable inwardly." Philip Hale, also, was correct in calling attention to its intensity of imagination as the composition's most salient feature.

On September 26th, 1912, Griffes copied out *Kubla* again and by October 3rd could play it by heart. The piece was heard sometimes thereafter by his friends and the students at Hackley. But an old doubt returned when he played it to Galston, during his New York visit, on the 9th of the following month. For Galston "thought that *Kubla* was essentially an orchestral piece." There the matter came to rest for a time, though evolution was momentarily sidetracked on the last day of the month when Schindler, acting as consultant for Schirmer's, "thought *Kubla* a remarkable piece — my best so far, and advised sending it in in its present form."

It would prove neither edifying nor instructive to follow in all the intricacy of their convolutions the further developments of *Kubla*. It was a thing picked up and put down whenever clues to its realization presented themselves. The general procedure is best indicated by Griffes's remarks on February 6th, 1915. "In the evening there was a lecture, but I didn't go down for it. I stayed upstairs and worked on *Kubla Khan*. Have changed and simplified it again. It improves every time." The next day he was recopying once more.

A significant influence in the progress of the composition was Busoni's opinion rendered the same year. *Kubla* was among the pieces that Griffes played the Italian composer during their fateful interview. "I think *Kubla Khan* interested him. He said there was very good Oriental atmosphere in it, and praised the theme. But he advised me to either do it for orchestra or make it shorter for piano. I myself had thought of cutting it up into two pieces." He was still uncertain. But after experimenting and exhausting all the remaining possibilities of *Kubla* as a piano composition during that year Griffes finally, on December 5th, "worked a good deal on a new version of *Kubla Khan* which I may fix up for orchestra."

Early in 1916 he started out on this tack. On February 7th he "wrote out in pencil the *Kubla Khan* orchestral sketch" and the next month played it to Mrs. Elliot. Other things intervened for a while, but on the 5th of April he worked four hours on the orchestral sketch, and again some more on the following day. On the 14th of April he completed it. It was from this orchestral sketch that he sometimes played to the pleasure and acclaim of Mrs. Elliot's circle of friends, to Helen Marot, Giovannitti, Lily Hyland, Barnhart, and others. On May 16th he began the orchestration and the next day "worked practically the whole day on the orchestration of *Kubla* and got a good start." In early June, Griffes played the manuscript to Arthur Whiting, who thought it too early for him to be doing a full symphonic score. Whiting also considered that there was too little rhythm in it, prescribed "Bach, rhythmical studies, and striving for more vitality and red blood," and by way of immediate stimulation lent him Forsyth's *Orchestration* and played Bach on the clavichord.

Off and on through 1916 there were glimmerings of hope for a performance of *Kubla*. Mrs. Elliot's friends were lacking in neither energy nor enthusiasm for the task of its promotion. At one time it was under consideration to press-agent Griffes at a protest meeting against the Irish rebel executions. Perhaps Ornstein or the conductor Adriano Ariani might be engaged to play *Kubla* under specially advertised auspices. Again, for a while it appeared that a wealthy New York woman would back a performance of it. Then the project lapsed.

Chapter XIII

It was not until now, in 1917, that a concrete first performance of the poem seemed imminent. Griffes's association with Nikolai Sokoloff during *The Kairn of Koridwen* had won him a devoted admirer of his music. "You may hear some of my music in San Francisco this summer if you are there," Griffes wrote Babe early in April. "Nikolai Sokoloff is to give ten concerts with the People's Symphony Orchestra of seventy men. He has asked for a work of mine, and I am going to give him *The Pleasure-Dome of Kubla Khan* if it is done. As an orchestral sketch it has been ready for a couple of years, but I never orchestrated it. Now I may rush it through. It wouldn't be done till July or Aug."

On May 7th, two days after the last performance of *Petrouchka*, he returned to the poem and spent the whole morning on it. He was still at it two days later when Babe sent him a newspaper clipping from San Francisco announcing *Kubla* for Sokoloff's concerts that summer. Nothing daunted, Griffes wrote an entirely new close to the composition on May 15th. Not only in San Francisco was *Kubla* announced, for *Musical America* of August 11th carried an item that " Charles Griffes, the young American composer, several of whose larger works were brought out in New York last winter, has completed a symphonic poem, *The Pleasure-Dome of Kubla Khan,* which will be done in San Francisco the end of this month."

The performance never came about. Individual parts had first to be copied out for the members of the orchestra, and this bulky and expensive job Griffes turned over to a copyist. When the score was returned there were so many errors in it that he had to set about restoring the sense himself, which proved almost as burdensome as the original labor. "His [Sokoloff's] season ended with July 30th, and my score reached him the middle of July so they couldn't work it up. I couldn't get the parts ready and copied out any sooner. I think myself that they found it a rather expensive proposition as it demanded more instruments than their regular complement and extra rehearsals. I think I can get it done this season here in the East, which is much more important."

Another reason for the delay in sending *Kubla* was that Griffes was also rushed with other work. On June 1st, the New York Community Chorus sang *These Things Shall Be* at the Hippodrome. In June also he had written to Rudolph Schirmer about the new songs. "I have some Chinese songs written entirely on the pentatonic scale which I intend to submit to the House soon." Another venture, an attempt to interest the Metropolitan Opera in presenting *The Kairn of Koridwen,* came to nothing as Griffes had correctly foreseen it would. ". . . The Metropolitan Opera House," he had written Babe, "is at present looking over the score with a view to its possible production there. But I don't really see how they could do it even if they wanted to. It is too different from anything their ballet corps has ever done. There is no real dancing in it at all. It is scored for eight solo instruments, flute, two clarinets, two French horns, harp, celesta, and piano, a combination which I think has never been used before by anybody." Nevertheless another ballet of his was to be produced that summer.

Adolph Bolm, as already mentioned, was organizing his own company of dancers, the "Adolph Bolm Ballet-Intime," which would present "choreodramas and comedies" and feature the talents of a number of exotic interpreters, such as Roshanara, Ratan Devi, and Michio Ito. It was for the last, a Japanese mime artist, that Bolm commissioned Griffes to write a Japanese dance drama.

The composer and his interpreter became good friends. "Do you know Ito?" he wrote Babe. "He is a strange boy — formerly an actor at the Imperial Theater at Tokyo, and now after contact with various European schools in Moscow, Dresden, etc., a very subtle dancer and pantomimist." Griffes also made the acquaintance of another participant in the Bolm programs, a soprano named Eva Gauthier.

With her ardent and untiring pursuit of everything new in music Mme Gauthier was then winning herself a niche in American musical life. Her programs may at times have been overcordial to the studied and merely clever, but they uncovered much that was best from abroad and at home and circulated like a fresh breeze through the mildewed caverns of the American concert halls. French-Canadian born, Mme Gauthier had early embarked on an unusual career, which is best described in a newspaper interview that she gave in 1923: "Fourteen years ago, when I was appearing in Europe, I knew nothing of the modern musical movement beyond what I got from *Pelléas et Mélisande*. I was familiar only with what Debussy had done. Soon after taking part in the English production of his opera, I went to the Orient; and I was one of the first singers to go there from Europe and regularly give concerts. I visited many places before I completed my Eastern travels, but I spent the greater part of my time on the island of Java.

"In fact I was in Java for five years, and during that period I learned something about the languages used by the islanders, and I studied their musical system and read their song lore. I sang there, too, with accompaniment of native instruments, which belong to the string, wind, brass, and percussion families, though they differ in structure from Western instruments. I was privileged to study with the best Javanese musicians, some of whom are very learned. . . . Besides sojourning so long a time in Java, I made visits of considerable length in Australia, New Zealand, the Philippines, and Japan. While in Japan I renewed the practice I pursued in Java of collecting original material. In particular I found a book of native music in which were things I liked, and I copied a number of them out, not knowing precisely what I should do with them."

In the second year of the war Mme Gauthier left the Orient and came to the United States. There, as she began to apprehend certain affinities between modern music and the music of the East with which she was familiar, she devoted herself to a fresh and skilled exploitation of the moderns. And she intelligently compensated her vocal limitations by the musical value of her programs. Not long afterwards she met Griffes. "I first met Griffes in 1917, when he was preparing a score for Ito, the Japanese dancer. . . . I gave him the melodies which I had copied in Japan." Her closing statement should also be given here. "To complete my observations about Orientalism in modern music and my association with it, I ought to say that all the material which I originally lent to Griffes I have given to Ravel." Mme Gauthier's other remarks about Griffes in this interview — apart from her association with him — are incorrect. For example: "He had been a pupil of Humperdinck in

Germany, and up to this time [1917] he had written in the old-fashioned German style."

As might be expected, Griffes showed Mme Gauthier his recent Chinese songs, and she was enraptured, planning to make use of them in the fall. She proffered the same appreciative collaboration that she would later to another American composer, in popular music, to George Gershwin and his jazz songs. For his part Griffes was fascinated by the fresh musical material that the singer disclosed to him and filled several little notebooks and scraps of paper with it, as well as with the fruits of his own intensive studies in the field. Lullabies, war songs, lance ceremonies, a Malay song from Sumatra, a Malay song from Java, Javanese and Indian and Japanese and Chinese melodies, carefully detailed notes on Eastern structure and development — he collected and mined them all. He acquired some fine Japanese prints and studied them with the same care that he lavished upon his technical blueprints of Oriental instruments. He limned out a melodic sketch of four verses to the four seasons, each with its complement: spring, cherry blossoms; summer, water; autumn, moon; winter, snow.

With thematic suggestions from Mme Gauthier and Ito, and with his own researches in Japanese music, Griffes was more than ready to undertake his ballet for Bolm. *Sho-Jo, or The Spirit of Wine — A Symbol of Happiness* was composed during July. The program book later offered a synopsis of the mime. " This is a legendary dance of Old Japan and illustrates the vagaries of a youth who smiles continuously and invites his friends to drink. In his happiness under ' the spirit of wine,' he has a vision of a beautiful maiden whom he desires and vainly attempts to ensnare. She escapes him, but his exhilaration continues, until exhausted, he drops to sleep." It was intended as a solo for Ito, who was assisted by Tulle Lindahl.

Griffes composed for it some of the most unusual music that

he was ever to write. To Frederick H. Martens, who was doing a piece about the Ballet-Intime for the October issue of the *New Music Review*, Griffes later gave a statement about *Sho-Jo* that is applicable not only to that composition but to all his other Oriental experiments — the earlier Chinese songs, the later Javanese, and the rest — as well. It is also one of the clearest pronouncements that he ever made on any phase of his art.

"It [*Sho-Jo*] is *developed* Japanese music — I purposely do not use the term 'idealized.' Cadman and others have taken American Indian themes and have 'idealized' rather than 'developed' them in Indian style. There is really nothing in them save themes; the harmonization, etc., might have come from Broadway. Modern music tends more and more toward the archaic, especially the archaism of the East. The ancient Greek modes, the pentatonic scales of China and Japan are much used, and there is little difference between the whole-tone and one of the Chinese scales. There is a striving for harmonies which suggest the quarter-tones of Oriental music, and the frequent employ of the characteristic augmented second, as well as of the organ point common to both systems. In the dissonance of modern music the Oriental is more at home than in the consonance of the classics. And all this I have borne in mind in the development of the *Sho-Jo* music."

Was there not a certain limitation upon the individuality of the composer in this "development"? Griffes later wrote Howard Conant of the Chinese songs: "It was most interesting work to me." But could it be something more? Could it be music? His answer was an unequivocal yes. For as Martens rightly pointed out, Griffes sacrificed too absolute a dependence on the letter of Japanese musical law to a broader working-out of his basic material. Or, in Griffes's words: "Whistler learned engraving from Japanese prints without sacrificing his own individuality. Japanese music should not be too largely infused with Western ideas and procedures; yet Michio Ito himself, who understands the music of his native land *au fond*, believes that it will gain in breadth of expression, that its beauties will be more widely understood if brought into a modified contact with Western art influences." He offered the score of his own *Sho-Jo* as a practical example of what this modified contact might mean. "My harmonization is all in octaves, fifths, fourths, and seconds — consonant major thirds and sixths are omitted. The orchestration is as Japanese as possible: thin and delicate, and the muted string *points d'orgue* serve as a neutral-tinted background, like the empty spaces in a Japanese print. The whole thematic material is given to the flute, clarinet, and oboe — akin to the Japanese reed instruments: the harp suggests the koto."

Without knowing it, Griffes was in effect fulfilling Bernard Shaw's earlier prescription for an emissary to American music, when Shaw had written: ". . . Since MacDowell began to compose, the Americans have shown an alarming facility in modern German harmony and orchestration, and the time has come for an Indian missionary — to show what can be done without the aid of as much as a common chord or dominant seventh, and with untempered intonation."

The mime was performed in August. Griffes later wrote Babe: "It was done a few times on the road and then for two weeks in New York as part of Adolph Bolm's Ballet-Intime program. . . . The number in question is *Sho-Jo*. The others to which my name is attached are arrangements only. I made no attempt to do Occidental music, used three Japanese folk themes, almost no harmony at all, and as nearly as possible only instruments similar to Japanese."

The three Japanese folk themes of *Sho-Jo* to which Griffes refers are as follows:

I. INITIAL THEME

II. DANCE OF INTOXICATION

III. THEME OF THE SPIRIT OF WINE'S DANCE

The other numbers mentioned were an Assyrian Dance — vigorously executed by Adolph Bolm — that Griffes orchestrated from music by a composer named Alexander Maloof, and *Sakura-Sakura*, a Japanese Cherry Dance performed by Tulle Lindahl, also arranged by Griffes.

On August 5th the *New York Times* announced: "The company will open in Atlantic City today, and play Washington later in the week. After six nights in New York . . . the organization will also visit Saratoga, Bar Harbor, Newport, and points of Long Island, the proceeds of the tour going to various war charities." There followed a list of the wealthy patronesses sponsoring the enterprise.

Bolm's troupe played at the Belasco Theater in Washington on August 9th, 10th, and 11th, and on the 20th opened at the Booth Theater in New York, where it had a two-week run. Performances were under the auspices of the American Ambulance in Russia. Besides the East Indian, Hindu, Japanese, Assyrian, and other such numbers, the repertoire included Saint-Saëns, Moussorgsky, and Borodin's *Prince Igor*, with Fokine's choreography in the last. The symphonic orchestra was under the direction of Marcel Hansotte. Mme Gauthier supplied a patriotic intermission with renditions of *The Star-Spangled Banner* ("the words weirdly juggled," according to one write-up) and *Hymn of Free Russia*. Indeed, of all the spectacles housed at the Booth in those two weeks perhaps none was more exotic than that of Mme Gauthier singing Francis Scott Key.

The ballets were presented to wild applause, and Bolm received a laurel tribute. The reviews also were favorably disposed. And the papers were beginning to watch for Griffes now, "whose songs and orchestral compositions," remarked the *Evening Telegram*, "have already received well-deserved praise." The *Globe* on the day after the New York opening said: "A feature of the entertainment was *Sho-Jo*, a Japanese mime play, in which Michio Ito and Tulle Lindahl appeared. The music, composed by Charles T. Griffes, on a basis of authentic Japanese folk tunes, proved especially interesting." The *Evening Sun* mentioned "Ito in his Japanese intoxication that came out of no Broadway bottle." *Musical America* said that "*Sho-Jo*, a mime play, music by Charles Griffes, was one of the most gripping pieces of the evening." The *Musical Leader* commented: "From the musical standpoint the detail which stood forth in bold relief was the orchestration supplied by Charles T. Griffes for a pantomime done by Ito and Miss Lindahl."

Although Griffes did not succeed in getting Schirmer's to publish *Sho-Jo*, the whole episode had been a feather in his cap. It was no wonder that he was unable to deliver the parts of *Kubla* to Sokoloff on time. Besides the ballet he had been occupied with the final proofs of the four William Sharp piano pieces, which came out in August. (Royalties from his other compositions, August 1916 to August 1917, were $23.78.) He invited Paul Rosenfeld up to the studio on 46th Street, which he was using again for the vacation, and played to the critic the *Clouds* dedicated to him. He also played from the score of *Kubla*, and when Rosenfeld asked him the reason for the Orientalistic passage, Griffes replied: "To give a sense of what was going on inside the Dome."

In addition to work accomplished Griffes had enjoyed the summer. He liked the people in the Ballet and deeply respected some of them as artists. They had all traipsed about together like a great family. "I have been in New York all summer with a great time, as usual. Spent most of the time with Bolm and the Ballet people. It has been one of the most amusing vacations I ever had. . . ." A highlight had been the jaunt to Atlantic City. There had been gay sun-filled afternoons on the beach, and intrepid explorations through all the byways of the resort. On one adventure "we all went to a Hindu 'psychic.' He read my character beautifully by palmistry and then told me of an advantageous change that would come into my life within two months. I am skeptical about that. To some of the other people he prophesied bad luck, and one in particular has had two very unfortunate things happen to her already since then, so maybe my good luck will come too. He foretold one other thing within a year which I hope will not happen." That which the psychic foretold within a year was marriage. And as to any advantageous change in his life within the next two months, Griffes had good reason to be skeptical. "In about ten days I shall be going back to Hackley," he wrote Babe on September 16th, "but am looking forward to it less than ever. However, it is too risky to break loose just now."

Babe was then in Sydney, Australia. "I envy you the opportunity to travel again — especially out in the Pacific. I am wild to go all over out there, but suppose I shall never get there. A couple of days ago I overheard a movie man in a restaurant telling some friends how cheap everything was in Los Angeles. At present I want to go to the Orient. Ito will take me back to Japan with him, where he says living is nothing compared to here. I am already very expert at eating with chopsticks. In town I go a good deal with Ito to a Japanese restaurant. One day Pod [Ethel Shoobert] and I went to Chinatown for lunch. We ate bushels of stuff, and I think Pod was violently ill for days afterward. It didn't affect me, but then I can stand anything. I think the Orientals are the only ones who know how to cook anyway."

But so much for dreams. It was back to the grind that month. In September, not long before his letter to Babe, Griffes had sold Schirmer's his three songs *In a Myrtle Shade*, *Wai Kiki*, and *Phantoms*, as Op. 9, and as Op. 10 the five Chinese songs, with *Impressions of a Traveller* left out and a Japanese song, *A Feast of Lanterns*, composed during August and September, substituted in its place.

Rudolph Schirmer, who had heard the *Five Poems of Ancient China and Japan* while on a recent visit to New York, received a letter from Griffes dated September 12th. "The reason for my writing you about them is to ask if they could be rushed through any way." They were going to be introduced by Eva Gauthier in November. ". . . I think they ought to be out by that time if possible. There are always many inquiries after a new thing immediately after its first performance. If people can't get it, they are apt to lose track of it, and do not ask for it again. I am sorry to bother you about this matter, but realize of course that only you can decide about such rush orders."

He had not forgotten his hopes of getting *Kubla* performed

in the East that season. On the 3rd of October he sent Walter Damrosch a note and, receiving a reply on the 5th, left the score with the conductor next day. Then he went off to tea at Eva Gauthier's, which was followed by a rehearsal of the songs.

On the 7th he got some new ideas for *Le Jardin,* and on the same day wrote to Giovannitti about copyright permission for *Phantoms.* Two days later he made a copy of *Phantoms* that he sent out for possible performance. All this while he conscientiously maintained the hours of practice incidental to his school duties. The procuring of outside artists for Sunday nights had become only an occasional task since the war. "It has been a quiet year in that respect anyhow," he had written to John Nichols, a singer inquiring about an engagement the preceding June. On the 18th Griffes started corrections on a second score of *Kubla,* and the next day wrote to Leopold Stokowski about it. On the 24th he sent it to Stokowski. But from neither Damrosch nor Stokowksi, though both these men later expressed real admiration for his work, was *Kubla* to have its first performance. It would have to wait two more years for that.

Mr. Schirmer had given the word, and publication on the Chinese songs went ahead. In early October, Griffes had still not decided on a title for the whole set. On the 16th he wrote Sonneck: "When the proofs of the Chinese songs are ready, will you telephone me here (Tarrytown 129)? I will come in town then that same day or the next one. . . . It will save considerable time as the mails are unreliable. If I could not be gotten to the phone to answer, you could leave the message." "No proofs yet of the Chinese songs?" he asked again on the 23rd. He was telephoned on the 25th and the next day spent most of the morning at Schirmer's correcting first proofs. Then with Ito and Miss Lindahl he visited the Century Theater where

Bolm was in rehearsal, went on by himself to Eva Gauthier's, and afterwards spent an hour with Miss Lindahl at the big Red Cross pageant at the Opera House. The next day there was another rehearsal with Eva Gauthier at 12. Afterwards, in the evening, he attended with some friends a New York Symphony concert, and on his way home ran up against a suffrage parade in which one of the bands was playing *These Things Shall Be.*

With all his chances to establish himself so much centered around these activities in New York, he could not help feeling that "any place in N. Y. would suit me. I am so tired of trains and giving up interesting evening engagements because I can't come in for them."

Eva Gauthier's recital came off on November 1st. It was a gala occasion. Besides Griffes's five songs the program included, for the first time in America, the *Trois Chansons* by Maurice Ravel; for the first time anywhere, three Japanese songs by Igor Stravinsky; and anteceding the Metropolitan's announced presentation of the opera, the aria "*Salut à Toi Soleil de l'Orient*" from Rimsky-Korsakov's *Le Coq d'Or.* Griffes accompanied in his own numbers. It was a program that inspired the *New York Evening World* to exclaim next day: "How the singer ever kept the pitch in such a medley is an unanswerable question. She even had the temerity to repeat one of the songs, and at least one hearer proudly realized that the music was the same as what she had just sung." As for Griffes, he stood his ground well even in such distinguished contemporary company: ". . . The real features of Mme Gauthier's program were the Chinese and Japanese inspirations of Charles T. Griffes and Igor Stravinsky. Of the two, Mr. Griffes adhered the more closely to the traditional scales of the Far East, and in general made his effects the more intelligible and hence convincing."

"This American composer has already given many proofs of his ability to appropriate and revitalize the Oriental spirit and the five examples of his work presented last evening were in his happiest vein."

Most of the other reviews in the newspapers and musical press were equally laudatory. "Nothing on Miss Gauthier's program was more interesting or written with a more winsome pen than *Five Poems of Ancient China and Japan* composed on the five- and six-tone scales by Charles T. Griffes, who appeared at the piano himself as accompanist in this series. The songs are of inherent beauty and indicate the fact that music which is regarded as the last expression of the day has its basic principles in the early centuries. Mr. Griffes has an unusual talent, and he had a fine interpreter in Miss Gauthier, just as she had an excellent medium for a phase of musical expression for which she is strangely well equipped."

Pitts Sanborn, in his review, especially commended the first three songs. "The first, 'In a dress of gaudy fabric,' really evokes the vision of a dewy morn. The second, 'Out across the waves,' imparts by the simplest means a sense of autumnal desolation. The third, 'The temple courts,' holds successfully throughout the curious combination of moods suggested in the central phrase, 'Come to the shrine while revolutions reign.'"

Two notices raised a question that Griffes had tried to anticipate. The *Christian Science Monitor* said: "These works, which indicate that the composer has studied Chinese melody deeply, are pleasant to hear and interesting; yet there is little of value, it may be surmised, in working in the restricted forms of the Chinese." The *Boston Evening Transcript* echoed the sentiment: "It scarcely seems worth while, indeed, to go to such trouble to avoid using certain arbitrarily condemned notes, but it reveals a laborious technical curiosity on the part of the composer, and much deftness of execution."

Griffes hastened to capitalize on his new success. To Schirmer's he sent a letter asking that clerks in the vocal department be instructed to inform prospective customers that the songs were expected from the press any day. For he well appreciated that music of such experimental character would have to be exploited at once if it were to bring him any money. (And in the end all his finicky alarms and ruses proved justified. From December 3rd, 1917, to January 1st, 1919, his total royalties on the Chinese songs were $16.87.)

Reviews of the *Roman Sketches* began to appear in December. The *Musical Monitor* found them to "exhibit a highly cultivated imagination, extremely fine taste, and a finely developed technique." A. Walter Kramer more or less agreed in *Musical America*, and added that the pieces were dedicated to Rudolph Ganz, Winifred Christie, and Paul Rosenfeld, "the last named being the critic who 'discovered' Mr. Griffes last winter in the late *Seven Arts*." Kramer's rancorous allusion to Rosenfeld's "discovery" was exemplary of a usual phenomenon on the musical scene. The fetish of "first performance" was perhaps its most prominent manifestation. Performers and conductors vied for the honor of first performance whenever it seemed likely to bestow personal glory upon them, and thus collected acts of discovery like scalps about their belts. A lamentable by-product was the near impossibility of obtaining other (musically necessary) hearings of such works from any but their discoverers.

Awaiting a final and messianic "discovery," Griffes meanwhile took more practical steps towards security. An affluent woman of his acquaintance who asked him to assist her in selecting a piano received a bill for $25. On December 11th he wrote his publishers: "What I wanted to ask you was whether the house wishes to make that five-year contract with me or not. It is entirely up to G. Schirmer whether they wish to keep a line on my output or not. If a contract is drawn up, I think the royalty question is best left out, as we agreed at our last discussion of the affair some weeks ago. It really has nothing to do with this and might only complicate things. Besides G. Schirmer's know that I am not going to make any exorbitant demands on them, and I expect they are not going to try to cheat me. Let me know what they wish to do." The brusque tone is indicative of the new approach he had found it necessary to adopt in business dealings with his publishers. The whole letter was simply another of his fruitless gestures towards establishment of outside lifelines on which he might depend, and Dan, whom he had consulted about it, advised him that he was well within his rights. Mrs. Ethelbert Nevin in her letter, already quoted, to Gustave Schirmer of the Boston Music Company had also pointed out: ". . . There has never been any contract written between you and my husband (which I confess has surprised me). . . ."

A few musical activities filled out the last month of the year. It was in this December that Griffes began the piano *Sonata* and also composed a setting to John Masefield's *Sorrow of Mydath*. The Ballet made a trip to the Wilbur Theater in Boston, giving *Sho-Jo* on the 7th. Its reception was a typical Bostonian smirk of lasciviousness. "The biggest excitement of the week was the three performances and a Saturday morning extra of Roshanara's Danse Divertissements, reminding Boston as they did of the glorious naughty days of the Russian Ballet. More than proper, it is true, these Divertissements would not have shocked the modesty of the furthermost dweller in virgin Maine." The music received slightly more dignified attention. "Perhaps the most remarkable of the divertissements was Michio Ito's mime play, *Sho-Jo*, with music by the very original, very daring Charles Griffes."

Griffes himself was in Boston for one day to attend some rehearsals. A reduction of the score was necessary, and Griffes, always particular about the manner in which his works were presented, replied to Henry Gideon, who later wrote him admiringly of the ballet: " The peculiar orchestration is one of its chief charms, and I hope sometime you will hear it done as it was meant to be."

The evening of his visit to Boston, Griffes accompanied his friend Arthur Shepherd to the home of Henry F. Gilbert, the well-known American composer whose avowed aim was to write " music which shall smack of our home soil, even though it may be crude." Shepherd later gave an expressive account of this occasion "which brought Griffes's art and attitude into sharp focus; this was during my residence in Boston. Charles, Henry Gilbert, and I 'got together'! Now it is obvious that two more diametrically different personalities than Gilbert and Griffes could hardly be imagined. I suppose that the only correspondence was the presence of the letter 'G' in both names. As an onlooker and observer I had a good time. Whether or not the other two (playing a similar role) were equally entertained I have no way of knowing. Charles played brilliantly his *Barcarolle* and *Scherzo* from the three *Fantasy Pieces*, Op. 6. One could easily discern the Gilbertian reactions: first an astonishment at the fastidiousness, refinement, and maturity of craftsmanship, then a characteristic grin of resentment and dissent from the aesthetic underlying this music. How could such hypersensitive art and technique subsist in an American carcass!? "

Griffes also intimated his dissent. "In the evening I got dragged out to Henry Gilbert's house in Cambridge," he wrote Bob. "I'm sorry now I didn't turn Gilbert down (he is one of the really famous Boston composers) and have a meeting with you."

Chapter **XIV**

ON January 22nd, 1918, Mrs. William Jay sent her famous letter to the founder of the Boston Symphony Orchestra asking for the dismissal of Dr. Karl Muck, its German conductor. ". . . In our opinion," she wrote, " even art must stand aside so that every possible influence can be brought to bear to terminate the war with an Allied victory." The subsequent commotion over Muck gave the inhabitants of the American musical world their cue. They had always preferred that " art stand aside" anyway, subservient to the performer's or conductor's personality, to the literary program of the music, and to anecdotes about its composition. They could now appear in public unabashed in their true guise. After the first public performance of Griffes's *Wai Kiki* and *Sorrow of Mydath* the critic for *Musical America* came right out with things in a review that did not even deign to single out the songs for individual mention. "The present course of worldly events has so altered values that sensitive folk no longer blench from the dire charge of Philistinism. One is not today an outcast and contemptible by reason of an inability to perceive a message of beauty in studied ugliness or significance in what arbitrarily professes to be recondite. Hence it will probably not be judged a sign of pachydermous insensibility to dismiss more than three-fourths of the new songs brought forward by this charming and artistic singer [Eva Gauthier] as ill-sounding and vacuous trash. It might, of course, be scrutinized at considerable length and diversely dissected. But altogether too much of this kind of thing is practiced." That was to the point enough. So was the rest of the review. Some of the music had merit. For example, and with almost contortive patriotism to the Allied cause: "The best of it was uncovered in the four Alsatian folk songs, delicately but unobtrusively harmonized by Gustave Ferrari — songs constituting in the Gallicism of their character a striking ethnological brief for the national allegiance of the 'lost provinces.'" But in general "the listener not pledged to the life and death defense of the ultra-modern yearned with the fullness of his being for ten bars of Haydn or five of Schubert." That it was no tribute to the art of either Haydn or Schubert to be thus comfortably ranged in public like a pair of old carpet slippers did not occur to their ardent devotee.

Such was the tone of American musical life in the war period — a welcome and deliberate lowering of artistic standards on every hand to a level even beneath what it had been in normal times. Not without point Griffes wrote Bob, away in training camp: "The mere serious recognition of a good thing means a good deal, and sometimes I very much prefer the appreciation of a layman to that of a trained musician." The alternative of redoubling and intensifying artistic accomplishment, of meeting the war's destructiveness with a renewal of creative energy, as had been suggested in the *Seven Arts'* supplement the year before, occurred to almost none. "Let us take measures to make ourselves for the first time thoroughly independent. America must begin a steady and slowly increasing mobilization in resource and in spirit, so that the day may come when we may go about our business assured that we need turn to no one when danger threatens us.

"If out of our crisis this emerges then we have converted a spasmodic reaction into a lasting good, and transformed a mood into living national power. Out of our momentary plight there may be born then the much-heralded, the long-dreamed-of America."

There were few American musicians or composers with sufficient faith in their powers to withstand the assaults of the time. Griffes was almost alone in his unswerving application to the requirements of his art, in his steadfast belief that his music was a factor of importance in the world. Whatever the course of outside events, it must follow the inexorable lines of its own development.

Schirmer's stated their view of music in wartime in the house bulletin. It was precisely what might have been expected. "We note with much pleasure the energetic manner in which certain public men and editors are defending music from the charge of being a war nonessential. Indeed, we have before us an article from a very influential metropolitan daily in which music is not only termed a vital war essential but an absolute necessity. This latter classification seems in perfect taste to us; because historical chronicles will show that whenever great stress and trouble have visited the world, music has always been the prime ameliorator of their balefulness. . . . And that our own government fully recognizes the efficacy of music to cheer, brighten, and invigorate, is convincingly assured by its recent order that all of our army and navy bands be increased."

There was such a waving of flags, such an establishment of bivouacs, in the Schirmer catalogue that Griffes's art seemed rather austere and remote beside the rest. In one broadside Percy Grainger was listed: "This celebrated artist, who endeared himself to the public by forswearing a brilliant musical career to become one of Uncle Sam's boys, is still further winning our admiration by giving many concerts in aid of the

American Red Cross." Another composer, Mana Zucca, "is doing much concert work, both vocal and instrumental, at the various training camps adjacent to New York. Her inimitable short songs, mostly humorous, are hugely enjoyed by the soldiers." Another, R. H. Woodman's "very latest work *To France*, will be featured in G. Schirmer's forthcoming brochure *Patriotic Music*." The claims made for Griffes on the same sheet seemed almost irrelevantly musical by comparison: ". . . music is ingenious . . . fine technical equipment . . . craft and color . . . truly skillful . . . modern in feeling."

In the frenzied rush of one and all to mingle their music with the red, white, and blue, Griffes's simple devotion to his artistic ideals was quite outdated. He could not help being a little skeptical about the antics of his fellow composers. Of Percy Grainger, for example, he wrote to Babe Shoobert: "He has a three months' furlough now to give concerts for the Red Cross. His uniform will be one grand advertisement — in fact it is all 'the last word' in advertising, though I don't think that is his only reason for joining the army."

Before long he would read in the *Musical Courier* an interview with Rudolph Ganz commending the new Griffes *Sonata* and tolerantly exonerating Bach, Beethoven, Haydn, Mozart, Schubert, Weber, and Brahms of being enemy aliens. On the other hand, Ganz maintained: "I stand firmly upon the idea that the works of the living German composers and naturally the use of the German language should be omitted from all concert programs." Mr. Ganz was standing very firmly upon the idea indeed. Early in the year the directors of the Philharmonic Society of New York had issued a statement that no living German composers would be represented on the orchestra's programs. Mr. Ganz concluded his interview with a prediction that the blood bath going on in Europe would prove a baptism for modern music, including American music. "I would like to add that the schooling of the young composers during the last fifty years has been so narrow that one can easily understand why some have become Bolsheviks and have thrown down all rules and regulations. This war will clear away all that is superficial. It will also deepen the emotion of every lover of music and every student, including the Americans. And, as in Europe, great men will be born out of the destruction of war. We know that the future glory of American music is in the hands of Providence."

Amid the veritable torrents and floods of balderdash that gushed from every side, Ganz's views were almost fair-minded and sane. They were at any rate lucid.

So far as Griffes was concerned the war made no difference in his attitude towards his German friends. "I haven't heard from my friends across the water for many months," he wrote Bob. "Someday I suppose it will be taken up again. In the meantime I imagine they feel the same towards me personally as I do towards them. I only hope the father isn't gone." "The father" was not gone, but the war had now snuffed out the incessant flickering of their correspondence. In a letter to Miss Broughton, written in 1920 after the composer's death, Konrad mentioned "the many years of enforced silence on both sides, during which each hardly knew whether the other was alive. . . ." He refers also to "a letter that I received from Charlie, a few months ago, expressing a point of view about the war and about Germany that was simply unbelievable coming from a person like Charlie, who knows our country so well, and that would have been absolutely shocking if it had not been explainable by the crazy newspaper instigation of an entirely hostile world against us, which nobody could encounter without being influenced."

That, considering his many liberal and socialist friends, Griffes should not have adopted the Marxian analysis of the war is not to be wondered at. They had been routed in utter confusion by the cataclysm. Some truly believed it the Armageddon from which world socialism would arise by the overthrow of capitalism. Others were pre-eminently occupied in working for or against immediate measures. Still others joined in the fray about a "war to make the world safe for democracy" or a "war to end all war." Their flurry and division had already been apparent in the election two years before when some had rallied to the support of Wilson. Griffes's own vote for the Republican Party had not ranked as any greater defection from the classical tenets of the circle. In October of 1917 he had learned of a new use that was to be put to his labor hymn and had communicated with Schirmer's to expedite the matter. "Harry Barnhart has written me that the committee on the National Song Book of the Soldiers and Sailors has decided to include *These Things Shall Be* in the collection. From whom do they get permission? G. Schirmer, me, or both? Perhaps they have already come to you about it. I understand that G. Schirmer buys the orchestration from me for $20 and band arrangement for the amount I paid for it myself, $12." He had thus signified his support of the country in wartime; and the incident had marked a formal break with his left-wing acquaintances.

Now his concern was simple and immediate. It was an unerring consecration to the growth and fruition of his art. Early in January 1918 he wrote Bob: "In the papers one day a rumor that the draft age would be raised to forty-five was mentioned, but probably these older men would be used in clerical positions. I am not going into things before it is necessary as I have a lot of things yet to do in my own career and I am not sure that the country needs me yet." And his next letter said: "I am working at new things all the time. It is the only thing worth while, and there is so much to be done. I have many things in mind." It is the only thing worth while. In a letter to Howard Conant he reiterated the same conviction. Discussing his latest music, he concluded: "I keep pretty close to this work. After all it is the only thing worth while, isn't it, to do something that somebody else hasn't done or to do it better than anybody else." There was nothing of cant or hypocrisy in the attitude. In his pocket Griffes carried always a bit of inspirational prose that reminded: "Know that you have a mission in life; that your work is important; that the world needs you, that you must do your best. Be alive with the fact that there is something in you — something that the world wants." It was perhaps naïve, even sentimental, in expression, but it stated exactly what he felt to be true. There was a war, but Charles T. Griffes's musical gift had its place too in the scheme of things. As Marion Clark later wrote, had he come to harm "his music would have suffered, and that would have been infinitely worse to him than death."

In June of 1917, when the war had threatened to encroach upon his own most sacred precincts, he had appealed directly to Rudolph Schirmer. "As I know, the house is on account of increased expense of paper inaugurating a new policy now of having smaller pages and cutting out extra covers of tinted paper such as were on my piano pieces in 1915.

"I don't know whether this policy is pursued in all new publications or not, but at any rate may I take the liberty of asking to have it set aside in this case [the *Roman Sketches*]. It seems to me that an attractive appearance undoubtedly has some effect on the sale of new works at the beginning, and under this heading should surely come broad margins and tinted covers. Pardon my making this special request. I think the unusual character of the pieces [would] also be most suitably matched by an individual cover."

Occasionally he visited Noble Kreider, who was in service

at Camp Merritt, New Jersey, and Kreider later recalled: ". . . On one of Charles's visits to me at Camp Merritt he spoke of the war with complete indifference, only expressing a hope he would not be compelled to go 'for if I do, it will be an end to my music.'" The threat of draft extension had already plunged him into prolonged and constant activity. There was so much to be done. Kreider, looking upon the pallid features and overworked frame of his companion, worriedly cautioned: "Too constant work will also do it."

His hopes of leaving the school and setting up as a composer, abandoned the year before, once again foundered on the rocks of wartime insecurity. Intolerable as the life at Hackley had become, it was the only means of obtaining some leisure in which to compose. A departure was out of the question now when the ravages of wartime economy were so general. He dilated upon these considerations, among others, in the letter to Howard Conant quoted earlier. It was dated January 5th, 1918.

"I am just now on my vacation but return to Hackley on Monday. We private school people are more favored than others — eighteen days was our holiday. I have made my headquarters here at my mother's apartment in Bloomfield, but I confess that the station has seen more of me than any other part of the town, as most of my time has been spent in New York. The cold has been terrific, and many people were forced to evacuate their houses for hotels, but I hope it is going to be better now. We were very comfortable here, fortunately. These shortages of coal, sugar, etc., are not so easily explained or excused, it seems to me. Surely there was never before such suffering from cold around here as these past days."

As to his own situation, ". . . people in the profession are glad of most anything certain now during the war. There is a great deal of hardship among smaller musicians just now. Concert engagements are few and not so well paid as usual. I am glad for my steady job, as dull and uninteresting as it is (between you and me, it is a deadly bore, but I have stuck it out for quite a sum of years now and shall not give it up in these uncertain times)."

On learning of Bob's enlistment he had been vastly relieved. "It was the only sensible thing to do," he wrote him. "Exemption chances are few, and nobody wants to be drafted under the conditions now reigning in camps." His next letter to Bob was dated January 10th, 1918. "It sounds awful when you tell of getting up at 5 o'clock, but I suppose your life now is about the most healthful and sane that you ever led. Late to bed and to rise never did anybody any good. I remember that you used to say that you would not mind a certain amount of military discipline here, so it is probably not irksome to you. When are you going to get snapped by some six for $1 photographer? I want to see how you look in your middy blouse and pants, go soon and send me one.

"Why did you go in for four years? I suppose there is always the chance to get out when the war is over if you want to. I was very much interested in what you told of your life there. Please do keep away from the women and booze. They can only harm you, and I am glad to know you are keeping shy. The next time I go in town I am going to get a box of tobacco and send it to you. You probably have all you want, but then a box from me may give you more pleasure."

The teacherly admonitions about "women and booze" were neither so hypocritical nor Machiavellian as they might at first seem. Griffes often felt obligated by his position as mentor at Hackley to drivel conventional bits of wisdom to the boys. He himself was the first to laugh at his apparent inability to strike a convincing note.

The letter continued: "I am not going to tell you anything

about Hackley because after all it is a dull subject. —— is engaged to ——, and I have taken over the ——s' table is all I can think of, and that isn't worth writing. We were all surprised at ——'s engagement. There are hopes for me now, aren't there? But a well-known composer whom I was talking with lately about such affairs told me never to get married for heaven's sake. He said it hampered a composer too much on account of bread-winning necessities, and he ought to know as he is married and has three children.

"I have had some rather interesting letters from a Belgian soldier with whom I got acquainted by proxy through a lady in New York. So far as I can learn, he has lost track of all his family and former friends during the war.

"We had a pretty cold time around New York lately. Many people have been forced to move out of their houses and into hotels or anywhere where they could get warm. I believe the school has plenty of coal."

He told about some new songs of his (the *Three Poems*) that Schirmer's were bringing out that month and ended: "I don't know whether you have any singing up there, but if you use the new Army and Navy songbook gotten out by the Government you will find in it *These Things Shall Be* by C. T. G. It was one of a very few modern American songs selected for the book."

There was another Elmiran represented among those "very few modern American songs." The words of *Keep the Home Fires Burning*, on page 21, were by Mrs. Lena Gilbert Brown Ford, she who had once read the chariot race from *Ben Hur* before a flickering tableau in one of Mrs. Fassett's spectacles, and who was to meet death in the air raids over London.

On the 27th of the month Griffes sent the tobacco. "Yesterday in town I got some Cake Box tobacco and am getting it off to you. It is very good and not too strong. I only hope it gets to you safely. Cigarettes shall be forthcoming also. Only do not inhale if avoidable. This seems absurd advice since inhaling is regarded as the only pleasure of cigarettes. That is, however, not true as I do not inhale and still enjoy them. Please do not eat too much and get *fat*. I can already imagine you toddling around in your middy suit looking like a stuffed sausage. So even [there] they smoke in forbidden places, do they. . . .

"I am very much amused at your observations about ——. I think you are mistaken, however, about the fire being dead. In fact, unless there is some hindrance on the other side, I predict a family. It may be a small one and attended with difficulties, but nevertheless there will be the attempt. . . .

"I had a letter from Arlo Garnsey a few days ago. He is at the aviation school at Memphis, living in a tent, with the ground covered with a foot of snow, having made only one flight, and very much dissatisfied with things generally. The latter of course is chronic with many of us. I do not claim to be immune myself — at times anyway. The routine stuff of every day is such a bore. Nothing much happens here to disturb the tedium. Three fellows have come down with chicken pox within three days, and I suppose more may come, but I hope not. The disease isn't serious, at any rate. Last night was to have been a dance here with the school band providing music, but I believe the band went on a strike. It is a habit of bandplayers. I am glad that bands and music still bring back to your mind the evenings in my room here."

The letter continued that he had been to rather more concerts than usual since September, "one reason being perhaps that tickets have been sent to me for so many things. I have paid for only three concerts this season. My three last songs [the *Poems*] came out at Schirmer's only last week. They are not my latest ones as they were written from one and one-half to two years ago. A publisher never keeps up with the output of a composer. . . . Among other things I have just finished a long work for piano [the *Sonata*]. I suppose it will be published sometime fairly soon, but I always let things lie around for a while before handing them in."

In January too he composed a setting to Fiona Macleod's poem *The Rose of the Night*, with its fascinating subject matter: "There is an old mystical legend that when a soul among the dead woos a soul among the living, so that both may be reborn as one, the sign is a dark rose, or a rose of flame, in the heart of the night."

On January 9th Miss Rosalie Miller had sung one of his *Rondels* in Boston. His piano pieces were heard in Chicago the same month. On February 7th Reinhold Warlich, baritone, whom he had known in Elmira, sang the Chinese songs in a recital at Wells College. The *Musical Leader* in a tardy notice of the *Roman Sketches* on the 8th spoke of Griffes. "More than any other American composer has he dared to free himself from tradition without overstepping the bounds of honesty and beauty. The schooled musician stands behind his work, which is interesting melodically and rhythmically as well as harmonically." The *Musical Observer*, in a nevertheless favorable review, disagreed. "All the numbers are conceived along lines of the so-called impressionistic school of writers, in which form, logical progression, and thematic development are thrown to the winds and replaced by what seems to be entire freedom in harmonic plan, spasmodic thematic treatment, and utter disregard of technical difficulties." Notices of the *Five Poems of Ancient China and Japan* appeared. The *Musical Courier* pointed out that the verses were bad translations and that the music to which he had set them "had more atmosphere and grace, more of the Orient in it than the texts themselves." The *Musical Observer* emphasized his technical achievement. "All the thematic material is characteristically simple, and from a musical point of view, very unpretentious. Owing to his musicianly skill and ability, however, the composer has turned what at first may seem barren Oriental tonal progressions into musical poems of very unusual type and fancy."

He was going forward with his things all the time. On February 11th he wrote Schirmer's and two days later stopped in to play *The Rose of the Night* and *Sorrow of Mydath*. They were accepted, Schindler and Sonneck suggesting that for business reasons it would be wise to substitute the first line as title for *Sorrow of Mydath*. Griffes secured Masefield's personal permission to use his poem, but the song was not published till after Griffes's death, when it came out under its usual title.

February 26th, 1918, marks an important date in the history of American music. On that day the piano *Sonata*, of which something more will be said later, received its first public performance. Begun in December of 1917, it was completed the following month, as Griffes had written Bob. The occasion of its première was an evening of compositions by Charles T. Griffes sponsored by the New York MacDowell Club. Griffes himself presided at the piano, and the concert, free to members and their guests, was attended by a large audience. In chronological retrospect the program included three of the early piano pieces; the Chinese poems, sung by Eva Gauthier; the *Roman Sketches;* a piano reduction of *Sho-Jo*, danced by Ito; and the *Sonata*, listed simply as " Sonata in one movement." *The Kairn of Koridwen* — as Griffes had informed Marion Bauer on the 4th — would have been too great an undertaking. " It would mean engaging ten first-class men and possibly several rehearsals. I am not quite sure now whether I want to undertake it or not. Also it would lengthen the program so much that some of the piano and voice would have to be out."

Griffes referred to the affair in a letter to Bob about " my latest stunt." " I wish you had been there. The King and Queen and about a dozen other people from the school were there. I had a wonderful audience, with a good many people standing who couldn't find seats." The reviews that followed, with one exception, gave no evidence that anything eventful had occurred. *Musical America* threw a wet blanket over the entire proceedings, giving credit only to the first three piano pieces and the songs, "already admired for their atmosphere." The *Sonata* "after ten minutes' wandering in the nowhere ends without any disclosure of musical beauty or tangible invention." The *New York World* in its report next day commented: "The sonata in one movement I would like to designate by some other name; but Mr. Griffes insisted to me that it was true to form." The *Musical Leader* trembled a little. " [The *Sonata*] breaks completely away from convention and belongs frankly to a field of endeavor that must be called experimental." One critic, however, listened to what was presented. In the *Christian Science Monitor* he wrote: " The work, though strange, perhaps, to some hearers, proves to be clear in structure, intense in feeling, and refined in expression." Griffes took note and was gratified.

There were other musical affairs going on in New York as well. On March 10th Griffes wrote Bob: "It looks terribly dreary outside just now to see the snow and wind again. It is dreary, and yet I am glad to sit here quietly for a change, as I have been in New York so much lately and am tired. Beginning with last Saturday I stayed in New York overnight, and went to a dress rehearsal of a new production at the Metropolitan Opera at 11 Sunday morning. I got back to the school just in time for choir at 4:30 (familiar sound, hasn't it?). Monday A.M. I went in again for the final dress rehearsal of the same opera at 11 o'clock and returned at 3. Wednesday I was in all day for several things, including first performance of aforesaid opera, after which I was up at Mrs. ——'s . . . house at a party given for the producer and some of the singers in the opera. I left there at 1:30 and of course stayed in town all night. Came up the next morning for a lesson at 11:35. That same evening I went down again to a box party at a concert. Yesterday I was again in for the day and came back again late, after being at the Neighborhood Playhouse. So I am today glad to stay home and would like nothing better than to sit all day in my room doing nothing. Only there comes again 'choir at 4:30' and service afterward. I believe Mr. Gage had difficulty in securing a minister today. Too bad he got one in the end! . . .

"Last night at the Playhouse they had two bills, a classical No drama and a Spanish play. The No play was done in Japanese style — namely, there was a small chorus at the side, part of whom said the lines of the play; others chanted in a low voice, and two others played Japanese drums. The story was partly acted out and partly danced by two No dancers in the middle of the stage — Michio Ito and Irene Lewisohn. All the characters had on Japanese masks, and the whole thing gave a most strange and at the same time wonderful effect. That brings me to the opera on Wednesday night, *Le Coq d'Or*, which was produced for the Metropolitan by no less than my old friend of last summer, Adolph Bolm. The singers and a large chorus sat stationary on what resembled bleachers at the side of the stage while the center was left completely free for solo dancers and a large corps de ballet who danced and acted the story. In other words every part had two interpreters, a singer and a dancer. It was one of the most brilliant productions ever made at the Opera. Bolm himself danced the principal part."

As this letter indicates, Griffes was not letting up in his endeavors to interest new people in his work. He had called several times in February at the Hotel Rensselaer, hoping to meet the new Danish soprano, Povla Frijsh. She was always out.

Finding her in one day, he played all his songs to her, and through Mme Frijsh, in turn, became acquainted with Marcia van Dresser, the American singer, and several others.

On March 23rd the Metropolitan Opera produced Henry Gilbert's *The Dance on the Place Congo*. Griffes, meeting Paul Rosenfeld on Fifth Avenue, enthusiastically described the *mise en scène* and advised the critic to hear it, but the latter's spirits were low, since he had been drafted and was about to leave for war. Rosenfeld could gather, however, that the event of the Gilbert performance had encouraged Griffes to believe that there would be a chance for the production of other American ballets. He was right. Griffes was hopefully negotiating that very project, among others. "I may orchestrate a ballet for the Metropolitan Opera House," he later wrote Bob, "and further may also in conjunction with another man write a new ballet of American Indian life with music based on original Indian songs. Further there is a bare possibility that some rich people interested may provide about $1000 for us to go out to Arizona for a month this summer and study Indian dances. This is all between you and me as it is unsettled, and I wouldn't want anybody else to know of it." Nor could the failure of these radiant plans dissuade him from promptly entering upon others.

The next few months saw no change in his status. On March 13th Miss Edna Gunnar Peterson played one of his compositions at the Ziegfeld Theater in Chicago. On the 30th there appeared a vitriolic review of his three latest published songs by A. Walter Kramer in *Musical America*. "'Three Poems for Voice and Piano,' Mr. Griffes calls these compositions. We are glad that he does not call them 'songs.'" The William Blake song was dismissed as "splendid." Then the review got down to business. "If this [*Wai Kiki*] be the music that he has felt from knowing this poem, then indeed is he the American Stravinsky, as he has been dubbed by his disciples in the nether regions of Greenwich Village! To us he seems to have missed the warmth, the languor of 'the murmurous, soft Hawaiian sea.'" "For doctors of music, for aesthetic dancers who constitute themselves authorities on modern music, for self-appointed music critics whose writing is as distinct as their knowledge of their subject is not, this song and the uninspired setting of Mr. Giovannitti's *Phantoms* will be masterworks before which they will prostrate themselves and about which they will wax enthusiastic. If ever there was a poem that clamored for rich and warmly felt music it is this *Phantoms*. Mr. Griffes writes for it an essay on the validity of the minor second as a factor of beauty in musical art."

In an article some years later Kramer expressed the opinion that Griffes might have been hurt by what he said on this occasion. Actually the situation was a good deal more complex than a single unfavorable review. The recent fiasco of the *Sonata*, which he had put so much store by, the apathy towards his latest songs, and the ambiguous reception that would be accorded the *Sorrow of Mydath* next month were adding up to an inescapable conclusion. He would face the same external barriers in his new independent development that he had earlier in the transition from a period of German influence to one of modern. But however people might howl, he had evolved a long way from the Griffes who had composed the *Lake* and *Scherzo*. One day Katherine Ruth Heyman, running into the composer at the Grand Central Terminal, spoke encouragingly of the growing popularity of his works. Griffes somberly replied: "Yes, but that's only my early work they play. Nobody understands what I'm doing now."

This is not to say that the customary pious twaddle and enthusiastic gush did not appear about the three *Poems* in the uncritical musical press. "The music throughout, with its restless rhythmic pulsations, tempo changes, and harmonic intricacies, proves the perfected musicianship of its composer, and justifies one in calling particular attention to the artistic value of his work."

Mr. Kramer's reference to Griffes's " disciples in the nether regions of Greenwich Village," whether by intent or unfortunate coincidence, was inept. For on the same date as his review there appeared a notice in the *Evening Sun* that Michio Ito, Tulle Lindahl, and Toschi Komori would dance at the Greenwich Village Theater on the following Sunday night, assisted by Mr. Charles T. Griffes, among others. It was, in fact, a series of three dance recitals on consecutive Sunday nights, beginning April 7th. The accompaniment consisted mainly of Japanese music, both traditional and by Koscak Yamada, assisting artist and Japanese composer. Griffes played one number, *The White Peacock*, danced by Ito, who not having believed at first hearing that the composition was by an Occidental did not consider it at all out of place on such a program.

On April 8th Griffes participated in the Second American Composers' Festival at the John Wanamaker Auditorium. Schirmer's had asked if they might count on his willingness to play three of his piano compositions published by them. Griffes consented, playing one from each opus. The programs began with *America* and ended with *The Star-Spangled Banner*. It was an American composers' festival for all but American composers. Wanamaker's, who sponsored the series and in whose auditorium it was held, derived free prestige. So did the music publishers whose share in the enterprise was advertised in captions at the top of the program. The composers " who have so generously given of their time and talents " received only verbal thanks by way of remuneration. It was splendidly typical of numerous other projects in operation to "aid the American composer."

Leslie Hodgson sent a note from Danville, Virginia, where he had played one of Griffes's compositions on April 16th at the Randolph-Macon Institute. On the 22nd Eva Gauthier sang *Wai Kiki* and the as yet unpublished *Sorrow of Mydath* in a recital at Aeolian Hall. The newspapers were cautious next day. Sigmund Spaeth in the *Evening Mail* wrote that "both of the new Griffes numbers showed an advance in the direction of ultra-modernism on the part of that gifted composer." In the New York *American*, Max Smith remarked that the two songs "disclosed genuine creative gifts." Herbert Peyser in his encomium of the Alsatian folk songs and the lost colonies, in *Musical America*, ridiculed Griffes altogether. "Over the tantrums of Messrs. Griffes . . . and the rest one prefers to draw the veil."

A cheering note sounded three days after the Gauthier recital, however, when Rudolph Ganz in a public interview flatly reversed the earlier verdicts on the *Sonata*. "Charles T. Griffes's new piano *Sonata*, which he played recently at the MacDowell Club, is free from all foreign influences. He is going his own way. . . ."

Chapter XV

GRIFFES discovered a new way to make money. Under the pseudonym "Arthur Tomlinson," proposed by Oscar Sonneck, he began to compose simple teaching pieces for children, which he sold outright to Schirmer's for lump sums. In April 1918 he received $90 for his *Six Short Pieces* by Arthur Tomlinson. *Six Patriotic Songs*, arranged for piano by Arthur Tomlinson and consisting of *America, Yankee Doodle, Marching through Georgia, The Star-Spangled Banner, The Red, White, and Blue,* and *Dixie,* brought him $100 at the beginning of May. His next batch of six, for which he received another $100, was accepted during the second week of May. Griffes suggested that they be called *Pictures of Military Life: Six Pieces Based on Bugle Calls* and appear separately. For commercial reasons, however, they were published as a set and titled *Six Bugle Call Pieces for Piano.* Schirmer's earliest designation of them as "American Bugle Calls in Easy Arrangements for Piano" had elicited the whimsical correction: "I see you had already found a title which is possibly better than mine—although I am not so sure about the 'easy.' However, that isn't so important in this case."

The Arthur Tomlinson compositions were a frankly money-

make them more suitable for quartet. The composer accepted these proposals most gracefully and set out to revise the piece. When he brought it back, it was still of extreme difficulty in rehearsal and did not produce the effect that he had anticipated. Nevertheless the Flonzaleys were convinced that there was something vital and arresting about the *Scherzo*. They decided unanimously not to be deterred by the few technical stumbling blocks but to go ahead with it for production at the earliest opportunity. A few days later, while Betti was at work preparing his schedule for the coming season, Griffes happened by. A new problem had arisen. Single pieces for quartet were exceedingly rare, and the *Scherzo* was not of sufficient length to stand by itself as a separate number on a program. "If I only had a slow movement by yourself," the violinist pointed out, "how much easier it would be to give your piece a fitting place." That very morning Betti had received from Washington a booklet containing a little collection of Indian and Negro popular songs. In glancing through them his attention had been immediately attracted by an Indian melody of haunting beauty, strangely evocative to him of "vast silences and nostalgic visions." It was a farewell song of the Chippewa Indians.

"Why don't you try to write a slow movement on this melody?" Betti suggested. "Seems to me it would lend particularly well to string treatment, and certainly it does not lack mood and character." Griffes was immediately aflame with the idea, jotted down the song in a notebook, and in less than one week returned with the draft of a slow movement intended as companion piece to the *Scherzo*. The "Lento," according to one acquaintance, Griffes later contended was of spirit rather than speed. This was the string movement of which Philip Hale was one day to write: " The first *Sketch*, based on a mournful theme, is singularly beautiful in the poetic treatment, in the dexterous employment of the instruments without a vain attempt to procure orchestral color. There is no anxious striving after effects, no desire to straighten the drowsy bourgeois in his seat, no effort to be original at any cost. The music is of a strange beauty, yet not remote, but warmly human."

Besides the string music Griffes had much else to do. His old friend Georges Barrère had requested him to compose a work for flute and orchestra that could be used in next year's concerts. Teeming with fine ideas for the project, Griffes resolved that it would not be a mere show piece. He was also planning to orchestrate the three Fiona Macleod songs. And in this connection he disputed with Schirmer's about a clause in his recent contracts. " It is further agreed that the Second Party [Schirmer's] has the right to publish practical orchestral and band arrangements of the composition covered by this agreement, and that such arrangements shall be free and exempt from all royalties." Now that he was contemplating the Macleod orchestrations he began to feel unprotected and discussed the matter with Dan. Schirmer's attitude was unequivocal and restated to Griffes in a letter from the assistant manager dated June 18th. " Mr. Sonneck says we had best cross our bridges when we come to them. As I told you, the added clause refers to those arrangements which we may make ourselves. Your share in any rentals which may accrue from the use of your own orchestrations is a matter to be settled when you shall have placed those orchestrations in our hands." He was now somewhat in the position of a novelist who has no financial or artistic proprietorship in the dramatization of his novels. If the novelist is also a dramatist, the analogy is complete. This clause would remain a bone of contention.

On the 27th of June, Griffes played at the Hotel Majestic for the New York State Music Teachers Association the same program that he had played two months before at the Wanamaker festival. "I am not a member of the association," he wrote Bob, "so you see it was as a 'prominent composer' that I was asked to do so." To Marion Bauer he later confided his impression of the concert as "rather a bore. . . . I think we all suffered more or less at being on the program at all."

The comment to Bob appeared in a letter from Hackley written two days after the convention. "You didn't expect to hear from me again so soon from here, nor did I expect to write from here at the time of my last letter." It had been necessary to do a considerable amount of composition work in a very short time. "So I decided at once to come up here where I am quite alone and have nothing else on my mind. I have been here since a week ago yesterday and leave tomorrow, having accomplished what I set out to do. Herr Schmidt was around till yesterday and —— likewise, but I never saw them except at mealtime. —— has been treating me to very nice meals, and the quiet of the place has been wonderful." He was still anxious about the draft. "At present there seems to be considerable opposition to extending the draft ages. I probably shall not wait in case it gets that far, but will step in some other way. I hear they are very anxious to have men go over to play in the camps, and are also looking for men who can speak German fluently. So you see I could get in on either of these jobs. Whatever it is, I shall go to France rather than stay here. Mr. Gage is expecting me back in the fall, and as it is now, I shall come back." Meanwhile he strongly wished to see Bob that summer. "Needless to say, I am hoping that you may be shipped from New York. Nothing could please me more than to be able to see you fairly frequently in that way. We could have some wonderful times together in town, especially in the summertime. My time and place in New York would be yours. I am counting strongly on having you. Let us hope the authorities don't disappoint me."

The summer began to pass all too fleetingly. At his old haunt at 12 West 46th Griffes worked away assiduously on his music. On July 8th he composed a setting to Masefield's *An Old Song Re-sung*, "a vigorous sea-song, full of the tang of the sea air and with a powerful climax — as sinister as it is powerful," in Mr. Upton's words. On the 17th Schirmer's sent Mrs. Sharp an order for six guineas in payment for the right to use the three Fiona Macleod poems. They paid half, and the other half was charged to Griffes. *Musical America* announced on July 27th: "Charles T. Griffes has just finished a new composition, a *Poem* for flute and orchestra. Mr. Barrère, who has seen the new work, has pronounced himself enthusiastic about it, and is preparing it for his next season's programs."

He saw much of Dan, with whom he planned a trip to Atlantic City that did not come about, and of Bob, who was temporarily stationed close to New York. With the latter, indeed, his affection overreached itself. The subsequent inner turmoil that he experienced is revealed in a pathetic letter that he dispatched soon after. ". . . As long as you are in N. Y. this is your home, and I want so much to make it pleasant for you. Perhaps I am too anxious, but you can pardon that. You know how much I care about you and how much it means to have you here with me. I can't bear that any of the time we have together should have any unpleasant moments."

Early in August, Griffes met Herbert Lansdale and his wife strolling down Broadway. It was a happy reunion after seventeen years' separation, and the three spent a good deal of time together while the Lansdales were in New York. Before they parted, Griffes, thinking back to a more carefree and un-dimmed period, said to his old friend: "You can't imagine what an inspiration it is to me to find you just the same after all these years." And Lansdale, seeing before him again the boy from Elmira, returned the sentiment.

August brought also an unlooked for variation in his sched-ule. There was a chance to make some money. Ito invited him to give performances with a Japanese troupe on the road. Half the net proceeds were to be donated to the Fund for Free Milk for France, and they stood to make some profit on the other half. Griffes accepted. He later described it in a letter to Mar-ion Bauer: ". . . I was out on a tour with a company of Jap-anese, giving performances for a French charity. We had three dancers (including Michio Ito) and three Japanese musicians (koto, samisen, and fué) whose music gave a very curious and exotic sound. The most interesting performances were at Washington and White Sulphur Springs, Va." From both these places he sent post cards to Bob. The first, from White Sul-phur Springs, was dated August 17th and said briefly: "Had a hot and dirty trip down yesterday, but it is very fine here, two palatial hotels and plenty of guests. Performance is tonight in open air, and tomorrow we go to Washington." The other was sent from Washington two days later. "Climbed [Wash-ington] monument (center of picture) among other things this A.M. Capital is about the same as Albany. Open-air per-formance will be rather chilly tonight, I am afraid. W. is lively now, but quite different from N. Y. C." On the 20th Griffes was back in New York, and on the 21st the troupe moved out to Plandome, Long Island, for overnight, returning to New York the next day. Then on midnight of the 23rd they de-parted for Manchester, New Hampshire, where they per-formed the following afternoon. He sent his mother a card on the 24th. "I return tonight by the midnight instead of later."

Griffes gave Bob a frank and amusing account of the whole adventure: "We had a nice trip in the South, many disagreeable things coming from mismanagement which made artistic performances impossible. But the people seemed to like it, and they made money for the charity. Likewise (and very important) we got our $25 each performance and all expenses. . . . Washington is a large small town but very homelike. We had some amusing hours, played double Canfield, about which the Japs were crazy. Got up and went to Chinese restaurants at 2 o'clock A.M.; stayed there until kicked out, returned home, and again played double Canfield until 4 A.M. Michio's chorines were this time (with one exception) distinguished for old age and bad looks. Otherwise they were highly respectable ladies eligible for any church sewing-circle. Our New England performance was at Manchester-by-the-Sea. . . . It was the best. It took place in the sunken garden of a magnificent estate just by the ocean. They took us for a drive afterward through Gloucester and Beverly Farms. It was an afternoon performance, and I returned to New York the same night in the sleeper, so of course didn't have time to see anyone." Griffes's share in the program had been the accompaniments to various dance numbers, including his own Wine Dance, and a part in the incidental music by Yamada to the company's presentation of *At the Hawk's Well*, the No drama by Yeats.

Between Southern and Northern swings of the itinerary, Griffes had written Bob: "I am sorry to lose so much time from N. Y. as I may have to move next week." The summer was practically over, and after all his fears and hopes the war had caught up with him. On August 27th, four days before President Wilson signed the Act providing for the registration of all men between eighteen and forty-six years, Griffes wrote Marion Bauer: "I hate to write such a late date at the top of my letter. . . . It means that my summer is almost gone. And summer gone means liberty gone now as I must either enlist within a few days (in case restrictions should be taken off) or be drafted. I haven't decided yet whether to wait for the draft or not. I hear the draft is to be vocational as far as possible, so maybe they will put me to doing something where I can be more useful than pulling a trigger. And again they may not see it that way. At any rate just now I can do nothing."

The letter also contained musical chatter. "I know the Ravel *Valses* very well. I used to play them a good deal. They are very beautiful though *raffiné* and *précieux* to the last degree, I think. That is the reason many people cannot like them. As for Ornstein, I am not sure about his being a primitive. I feel that he may be one in *The Wild Man, Moods*, and the *Dwarf Suite*, but his *Impressions* I don't think belong to that tendency. The end of June I was around at his studio several times, and we had some interesting talks. He is planning some intimate recitals with special programs for this winter, on one of which he wants to play my *Sonata*, but I doubt if they materialize. To come back to the 'primitive' idea, you may be right. I would like to have a perfectly exact definition of the term first. What makes me think that O. is not really a primitive is that the music he writes now is not at all of that type. At the convention he played a pretty salon waltz that he had written a week before."

Griffes summarized his vacation's work: "The summer has passed here very quickly and agreeably. I have had one of the pleasantest summers I ever spent in town. I might have worked more, but then I have not been quite idle, and anyway I do not regret the time spent otherwise. I wrote a second and third string quartet movement so that the quartet is now complete. I think the slow movement is the more successful of these two new ones, and for the present I am sending only that one to

Mr. Betti to look through. He was kind enough to ask me to send him at once whatever I did. Then I have started several sketches. Aside from that I have been orchestrating my *Poem* for flute and orchestra and the accompaniments to three new songs (which I think you do not know). Marcia van Dresser is going to sing them in November with the Philadelphia Orchestra in Wilmington and Philadelphia, and also both Maggie Teyte and Povla Frijsh have said they wanted to do them with the orchestra. Schirmer is printing them with piano."

His assertion that he did "not regret the time spent otherwise" was from the heart. "I had in some ways the pleasantest summer I ever had in town," he wrote Bob, "to which your visit contributed not a little, my dear boy. And if it was my last one in New York, I am satisfied that I spent it thus."

He had closed his letter to Marion Bauer with the information that he must vacate his apartment the following week — "Now I am just hurrying to get things done" — and would remain at his mother's "till school opens (Sept. 26th) or draft comes."

He left 12 West 46th for Bloomfield on the 3rd of September. Two days later he participated in the National American Music Festival at Lockport, New York, accompanying Miss Louise Lancaster, soprano, in three of his songs, *Come, Love, across the Sunlit Land*, *La Fuite de la Lune*, and *Wai Kiki*.

But by then the ax had fallen, and in the second week of September Griffes went to Washington to see if it were not too late to mitigate the blow by enlisting. While there he visited Towsley and his wife, who were now living in Washington. On September 15th he wrote Bob of his efforts: "Of course I expect to go now in some capacity. I told the King I would start them off anyway. If I go as a private, it seems that I must surely be called in Nov. at latest. Any other capacity will probably take me by then. I was in Washington last week and offered myself as interpreter, musician, or private. The Navy Intelligence said they could do nothing as all enlistments were closed; at the Army Intelligence, however, they said they needed men with my language qualifications and wanted me to be examined at once for the Overseas Interpreters' Corps. I postponed the exam from an immediate one at Wash. to one at Governors Island within a few days probably. If I rate well, some commission will be forthcoming, and I go to the front at once, or as soon as called. I don't know how stiff the exam is, but I am glancing through the German dictionary and taking conversational French lessons in town. I shall also tell them of my Italian. There remains still the music to be investigated, and that I must do at once. My musical friends want to get me in as band-leader or, better, instructor, where I shall be stationed on this side and can keep up my touch and connection with musical life here. It is all unsettled. At any rate I shall store my things at the school, and my position will be open to me on my return. —— and —— are of course also threatened with immediate call but are going to await things. I think the school has a good enrollment, and W. B. has been advised officially to keep enough teachers there to run the school as usual, so maybe everybody will be exempted (if they wish to be)." He ended on a familiar reprise: " I have many things to finish up before going off anywhere."

He remained uneasy about his prospects. On the last day of the month he made a second trip to Washington and stayed three days. Returning, he sent Marion Bauer a note: " I don't quite know how things will turn out yet, but I hope to be in France before very long. Just now I can only wait to hear orders. In the end it may just be the regular draft."

Griffes passed his examination for the Military Intelligence Department in France with a good mark and was assured of a first or second lieutenancy. Through a month of suspense he awaited final information and sailing orders, to the very end pulling every string at his command. Early in November he wrote Howard Conant for assistance, and on the 7th Conant helpfully sent a letter of recommendation to Captain Howard R. Whitney in New York: "He is a young man possessing the highest sense of honor, quiet and unassuming, thorough in his work and painstaking in details. . . . Mr. Griffes is a candidate for the Interpretation Corps." On November 11th President Wilson announced the Armistice to a joint session of Congress.

It was over. Griffes sat back and began to look upon the future as a living thing once more. Rudolph Reuter, the eminent Chicago pianist, performed one of his compositions at The Playhouse in Chicago on November 24th. Griffes sent a note inviting him for a visit when next he should be in New York. Ganz played something of his at the Grinnell School of Music in Iowa on December 7th, and Heinrich Gebhard, the prominent Boston pianist, also played two of his things at Steinert Hall in Boston on the 10th.

There was a block party with dancing and other festivities on Fifth Avenue between 42nd and 43rd Streets. Griffes met Dan, and they celebrated hostilities' end together. Having tutored intensively in French for his military examinations, Griffes could carry on a moderate conversation in the language and now began to reap the benefits by attending the French theater once a week — "chiefly because I have passes," he wrote Babe Shoobert.

Royalties from August 1st, 1917, to August 1st, 1918, had been $43.79. His activities began to revive. To Babe Shoobert he wrote on December 19th about the "three songs to beautiful poems by Fiona Macleod. The original conception was for voice and orchestra, but Schirmer's have published the piano version. There is a possibility that the very first performance of them may be Marcia van Dresser with the Philadelphia Orchestra, but at present it is uncertain on account of a squabble about her dates which may cause a cancelment of them. Mme Gabrielle Gills and one other are going to sing them with piano in New York this winter. Also Maggie Teyte may do one at least with orchestra." That nothing might go amiss with his fond hopes for these three songs, he dedicated them to Marcia van Dresser, Gabrielle Gills, and Povla Frijsh.

He had still other irons in the fire. "The Flonzaley Quartet intends to play two pieces for string quartet which I wrote last year, and either this year or next Georges Barrère will play with the orchestra a *Poem* for flute and orchestra which I wrote for him. Damrosch has it in mind. And now is that enough of myself? Oh, I forgot, I am giving another recital of my work in February (probably the Letz Quartet and Marcia van Dresser assisting)." He was forward-looking rather than optimistic about his things. "It is uphill work with my stuff, but the piano pieces seem to be getting a start. Half a dozen well-known pianists, including Ganz and Ornstein, are playing various ones this season. Harold Bauer has also told me that he intends to play my new manuscript *Sonata* next year."

Griffes explained his presence at the school: ". . . I came back here in September to start off the year for them, and here I am still. At first the thought of staying here another whole year seemed unbearable, but in some ways I am lucky to have a steady job when so many musicians are up against it. My class up here is larger than last year, but oh! how they bore and weary me! I am keeping on my own work pretty steadily."

So the year that had stirred with such dark urgency throughout finished like every other. Describing to the annotator of the Philadelphia Orchestra program books an orchestral *Notturno* that he had composed in this year, Griffes himself afterwards provided perhaps the best description of the year as a whole. " The mood and color are very somber, expressing the gloom of night. After the opening there is a passage expressing a mental anguish and struggle, followed by a passionate climax. Then comes a passage expressing momentary rest, followed by a slipping back into the original mood. After a sound of distant horns the piece closes with a few somber chords."

Yet it was a wonderful year. Under the threat of departing before his work was done, and despite innumerable obstacles, he had turned out unceasingly the majority of his greatest works. The *Sonata*, the string music, his finest songs, the *Poem* for flute and orchestra, the *Notturno* — with a sure instinct, one after another, he had piled them up in the very face of danger. And he had justified his belief in a creator's true mission.

Chapter XVI

GRIFFES started 1919 in new desperation. He had returned in September to help begin the music classes, "and here I am still." Well, he would make it his last year there. In whatever time could be winnowed from school routine he would expand his musical contacts, propagandize his compositions, and create fresh things. If independence could be won, he would win it. More than ever now, as he hastened about from one pursuit to another, he seemed to fulfill Arthur Farwell's description of him as "one of Maeterlinck's 'predestined,' who know that their time is short to do what they have to do." Any gaps in his busy routine were more than welcome. Once invited to dinner at the home of Manton Marble, Schirmer's assistant manager, he arrived early and seated himself in a rocking chair on his host's front porch where he was later interrupted rocking to and fro in gentle contemplation.

Through January he made the dizzying rounds of the musical metropolis trying to interest all and sundry in his work. Suppers with Dan came as interludes in this program, and he fell in the habit of riding out with the policeman when he changed stations. There were worth-while concerts, the New York Philharmonic, Prokofiev's recital for the New Music Society, and *Monna Vanna* at the opera, which he attended with Marion Bauer. He kept up his practicing at the school and cultivated new friendships. In the latter connection he now found sympathetic companionship with an eccentric Frenchman who had come to Hackley as a substitute teacher during the war. The man was temperamentally incapable of maintaining order in a preparatory school classroom and might often be found snowed under a barrage of chalky erasers after defeat. Moreover, this teacher was visited every other day by a friend with a German accent who left a small black bag, and this together with the fact of his presence at Morgan, New Jersey, on the day of the famous bombing had convinced some of the faculty members that they were harboring an authentic saboteur in their midst. Facts later proved them more excitable than discerning. So far as Griffes was concerned, the fellow's company afforded an excellent opportunity for linguistic improvement, and with French thus under professional guidance he turned now to Russian and Chinese.

He was perforce brusque and curt with the Hackley boys and became ardently disliked by some, but there were others who were his friends — Edward Crandall, Fontaine LeMaistre, Frederick T. Lewis, Chester P. Thomson, Garrison Sherwood, Frederick Smith, and other boys interested in music, the stage, art, literature, and the Orient. (Young Smith, who had traveled a good deal, had lived in Hong Kong for three years.) And Griffes's pianism enchanted the whole school — especially when he played his own pieces — so that when he ended his Sunday evening recitals with Nevin's *Good Night* as a tacit reminder, his auditors were reluctant to depart.

He visited the Garnseys', where a friend told of Arlo's death in a transport epidemic. Marion Bauer invited him to Mrs. Elizabeth Sprague Coolidge's, where he heard the Berkshire Quartet sponsored by that patroness of chamber music in

America. He also escorted Miss Bauer on a visit to Victor Wittgenstein, for musical discussion. He attended a concert of the Philadelphia Orchestra with the Bolms in their box, and later a recital of the Flonzaleys, with Marion Bauer. On January 23rd Rudolph Ganz played something of his at Aeolian Hall, and Griffes managed that too. During the interims between lessons at school he read Loti's *Mon Frère Yves* and liked it very much. There were several stray meetings with Adolfo Betti about the performance of his string quartet, the parts of which he had finished copying on the 20th; and meetings with Edgar Varèse, who, having secured the necessary quota of society women to back a New Symphony Orchestra for the dissemination of modern music, was now considering a presentation of *Kubla Khan*. This was not to be.

The *Sonata* had not as yet found a performer either. Through Marion Bauer, Griffes had secured an appointment the year before with Harold Bauer and had even been excused from Sunday chapel service in order to go into town and play it to him. In an interview in *Musical America* for January 11th, 1919, Bauer had praised the work in glowing language. "It is a splendid piece of writing, broad and noble in outline, full of meaning, subtle in atmosphere. It will not attract the crowd — it is technically very difficult — but it will deeply appeal to the serious musician. From a man who can write such music we may look for even greater things." On the 29th at a party at Marion Bauer's attended by the Flonzaleys, Heffley, Mrs. Elliot, and others, Bauer played the *Sonata* to Griffes, who could not at first conceal his astonishment at the other's interpretation. Yet he was at long last beginning to accept the differences between a composer's vision of his work and a performer's application.

Also present at the Bauer gathering was a young French composer named Darius Milhaud who was stopping in New

York on his return from Brazil to Paris. Griffes took a fancy to the man and his music, and on the 1st of February spent an afternoon with Milhaud, during which they exchanged compositions humorously inscribed to one another. The day before Griffes had written the Frenchman a brief note of introduction to Schirmer's. " This note is to introduce to you M. Darius Milhaud, of whom we were speaking this morning. He has some English songs in manuscript which it might interest you to see. He would be glad to show them to you." Before parting Milhaud sketched for Griffes a new ballet he was composing and introduced him to Paul Claudel.

Schirmer's urgently requested some new compositions by Arthur Tomlinson, "which makes me laugh," wrote Griffes. He played his *Sonata* at Heffley's before the students. Bolm gave him a ticket to *Le Coq d'Or*, and after the opera he rode out with Dan. He went to hear the Flonzaleys play the new quartet by Loeffler, and visited rehearsals of *Petrouchka* at the Opera. He met his friends Ito and Yamada once in a while, and attended *Pelléas* with Mrs. Elliot. On the 6th of February he took time out and made changes in the *Poem* for flute and orchestra, and the next day almost finished a new version of *Sho-Jo* that he had been working on and that was intended to meet the instrumental requirements of the average symphony orchestra. He attended a concert by Harold Bauer and kept an appointment with Yvette Guilbert, but on the 9th worked some more at *Sho-Jo* and finished it on the 10th. Two days later Winifred Christie played some of his things at Aeolian Hall (she had also played them at Jordan Hall in Boston four days before), and Griffes brought one of his pupils to the recital. Rudolph Ganz sent word from California that he had played Griffes at Palo Alto and Oakland with success.

During all the second week of February he worked intensively at a large job of musical ghosting that he had undertaken for Sacha Votitchenko (who was planning a concert with orchestra) and completed it finally on midnight of the 19th. His fee was $100, and Votitchenko also bestowed upon him a dubiously legendary ring of rubies as a token of esteem.

On the 21st Griffes began the orchestral score of a *Nocturne* drawn from his *Sonata*. The next day he visited Mrs. Bolm, with whom he always enjoyed conversational practice in French, and after some musical rounds finished up at his friends', the Bancrofts'. On the following day, a Sunday, he assisted in a war memorial service at the school, then went in to New York — there wasting all his time on some parents whose prodigy he was trying to interest in lessons, and on that account missing Votitchenko's concert, where his piece was played, after Count Tolstoy had impressively introduced the program. Monday morning he spent two hours at Harold Bauer's and in the evening heard the Flonzaleys at the Mac-Dowell Club play the new Loeffler quartet and some Bloch. School work tied him down thoroughly for three days, then on the last day of the month he finished his orchestral *Nocturne* and worked at an orchestration of *Clouds*. Varèse, who approved of Griffes's music and fostered it, had already announced the *Nocturne* for the first concert of the New Symphony Orchestra and wished to play *Clouds* on the third, along with Satie and Busoni. In the end neither of these compositions was to be performed by the New Symphony, owing to a dispute between Varèse and his sponsorship that soon culminated in the dismemberment of the Orchestra. According to Varèse the difference was over his refusal to include an abhorrent potpourri on one of his programs, as suggested by the most influential of his patrons. Whatever the cause, Griffes was obliged to look elsewhere finally for a hearing of his two symphonic sketches after many wasted conferences and rehearsals with the New Symphony.

March began thus with hours of conference with Varèse, the usual visits to singers, and a party at the composer Richard Hagemann's, where Griffes could reach several people who counted. On the 5th he met Nikolai Sokoloff and arranged to send him the score of *Sho-Jo* for a concert in Cleveland.

At the Beaux Arts Restaurant he often lunched on Wednesday afternoons with Emerson Whithorne, another American composer, whom he would lecture on the dangers of his urban life, advising sports, and tennis in particular, of which Griffes himself was very fond. At one of these lunches Whithorne first introduced him to James Huneker, and Godowsky also was present at one or two.

Marcia van Dresser had straightened out her dates, and Griffes was looking forward to a performance of the three pieces for voice and orchestra. There were many rehearsals with Miss van Dresser. He had also managed to place the pieces in their piano accompaniment version with Vera Janacopulos, a young Greek-Brazilian soprano, who was planning her second New York recital, and there were additional hours of practice with her. On March 9th he wrote to Reuter and suggested that Reuter do a piano roll of the *Scherzo* for Duo-Art. "A number of dancers have wished to use it and asked if there were a roll of it." Contemporary dancers were just beginning to discover the early pieces, which would prove a calisthenic teething ring for a whole generation of dancers like Ted Shawn, Ruth St. Denis, and Doris Humphrey. Griffes might well address his request to Reuter, who was proving a most sympathetic champion of his art.

He attended another evening at Mrs. Coolidge's, where the Berkshires performed again, and there were more rounds, more new acquaintances, and more disappointments. He began to familiarize himself with modern Italian music, attended a recital of Eva Gauthier's with Mrs. Elliot, played his three Macleod songs to Walter Kramer, who found them admirable, and continued rehearsals with Marcia van Dresser and Vera Janacopulos. The pianist Artur Rubinstein praised his music. He attended rehearsals of his string quartet by the Flonzaleys. In all this New York activity Marion Bauer's provided a haven of shady comfort to which he could repair for rest, and he gladly took advantage of the privilege. Occasionally he stole time out to visit Dan's home for dinner and would shock his friend with tales of the corruption rampant in musical circles. For example, the music critic whom Dan happened to admire most among newspaper writers on the subject had offered Griffes a frank bribery proposition. So it went.

On Saturday afternoon, March 22nd, Vera Janacopulos gave the first performance of the three Macleod songs in a recital at Aeolian Hall, with Griffes at the piano for his own numbers. Another modern composer, one of Griffes's new friends, Serge Prokofiev, also accompanied Miss Janacopulos on the same program in three of his own songs presented for the first time in America. "My songs had great success," wrote Griffes. Almost anything of his that was performed had great success now; it was one happy augury that might be counted upon. Even those like his student Frederick Smith, who attended the concert with his mother and later wrote of Griffes's songs in his diary: ". . . I must confess that it was a bit too modern for me," even those skeptics were compelled by something powerful and sincere in this unfamiliar music. After the recital Griffes sipped tea with Miss Janacopulos, Prokofiev, the Bolms, and others. So far as the press was concerned, it re-echoed the audience's fervor. The *Evening Mail* singled out " Charles Griffes and his strangely delightful melodies " in a brief review. The *Musical Leader* said that " perhaps the deepest of the songs were those by Mr. Griffes, who writes with significant power and great reserve force." And *Musical America,* whether through careless writing or genuine misapprehension, extolled *The Lament of Ian the Proud* as one of the finest pieces of music Prokofiev had ever done.

The day after the Janacopulos recital Griffes attended a reception and a dinner where he could meet several prominent musicians. The day after that, Monday, March 24th, Marcia van Dresser performed his songs at Wilmington, Delaware, as they were originally conceived with orchestra. Griffes took an eight o'clock train for Philadelphia in time for a ten-thirty rehearsal with the Philadelphia Orchestra, spent the afternoon in the city, and caught the six-fifteen train to Wilmington, where the concert took place at eight-thirty. He was pleased with Miss van Dresser's performance but considered that the men had not rehearsed enough. Stokowski was indisposed, and Thaddeus Rich, assistant, conducted in his stead.

On the following day, Griffes relaxed, and practiced some. He had to keep up with the growing circle of pianists and singers whom he coached and on whom he must depend when he gave up his school position. On Wednesday, the 26th, he worked with a few, visited Winifred Christie, and called upon Percy Grainger, whom he tried to interest in the *Sonata* by playing it through twice. The response was not very heartening, for, as Grainger frankly acknowledged in later years, " I think I was a little stunned by what seemed to me its austerity. And then, I have always hated piano music and probably sat wondering why such a fine composer as Griffes should waste his time (as it seemed to me) writing for such an unworthy instrument as the piano. Or maybe I was just waiting to digest my impressions of the *Sonata*. At any rate I said very little. . . ." The same evening he played his things to Harold Morris, a young pianist-composer, and at length requited himself for whatever disappointments the day may have contained by riding out with Dan at midnight. In the days that followed there was another concert by Prokofiev, and meetings, suppers, and rehearsals with musicians like Godowsky, Rubinstein, Varèse, Yamada, and others, and still more rehearsals with Marcia van Dresser, who was to participate in the second evening of his music at the MacDowell Club, which eventually took place on Wednesday, April 2nd, at eight-thirty, under the auspices of the Modern Music Society of New York.

The concert began with Griffes's playing of the *Sonata*, which was followed by Marcia van Dresser's singing of the three Macleod songs, then the four *Roman Sketches* played by Griffes, and finally the two pieces for string quartet by the Flonzaleys. These works were gratefully received by an audience that had already heard evenings of Loeffler, Bloch, Yamada, Henry F. Gilbert, and others. "The audience manifested great enthusiasm and interest," said the *Musical Leader*, "and many seemed to realize that in the work of Mr. Griffes there is manifestation of a school of American composition with the courage of its convictions, sincere and of high ideals." Paul Rosenfeld, who was present at the recital, saw Griffes, on leaving, and years later reconstructed the incident. "I am in the company of Ernest Bloch, and we go up to Griffes, or rather come across him sitting broodingly in a corner. I have the sense that he has become maturer and feels things opening up within and for him. . . . We speak to him for a moment and to Archambeau (a member of the Flonzaleys). Now that I look back it seems to me that he might have been sick already at this time. But at the time I had no inkling of it, if indeed he was sick; I merely had the impression that he was looking more serious and deeply concerned."

The press reaction paralleled that of the audience in many respects. But the critics were not yet ready for the *Sonata*. Partly it was because, as the *Leader* pointed out in its tribute to the piece, "It is difficult to grasp at a first hearing . . ." and partly because there was undeniable truth in *Musical America's* assertion that "not a very forceful player, Mr. Griffes lent no particular dignity" to its performance. Harold Bauer on first hearing the *Sonata* had expressed a desire to push Griffes off the piano bench and show him what could be done with the last two or three pages. Griffes himself would probably have reiterated what he had written of the earlier German sonata: "I certainly never thought of my own hands when I wrote it. . . ." Nevertheless among serious musicians in the audience it created high excitement and the wish for a second hearing.

The days following on his program for the Modern Music Society were crowded days again for Griffes. There were rehearsals with Varèse and the New Symphony, renewed visits to musical personages with manuscripts under his arm, and an evening of heated musical argument with Harold Morris and John Powell.

His continued experience in the upper stratum of American musical life, the constant scraping away at his youthful purpose, had left him bitterly disillusioned with the whole scene. In one of his letters to Reuter, dated April 8th, he referred to "the very tiny group of men in America who are really looking ahead and have the courage to follow convictions. They can be counted on the fingers of one hand almost." Now a new adjective became part of his working vocabulary — "furious" — and more and more things made him "furious" every day. He began to draw invidious comparisons between other American composers and himself. They married money. Or they inherited it. Or they went into business and amassed enough money so their future was secure and they could afford to compose. Or they did anything but get stuck away in a miserable hole of a boys' school without a future or a real vocation. Sometimes he chided himself that with his good head and tidy management of personal expenses he had not gone into business himself. Perhaps then he could have made a go of things and created music in his leisure. In these despairing moods, he would occasionally prevail upon one of his outside pupils to remain for dinner after the lesson because "I'm so terribly blue."

He worked on. In the letter to Reuter quoted above, he mentioned: "I have been sketching out some rather experimental short pieces for piano which I will show you if you come to New York this month. They will be at your disposal as well as the *Sonata*." These were a group of five pieces to be played in succession that he had worked on during the fall. Only the first three are in any finished condition, and their date is probably January 30th, when Griffes composed the bulk of this work. Like most of Griffes's later music — the *Sonata*, the *Poem*, the "Pieces for String Quartet" — they were to bear an abstract title and were to be called simply *Five Pieces*.

The letter ended with real gratitude to this pianist who did not need to be coaxed or cozened or rewarded but who felt an entirely spontaneous admiration for Griffes's music that he signalized by performance. Reuter pushed his things everywhere and was in fact to play him in Decatur, Illinois, on the 17th of that month. "Your real appreciation and understanding are a joy."

Mrs. Elliot had acquired two young pupils, Katharine Cornell and Ann Parke, who had come to the big city from Buffalo to make their way in the world. Griffes was recommended to Miss Parke by the alert Mrs. Elliot as an excellent coach both for learning his own songs and for French diction, and Miss Parke had begun studying as one of his private pupils. He enjoyed visiting the two girls in their flat, so that it became in time something of a refuge on his busy, hurried jaunts to New York. Miss Parke always made him welcome, bidding him lie down for a nap, or have some tea, or work away informally at his manuscripts. It was a welcome hideaway from the nuisance of engagements that piled up.

They continued to pile up for the rest of that month. There were teas at the MacDowell Club, meetings with Morris, Powell, Marion Bauer, the Sutro sisters — Rose Laura and Ottilie (a piano team whom he tried to interest in his early two-piano arrangement of Humperdinck) — Whithorne, Schindler, and Frederick Jacobi. With Jacobi, a gifted musician, he had become acquainted early in the year, and had several times invited him to Hackley. Occasionally Griffes would meet with Jacobi and his wife for all-day hikes along the grassy aqueduct running parallel with the Hudson in the neighborhood of Ossining. With Eva Gauthier he attended a concert of the Salzedo Harp Ensemble, and two weeks later dined with Salzedo, who was interested in having him compose something for the group. On April 14th he began three Javanese songs for Mme Gauthier, then read some Frank Harris. The next day there was a concert by the Letz Quartet, followed by a gathering at Mrs. Coolidge's, which he attended with Rudolph Ganz. There were more days in which he made the musical rounds, and attended gatherings like the concert of flute, harpsichord, violin, and cello at Arthur Whiting's. He played to the Lewisohns and others at Mrs. Elliot's. He played his *Sonata* and more of his pieces to Artur Rubinstein, and a few days later heard some Medtner and Ravel from Rubinstein in turn. He conferred with Ivan d'Archambeau and Adolfo Betti. He played his *Sonata* and other of his pieces at various wealthy homes and at musicales. At one gathering Ann Parke assisted with a rendition of *Symphony in Yellow* and three of the Chinese songs. He spent a good deal of time rehearsing the *Poem* for flute with Georges Barrère. Arthur Shepherd was in town, and Griffes took him to a favorite Oriental restaurant, whence they ad-

Late portrait

journed to Heffley's studio, so that Griffes could play his *Sonata*. On as many of his expeditions to New York as possible he rode out with Dan, and together they often planned a trip of escape to Boston.

On May 5th he made a great many changes in the *Sonata*. He tried showing his orchestral scores to concert managers and others of influence, seeking to enlist their aid in a placement. Then more teas at the MacDowell Club, more brief snatches of companionship with Marion Bauer and Mrs. Elliot, more musical rounds—some with Noble Kreider, who was in town—and more disappointments. On Sunday, May 11th, he played the *Sonata* to Harold Bauer, who expressed himself as pleased with the new changes, calling them improvements.

It was discouraging to have to continue on the rounds like any novice, subject to the same disappointments and the same boredom of the preceding years. Harold Morris, an acquaintance of this period, later recollected a typical occasion, in a lecture at Duke University. "Some friends planned an informal recital at which Griffes, John Powell, the Virginia pianist and composer, and myself were to play some of our latest works. Griffes planned to play his revised piano *Sonata*. A composer unknown to us, on hearing of the plans, asked if he might play also. The hostesses consented and placed the 'intruder' first on the program. Coming with an armful of manuscripts, he continued to play and play until 11:30, until the hostesses were baffled and shocked to tears. Finally, at 11:45 Mr. Powell whispered to us he was going to faint, which he did so realistically that the party quickly broke up. An ambulance had been called for Mr. Powell, but he wisely had departed. It was the last time any of us saw Griffes. . . ."

On Sunday, May 17th, after a dinner at the Bolms', Griffes took part in a discussion with them and Hugo Riesenfeld about a new opportunity that had arisen. Riesenfeld had recently assumed the post of musical director for the Rialto and Rivoli moving-picture theaters and, having as a first step decided to elevate the importance and quality of the noncinematic portions of his programs, called in Adolph Bolm. Already in an interview in *Musical America*, for April 5th, Bolm had hinted at Griffes's possible inclusion in the enterprise: ". . . Now I am doing a series of short ballets at the Rivoli Theater with Hugo Riesenfeld's co-operation. Toward the spread of art this is a great impetus. For Mr. Riesenfeld, with much vision, is giving his audiences, made up of the average public, bits of the finest type of music. . . . The series of ballets which I am giving are short and simple, but are meeting with much success and are acquainting the audiences with a new type of art." In the same interview he suggested that "the splendid suites of Mr. Griffes" might make exquisite ballet material.

It was *The White Peacock* that they were now discussing as a number for the Rivoli. The piece had already shown itself an effective dance composition when Ito had danced it the year before, and as a piano work it had begun its long popular career. "The most popular of the four [*Roman Sketches*] is *The White Peacock*, which has been played quite a good deal," Griffes had written Babe Shoobert the year before. The ballet was scheduled for June, and Griffes, grateful for the new commission, took whatever time he could to prepare the orchestral version of his piano piece. He went for occasional strolls, took some photographs for diversion, and studied the score of Stravinsky's *L'Oiseau de Feu*. On May 21st he brought Eva Gauthier the Javanese songs, which were by then complete. Otherwise he worked quite steadily at Hackley on *The White Peacock*, venturing into New York only for lessons or conferences at the Rivoli, which he would follow by rehearsals with Barrère or meetings with Dan. On June 5th he completed the orchestration of the *Peacock*, at a table in the music branch of the Public Library — where Otto Kinkeldey, the librarian, observed him hard at work — then delivered the score to the theater. After a few days, during which Griffes taught, practiced with Barrère on the *Poem*, and attended a gathering at the Sutro sisters', the first rehearsal of the *Peacock* was held at the Rivoli on Sunday, June 8th. Immediately afterwards Griffes dined on the matter with Riesenfeld at the Friars Club. Off and on during the next two weeks he would stop in to rehearsals whenever he could get away from the school, and at one rehearsal discussed with Georges Barrère the possibilities of *The White Peacock* for the Barrère Little Symphony. He seemed a bit worn but glad of the chance to obtain his music a hearing through the large orchestra at the Rivoli.

That he would have to turn elsewhere than to the returns on his published compositions there was no longer the slightest doubt. The three Macleod songs had appeared in Schirmer's spring catalogue and had, during April and May, been very favorably reviewed in the musical press: ". . . It is remarkable how well Mr. Griffes has reduced them for performance with piano." Yet how much would they bring? Towards the close of May he had heard from Sonneck about the maximum that Schirmer's would pay for even the two latest Arthur Tomlinson sets (*Six Pieces for Treble Clef* and *Six Familiar Songs*), which he had left with them after seeking to raise the price. "Well, I told you so. Mr. Schirmer agrees with me that the sales would have to be very large before we could possibly get our author's fee back on such pieces selling for so low a price and with such discounts. It is utterly impossible for us to buy the sets for anything like the sum mentioned by us. Our maximum would be $100 for both sets together, or $50 for each.

" I am holding the manuscripts here until I hear from you." He relinquished them for $110 in June.

The ballet, listed as a "tone poem by Charles T. Griffes," and staged by Adolph Bolm, with the orchestra under the direction of Erno Rapee, was presented at the Rivoli for the week commencing Sunday, June 22nd. It was a solo performed by Miss Margit Leeras in a costume with a specially designed mechanism in the construction of the peacock's tail, which was built of slender steel rods, manipulated at will by the dancer. The choreographic number was sandwiched between the feature picture, *Secret Service,* a Civil War drama, and a Mack Sennett comedy. Griffes received valuable publicity in the advance write-ups occasioned by the production, and his subsequent notices were mostly favorable. "Rivoli Shows Patriotism," glibly sang the *Morning Telegraph* with unconscious insult to the composer, whose American citizenship was scarcely the qualification at issue. Other reviews were as favorable, if for different reasons. "*The White Peacock,* of which Mr. Griffes made a filmy, exquisite orchestration, was a new departure without concession to the dancer or to the public; it was the first time they had interpreted a special piece of music, instead of adapting music to fit the ballet; it was also the first time they had used ultra-modern music at the Rivoli, and the response was both astounding and encouraging. It made one hope that this same work would be repeated during the coming winter season, and that music of similar character would be heard often in the same environment." The *New York Times* referred to it as "an attractive number," the *Globe* as "an exquisite fantasy," and elsewhere it was called a "remarkably beautiful dance number." The *Evening Sun* dissented: ". . . Margit Leeras endeavored to express the composer's thoughts. Judging from the general emptiness of this Adolph Bolm divertissement Mr. Griffes had little or no ideas to express."

Griffes attended the performance several times during its

run, often accompanied by students, whom he treated to a visit backstage to meet the dancer and to inspect the mechanically ingenious tail of her costume. At the end of the week he pocketed $50 in royalties from the Rivoli.

Since the time of its first performance in 1919, *The White Peacock* has moved rapidly forward to a permanent place in the repertoire of American music, remaining, after *Kubla*, the most popular work by its composer. A striking account of the effect of the composition was published in 1941 in a powerful novel entitled *This Finer Shadow*, by Harlan Cozad McIntosh, the tormented American writer, who had ended his life the year before. McIntosh, who was himself much taken with the piece and who constantly played a record of it while engaged on his one novel, used *The White Peacock* to symbolize the homosexual obsession brooding over the life of his principal character. Another character, the heroine, listening to this music, becomes indistinctly aware of it as an embodiment of the threat to the man she loves.

"The concert hall quieted. Conversation hushed.

"The White Peacock, sorrowful and majestic, appeared in the faint light. Winding through deep white reeds, brushing through ghostly ferns, he approached. Wading the moon-puddles, breaking the mist with silver feathers, he looked at Deane. Holding his white throat into the stars, moving the fallen petals, he sang to her — sang a clear, demanding song of his remote, pale island. Deane shivered under the soft notes, loosening her gown. The White Peacock, his snowy tail drifting over the moon-flowers, lifted his scarlet eyes — lifted his eyes through clouds and placed each strong tone against her. . . . The music changed tempo. The white bird screamed shrilly, his bright whistle falling through glissandi of sound. The exquisite melody rose into the wind, hesitated, and dropped murmuring into the white sea. . . . The White Peacock faded in the fluid light, became distant — Deane, following with her arms the receding shadow.

"The music died. People moved in their chairs and the subdued whispers grew into applause. . . ."

In addition to *The White Peacock*, it was probably during this spring that Griffes composed for Caroline Beebe and her New York Chamber Music Society the three chamber works arranged from his *Lake at Evening*, *Vale of Dreams*, and *Night Winds*. He had attended several rehearsals of the Society, playing as a member and listening attentively, so that his arrangements might escape the peril of sounding anti-chamber, and at the same time convey all that he wished in point of balance and color. When the copyist returned the final score to Miss Beebe with the legend "for orchestra," Griffes smiled and requested that she change it to "for double quintet and piano."

After the Rivoli production, summer was upon him, and Griffes, at 12 West 46th as usual, continued with private lessons well into the vacation period, intending the total of his $4 and $4.50 rates per lesson as a financial reserve for the coming year. He was also busy plotting out the preliminary sketches of a new work commissioned by the Lewisohns for the Neighborhood Playhouse. In the spring they had decided upon a pageant based on Walt Whitman's *Salut au Monde*, which would combine pantomime, dance, lighting effects, music, and choral speech. It was to be a sort of culmination of the Neighborhood's "festival" tradition. They had already worked out a libretto, adapting music by MacDowell and Marion Bauer to their purpose, and had even held a skeletal rehearsal, when Griffes got wind of the enterprise and, passionately concerned, sought the commission. At first the Lewisohns were reluctant through a partial uncertainty whether his gifts were appropriate to the kind of thing they had in mind, but after discussing the matter thoroughly from every angle and insisting upon the stark simplicity that they wanted, they agreed that Griffes should handle the music. He felt a slight embarrassment in the circumstance that his friend Marion Bauer might have lost out on it, but she assured him that she had not had enough experience with orchestration at that time and, goodheartedly professing complete indifference to the project, wished him Godspeed.

In the second week of August Griffes wrote Miss Bauer, who was staying at the MacDowell Colony in Peterboro, New Hampshire, about his summer activities. "From your letter I see that you are for the time really at peace with the world. That is a good state of mind occasionally. As a permanent condition it might be a bit soporific. However, I know what you mean about New Hampshire fields. I have driven about the state many times, and I always feel an extraordinary sense of simple peace and beauty that takes me far away from the struggles of existence. It is perhaps the most real 'country' that I know of." As to the MacDowell Colony, he continued, he did not know much about it, although what music he had heard from that source frankly did not impress him. ". . . You may be amused to hear that I have, temporarily at least, cast out the second of my two quartet pieces and written two more, both based on Indian themes like the slow one. So I have 'a set of three.' They worked out very quickly. The Lewisohns were in town for a few days this past week. We had several conferences. I have already worked through a few places. It is an interesting problem. But oh! what will you Whitmanites say! You will be interested to hear that Stokowski of his own accord sent for the score of *Kubla Khan*. Whether that means a performance, I don't know. *Qui sait?* At any rate I am rescoring certain passages from a second copy which I have. In between these bigger things I occasionally put a few touches on the Javanese music I spoke of sometimes. I want to make some short piano pieces in the same mood (thematically also), but in America people always label you and then you can't get away from it. I don't want the reputation of an Orientalist and nothing more. There is a very beautiful exhibition of batiks in town now which is bringing Java into people's minds. Gauthier has some very nice pieces in it. . . . I am very unhappy that the summer is passing so quickly — when I allow myself to think of it at all. I think it will finish by being a much more profitable summer to me than last. I have hardly read anything, only Huysmans's *En Route*, and a rather dull book on psychical research. Mrs. Elliot just left town last Tuesday and is now up near Woodstock, N. Y. The weather in town is very comfortable, and I see almost nobody, which is agreeable. I enjoy wandering about town with no engagements hanging over my head."

A week after the letter to Miss Bauer, Rudolph Reuter arrived from Chicago to play at the New York Stadium, and, as he later recollected, " Griffes came with one eye bandaged up — having given himself severe eyestrain from copying his orchestra and chamber music parts. I asked him to come to a restaurant with me after the performance, and he did, but stayed only a little while, as he said that he had more copying to do, with the one good eye, and that it would probably take him until four in the morning." The long strain was at last beginning to tell. Towards the latter part of August, Griffes felt tired and run down, coughed somewhat, and was afflicted with a general sense of malaise. It was nevertheless time to be thinking of a return to Hackley, for he was in no better position now than before to shrug and follow the prompting of his desire. Over the last few years he had kept an infinitesimally detailed, scrupulously complete account of his personal expenses, listing every item as he copied it from the day-to-day record scattered across calendar leaves, bits of newspaper, program books, and even — overrunning the staves and crowding out the music — his manuscript paper. Stamps, newspaper, train fare, lunch, chocolate bar, tea — everything was carefully noted and set down. The cost of his suits, shoes, underwear, ties, collars, shirts, hats, socks, and repairs was entered in a separate notebook. Although he loved and needed books and music and had never unwarrantedly skimped on these, his purchases were otherwise circumspect and requisite.

Parallel to responsibility and to these personal expenses was the list of earnings for the last three years, which he now brought up to date. October 1916 to October 1917, covering school salary, *Koridwen* music and royalties, *Petrouchka* salary, Schirmer royalties, private lessons, ballet for Bolm — $2293.30, of which the substantial item was his $1600 at the school. October 1917 to October 1918, covering school salary, Schirmer royalties, money received for the arrangements of *These Things Shall Be*, fee for selecting a piano, sale of the three Tomlinson sets — $1980.78, of which the substantial item was his $1600 at the school. October 1918 to summer 1919, covering school salary, private lessons, orchestration fee from Votitchenko, the two Tomlinson sets, royalties from the Rivoli — $2087.29, of which the substantial item was his $1700 at the school. Griffes returned to Hackley in the fall.

Chapter XVII

RUDOLPH GANZ on first hearing the *Sonata* adjudged it the finest abstract work in American piano literature. This was also the opinion of several other contemporaries, and posterity has seen no reason to alter the verdict. The *Sonata* remains today a solid and formidable landmark in American music — though more generally respected than understood, and with a greater reputation than audience. This is because it is a difficult and original work that must be comprehended in its own terms. (The one noticeable influence is that of Scriabin, with whose music Griffes was indeed familiar, as also with the biography by A. Eaglefield-Hull.)

The present chapter is devoted to an original interpretation of the *Sonata* that may help to clarify its meaning. There is no use in pretending, however, that the work is not difficult or that it will yield its beauty to any but an attentive listener. The analysis that follows is intended for the serious student, but the layman equipped with records may also, by judicious skimming, follow the outlines of the discussion. For his benefit the harmony of the *Sonata* — possibly one of Griffes's chief interests in it — is not considered, harmony being a difficult subject to present in simplified form. The marginal notations give first the numbers, in the score, of the measures that are referred to,

and second the approximate place of these measures, to nearest sixteenth of an inch, on the recording by Harrison Potter.[1]
The Roman numerals I–IV indicate the side of the recording;
and a $+$ or a $-$ indicates a slight degree more or a slight degree
less than the figure it adjoins. $\frac{77-79}{\text{II}:}|\text{I} \longrightarrow \text{I}''\text{I}+$, therefore,
means the passage that may be located in the score at the sev-
enty-seventh to seventy-ninth measures of the movement under discussion, or that may be heard if the needle travels, on the
second side of the recording, from a distance a little less than
one inch from the outermost groove to a distance a little more
than one and one-sixteenth of an inch from the outermost
groove. The record measurements have been obtained by means
of a special slide rule for this purpose included with B. H. Haggin's *A Book of the Symphony*, but an ordinary tape measure
will serve the reader not having access to one of these devices.

The *Sonata* is a three-part work of fifteen minutes' duration.
It has no pianistic ambitions, and its form in the large does not
essentially depart from that of the romantic sonata, except for
omitting some repetitions. The creative effort is uniquely directed towards a novel tonality, and towards a unity rooted in
the identity of the characteristic intervals appearing in the different themes. A profusion of semitones and tri-semitone melodic jumps imparts the distinctive flavor to the tonality employed. The reader is advised to set his ear on catching this
flavor, and to try to enjoy it. It can be done. He will derive
much pleasure from recognizing how closely related the themes
will sound, despite entirely different melodic outlines.

I. *The tonality*

It is in the Griffes *Sonata*

(T) $\qquad$ \C♯DE♭.F./ . \G♯AB♭..C♯/,

---

[1] See Appendix IV.

and consists of two almost congruent tetrachords. F is the rebellious note; F♯ would yield complete congruence. (A dot indicates an interval of two semitones, two dots that of three semitones; adjacent letters stand for notes separated by one semitone.) There are four semitones in the scale (which is a good deal), and two tri-semitones ("augmented seconds"), which have a reputation for being extremely distinctive (Jewish, Arabic, Persian music); two of them are quite plenty. There are fifths on all the degrees of the scale (except F), owing to the congruence of the tetrachords; the fifth may be expected then to retain its harmonic significance.

It is evident that the position of F is by no means rigidly enforced by the structure of the scale; in fact, F♯ would perhaps be more attractive. Griffes uses F♯ almost as often as F, although not quite. One might take the view that the fourth degree of the T-scale is rather floating — the leeway to the right of F is inviting.

For variety it might be natural to take advantage of the leeway to the right of B♭ and to moderate the jump B♭–C♯ by using B instead of B♭. Griffes does that often, and one may call this modified scale T'. The relation T—T' is not without resemblance to that between the major and minor modes.

If one agrees to disregard the difference between F and F♯, there are four scales of the type T, closely related to that starting with C♯; "closely related" meaning having four tones in common. Two of them are obtained in the traditional way, on the basis of the quintic relationship:

$$(T_5) \qquad G♯AB♭.C^{C♯} \quad . \quad D♯EF..G♯,$$
$$(T_4) \qquad F♯GA♭.B♭^B \quad . \quad C♯DE♭..F♯$$

Two others are obtained by moving the scale one semitone to the right or to the left:

$$(T_2) \qquad DE♭F♭.G♭^G \quad . \quad AB♭C♭♭..A,$$
$$(T_{-2}) \qquad CD♭E♭♭.F♭^F \quad . \quad GA♭B♭♭..C$$

T_2 and T_6 are encountered in the development section of the first part (by the side of the scale starting with G), but the bulk is in T and T′, and it is truly remarkable how strictly the tonality is preserved throughout the work.

It is evident that the system of musical notation based on the conventional scale is entirely unsuitable to the tonality T. All the rules of orthography (and especially those of enharmony) had best be abandoned altogether. The notation used by Griffes is a poor attempt at squeezing his music into the customary frame of the major-minor tonalities. His orthography is therefore highly confusing and might better be disregarded. Above all, there is no foundation for the signature ♯. Already ♯ would be much more expedient, but the rather unconventional ♯ would in fact be the most practical and the easiest to read. The number of accidental chromatic signs would then be surprisingly small. It seems that Griffes (afraid of his own daring?) tried to pretend that he was remaining the whole time — in spite of all — in the domain of some general, underlying tonality. How else account for the F major signature?

II. *The themes*

An intimate acquaintance with the themes of the *Sonata* will greatly help the reader to understand it. They are given in the order of their appearance.

FIRST MOVEMENT

Note the abundance of semitones (and their inversions); they are marked by ⌐⌐ . Note also the augmented seconds B♭–C♯. The G♯ sounds strange after the D minor key has been established by the first element of the theme. The last element — bringing the theme to a singularly abrupt ending — sounds, with the down-glide F♯–F, like very sorrowful resignation. The first and second elements of the theme are much used in the elaboration.

a'

26–27
$\text{I:}\,|\,\text{1}''7+ \rightarrow \text{1}''8+$

A fellow theme of *a*. Its first five notes differ in time-value only from the eighth to eleventh notes of *a*; the rest is an intensification of the final element of *a*. A strongly Scriabinesque theme, especially with its actual harmonization. In contrast to *a*, it seems rebellious in character.

c

31–32
$\text{I:}\,|\,\text{1}''11+ \rightarrow \text{1}''12+$

Derived through decomposition of one of the fundamental chords of the *Sonata* (E♭–B♭–F(♯)–C♯), this theme — against a background of the same chord — is used for the coda. Energetic, active.

b

36–38
$\text{I:}\,|\,\text{2}''1 \rightarrow \text{2}''4$

Tonality T′ (B for B♭ *passim*; it should be B, not A♯). Note the sound of the B-natural following immediately the B♭ minor chord of the first measure (just conceive C♯ as D♭): rather peculiar — hesitant. This is the "soft" theme. Incidentally, the introduction of B-natural means one more semitone.

d

77–79
$\text{II:}\,|\,\text{1} \!-\!\!-\! \rightarrow \text{1}''1+$

This theme accounts for about one-third of the development section. The semitones G♯–A sound very pungent after the G minor established by the preceding notes. This feature is preserved at its subsequent repetition (A–B♭ after A major).

It is a "progression theme," enduring unlimited repetition and therefore suited to bring about the climax leading to the re-capitulation.

SECOND MOVEMENT

e 1–6
III:|0 → "6

A simple chant whose only ambition is to stand completely in the T-tonality. Do not be misguided by all the flats. Their purpose is probably to misrepresent the theme as a polite E♭ minor for the convenience of critics.

The motive

f III:|1"2

etc. going down

is embodied in the following themes f_1–f_4. Since it occurs in strong positions, all these themes sound related, even if it is not at once obvious why. This device, not new and not too different from that of variations, is a favorite with Griffes. The occurrence of the motive f is indicated by stars.

f_1 22–24
III:|1"2 → 1"5

f_2 23–24
III:|1"3 → 1"4

f_3 (a direct variation of f) almost pure Scriabin

                                28–29
III:|1"6+ → 1"8

f_4 (a soft and tame embodiment of f)

                                38
III:|1"14 → 2

Here the second note is a tone (instead of a semitone) higher than the third note (this refers of course to the notes with stars); their values are changed, and developing notes are intercalated. Still, if the motive is well established in the ear, the F–G♯–F–F, with all the strong F's, cannot remain unrecognized.

THIRD MOVEMENT

g

There is nothing special to remark about this theme (except, perhaps, that what Harrison Potter plays on the recording is with the bars moved one-eighth to the left and in ¾ time, which sounds more interesting than the authentic version). The B♭ prevents it from being a polite A major. Aside from that it might as well be Haydn. The rhythmic figure of the first five notes is important.

g′

The first two measures are a rhythmic rearrangement of the first two measures of g; the two following just a continuation.

h

There is in the whole *Sonata* no other measure in which the T-tonality would speak up so powerfully as in the first measure of this theme. The first tetrachord C♯–D–E♭–F appears here in all its éclat, and, as if that were not enough, the left hand throws in the chromatic triplet C♯–D–E♭. The whole section following this theme is an orgy of that chromatic triplet. The following theme h′ is much the same thing. It uses the other chromatic triplet.

h′

III. *The anatomy*

First movement: Feroce. Allegretto con moto.

Sonata form. Outline (each sign stands for two measures):

.... Introduction: Feroce

aaaaaaaaaaaa'a'a'ccbbbbbbbbbccc Exposition AA'BC (C — coda theme). Allegretto con moto

aaaaaaaaadddddd Development

aaaaa'a'a'a'bbbbbccccc Recapitulation AA'BC

0	1–4	A sharp figure (its rhythm reappears in the third movement) derived directly from the scale acts like a call to attention. Stated once, it is repeated after a short pause an octave higher, and after the same pause, again an octave higher, four times in rapid succession.
"4	4–9	Then the theme *a* is announced by its first element (a very classical procedure) and is echoed twice in the bass. A scale-like sextuplet, repeated twice, introduces the Allegretto con moto,
"8+	9–11	and two more of its repetitions form the background for the first measure of theme *a*. Its second element is used as
"10	12–14	material for a short (three-measure) elaboration. The theme is stated again
"13	15–16	with a change of rhythm (and harmonization) in its second half, which is
"15	17	once more repeated in a different T-tonality; then it is restated in the origi-
1	18–22	nal tonality in the bass, then again two

1″5	23–25	times in T_2, and dismissed in three measures of runs that lead up to the fellow
1″7	26–29	theme a' stated twice in succession.
1″11	30–34	The following six measures use the coda theme c to bridge over to theme
2	35–38	b, which is contrasting a in the usual way. Note the simple fifth of the accompaniment, the basic harmonization of the *Sonata*. The theme has one bar of 10/8 between two bars of 12/8; the effect
2″8	39–44	is not very telling. Theme b is repeated twice, with its last element changed each time. After the third repetition a
2″9	45	brilliant measure in octaves (contrary motion) — perhaps the best sounding
2″10	46–48	measure in the *Sonata* — leads to a forte repetition of the theme in a heavy
	49	harmonization. An extra cadence-like
2″13	50–58	measure ends in the basic chord B♭–F♯–G♯–D, against whose eighths the
2″15	53	coda theme is sounded once, the chord is broken up twice, and followed by
3—	54–56	the octave succession E♭–D–C♯ (chromatic triplet) –B♭–G♯–A, almost step for step down the T-scale. (Why G♯–A and not A–G♯? Probably to make the A pass for a nonexistent dominant of the imaginary tonic D.)

The development section is in two parts. The first is a study of the possibilities of the chromatic triplets. The

0	57–60	initial measure of the development (la-

beled Tempo I°) boldly brings the triplet G♯AB♭, broken up into G♯B♭ and
A, all by itself: a soft challenge, marked
"pedal." In the next measure it serves
as a harmonic background for theme *a*,
which is now provided with a tail-like
ending, a low rapid triplet followed by

"3   61–64   a trill. Those four bars are now repeated, an augmented fourth higher,
but strictly in a T-tonality. The theme

"6   65–67   *a* is restated in T_5 (a fifth higher) in
the bass, and then in T_4 (a fourth
higher) in the middle register, both
times against a milder harmonic background.

          70   A measure of runs paves the way for
a six-measure section beginning with a
restatement of the first half of theme

"11   71   *a* in the original tonality in the bass,
against the second tetrachord (G♯AB♭
.C♯) cast in the same rhythm as the
mentioned tail-piece in the fourth bar
of the development, a triplet in six-
teenths followed by a trill. In the fol-

"12   72–76   lowing measures the same idea is
pursued. Fragments of theme *a* are
combined with the "tail." The latter
dominates this section entirely, and two
repeats of the "tail" with the trill amply prolonged bring it to an end. The
joy at the chromatic triplet of the tetrachord seems to be the main incentive
of that passage.

I	77–88	The remainder of the development is new material. Its role in the development section is not clear. It may be viewed as an independent twelve-measure prelude consisting of a climactic treatment of theme *d* against a basically constant harmonic background, varying only in its rhythmic design.
I″3	89–114	The recapitulation is hasty and closely follows the exposition. The
2″10	115–118	coda theme *c* is then sounded twice, and the E♭–B♭–F–C♯ is sounded in various triplets in a rather redundant cadence before it settles on E♭–B♭–F.

Second movement: Molto tranquillo.

Free in form, but not unrelated to the two-part lied form with coda. Outline:

eeeeeeeeee Repeated theme *e*

f₁f₁f₁f₃f₃f₃f₄f₄f₄f₄f₁f₁f₁ Pseudo-variations (3) falling back on the first

eee Reminder of *e*

hhhh Coda

o	1–6	Theme *e* is stated in simple harmonization, in ⁴⁄₄ time.
″6	7–10	Theme *e* is stated in ⁵⁄₄ time against harmonic fifths moving in ¾ time, a fine polyrhythmic effect.
″10—	11–21	The first ten measures are repeated with some changes in the melodic line (inversions) and the harmony; they

		may be considered a variation on the theme *e*.
1″2	22–27	The right hand plays f_1 while the left offers striking counterpoint f^2 based on the motive *f*. This fades out on basic harmonies: one "variation."
1″6+	28–29	The second variation on *f*: almost pure Scriabin, both melody and harmony. The motive *f* stands out strongly in the highest spot of the melodic line.
1″8	30–31	The variation is repeated one fourth
1″9+	32–35	higher. A third repetition (two semitones lower) with rhythmic changes follows, strongly tinted with echoes of motive *f*, and fades out in basic harmonies.
1″12	36–43	The third variation is soft (cantabile) and marked "tranquillo." Against waving triplets in fifths (B♭–F) flows a wistful melody whose relationship to
2″2+	44–49	motive *f* cannot be missed. It steers into a variety of f_1 (always against the same harmony), thus producing a cyclic effect.
2″8	50–55	This effect is strengthened by a repetition of *e* (in octaves).
2″13	55–71	A short coda in ⅝ time, dominated by the chromatic triplet, prepares the following movement. It goes accelerando from the dreamy last notes of theme *e* to some furious triplets, virtually repeating the whole time the rhythm ♪♪|♪.

Third movement: Allegro vivace. ⅝ time.

Sonata form (without recapitulation). Outline (one sign for
four bars):

ggggggg′g′g′g′hhhhhh Exposition 1
gggggg′mmmmh′h′h′h′ Exposition 2
g′hmmf f f f, *nnnnnnnn h′h′h′h′* Development
hhhhhhhhhh Coda (Presto)

> This movement is cemented together
> by two elements: the rhythmic figure
> ♪| ♫♫ ♪ (which shall be denoted by
> R), expanded sometimes to ♪| ♫♫ ♫
> (R′); and the chromatic triplet.

0	2–6	It starts with the theme g whose first five notes form Figure R.
″1+	7–10	Keep your ear on it. The theme is echoed twice, then
″2	11–14	repeated. As an outgrowth of it comes
″3	15–18	a figure k of broken chords (in triplets) sounded against the figure R
″4	19–20	twice in succession, then once more against a ¾ rhythm, and
″4+	21–24	this section ends in four bars of a triplet trill.
″5	25–32	A ¾ variation g′ of g against the figure R alternating with R′.
″6+	33–36	g′ is repeated in abbreviated form, and
	37–38	a triplet trill leads to a close of this section
″8	39–42	by R repeated four times as the fourth B♭–F.

″8+	43–46	*h* is stated against the figure R realized alternately as a chromatic triplet, and in constant chords.
″9	47–50	It is then repeated an octave higher.
″10	51–54	The strong part of *h* (the first six notes including the chromatic triplet)
		is stated again twice against R′, then
″11	55–58	climaxed up to a repetition of *h* in thick harmonization, and
″12—	59–62	again climaxed up to an expiration of theme *h*, and of Part I of the movement.

		Part II (Exposition 2) follows essentially the pattern of Exposition 1. The
″13+	69–92	measures are repeated without substantial changes. Instead of variation *g′*
1″2	93–108	there is a harmonic episode *m* in runlike triplets against a bass in climbing quarter-notes, a touch of brilliancy in
1″4	109–112	it. Then *h* appears in a rhythmically different form (♪| ♩ being the rhythmic
1″5—	113–120	pattern). This is repeated twice, and
1″6+	121–124	ends up in figure R, as *g′* did.

		The measures 126–167 are not easy to rationalize. One way of viewing them is as a development section of the sonata form. That is the view adopted here, and some corroboration will be found below.
1″7	126–129	These measures are related to *g′*

by the rhythm of the theme

, by its semitones,

and by the figure in the bass followed by the figure ♫ ♩..

1″8	130–133	These measures are obviously related to *h*.
1″9—	134–141	These measures are related to the harmonic episode *m*, 93–108, or rather to its last bars. This is not entirely certain.
1″10	142–150	A faithful reproduction of 37–47 of the second movement ($f_4 f_4 f_1 f_1$), except for the last four bars, where the counterpoint of *f* is applied and then followed by figure R low in the bass, *quasi tympani*.
2″2	151–167	These measures are marked Lento (¾) misterioso. It is a mystery how they got here. The theme

159–

161 climbs up steadily from the bass to the treble, climaxing and thickening in harmony, with occasional cannon episodes. It is repeated four times, with a climax based on its last bar (a semitone again).

2″14	168–183	This "development section" closes with a short elaboration of both *h* and *h′* and does not require any explanation.

3″1   184–223   The coda is marked Presto and based entirely on *h*. Note the thick, rich, dry harmonies, with almost no emotional content. The bass is syncopated against the right hand, and the general effect is that of rushing eighths in ¾ time. The chromatic triplet has the time of its life. The movement closes with the conventional accelerando, with the conventional effect.

The Griffes *Sonata* is exceptionally pure, absolute, uncompromisingly unemotional music, with not a cheap bar in it. The sound and the rhythm are the only rulers here; no imagery could be associated with the composition. It is the first major utterance in American music.

Chapter XVIII

GRIFFES's tiredness of August carried into most of September and the months that followed. But there was work to be done.

On September 8th he signed a contract with the Aeolian Company to record his compositions for the Duo-Art Pianola. He was to receive $75 apiece for six to be recorded within the first year, and the agreement extended for five years. Schirmer's according to a clause in their contracts must pay him "Fifty (50%) per cent of all sums it may receive and collect as royalties or payments in full, for the licenses it may grant to the manufacturers of . . . mechanical instruments. . . ."

A week or so later he received two communications on the same day that also summoned forth a renewal of energy. Miss Arthur, representing the Lewisohns, wrote him on the 16th to confirm the agreement under which he was tackling *Salut au Monde*. "You, as I understand it, are willing to undertake the composition and play in fourteen performances on the same terms as were made with you for *The Kairn of Koridwen*. We are suggesting four hundred and fifty dollars as a lump sum to cover the composition, the playing of the performances, and the necessary rehearsals — two hundred of this you are to have as an advance, should you desire it."

He was already some way along in his sketches to the libretto, which, like the earlier Lewisohn production, effloresced into murky cosmism in some passages and offered splendid opportunities for imaginative feeling in others. " Out of the darkness there comes a slight stirring — sounds of peace and plenty, reminiscent of pastures, and plowmen, the metallic clang of building, the cries of the fisherfolk, the ordered creative forces of modern industry, the color and light of modern art — all brought together in progressions and harmonies that have form and direction." ". . . A rhythmic progression of human effort in various stages of civilization, tending upward in spiral lines toward light, beauty, harmony. The scientist, the artist, the agriculturist, and laborer — the builders of the world carry on life with an ordered plan and bear their burdens with a vision of the future." ". . . Youth gazing beyond a dawn-colored sky into a world of unchecked images; below them, workers, children, and planners dancing, while the air is filled with petals of fragrant blossoms and the sounds of joy and harmony." It was the happy vision of a social future that almost perfectly synthesized Walt Whitman and Mrs. Elliot. " Wait till you hear *Salut*," Griffes told Marion Bauer, " you'll be surprised how diatonic it is."

The other communication of the same date was a post card from Georges Barrère. " I am working hard on the *Poem* which I will play in Aeolian Hall with the N. Y. Symph. on *Sunday afternoon, Nov. 16th*. Help!! Am back in town." The card gave his address and telephone number. Barrère had appreciated almost at once the true value of this lithe and mature work that his friend had composed for him. It was no wonder that he inscribed to Griffes the preceding June: "If you want real good music ask Charles T. Griffes — he can write it for you if he wants — and he will for his most sincere friend, Georges Barrère."

Other, and perhaps more important, projects were also shaping up. Towards the end of August or at the beginning of September, Adolph Bolm had interested his friend Pierre Monteux, new conductor of the Boston Symphony Orchestra, in *The Pleasure-Dome of Kubla Khan*. Monteux and Griffes were reintroduced at the Bolms' studio on East 59th Street, where Griffes played through his old score to the French conductor. Mrs. Bolm later recollected the event. "When Charles, very nervously and shyly as usual, arrived, he and Monteux sat at the piano in the adjoining study and played *Kubla Khan*, the sound pouring out into the space vibrantly. Monteux, after it had been played through with stops and discussions . . . , expressed his delight with the score and on the spot proceeded making arrangements with Charles, who beamed with an inner joy. When Monteux left, Griffes sat silently for a while as if he were in a daze and exhausted."

Stokowski, too, had now shown an interest in his music and had scheduled four of Griffes's other pieces for early presentation by the Philadelphia Orchestra: the 1918 *Notturno; The White Peacock*, already performed at the Rivoli; *Clouds*, from the 1916 piano composition; and *Bacchanale*, from the 1912 *Scherzo*. These also must be revised and parts prepared.

Nor had Griffes relaxed his efforts to secure the piano *Sonata* a performance. Despite the increasing popularity of the work among musicians, it had not as yet been listed on any programs. Meeting a friend who had known of his hopes, Griffes complained bitterly, in the manner of a disappointed child: "You see, Harold Bauer hasn't played my piece after all." He began making new copies and sending them around.

The tasks at school were now harrying beyond words. He worked at his own things every minute between duties. He had almost no time for pleasure except during his trips to town on business. But in spite of all, his natural good humor was unaffected. He was still irrepressible. On September 22nd Frederick Smith noted in his diary: "Mr. Griffes took me down to Chinatown to have dinner in a Chinese restaurant. One of the dishes was described as 'pungent' something or other, and he ordered it just because he liked the work 'pungent.'"

His sister Florence visited him two days later, and he dug up some iris roots from around his studio for her. There was one variety that he especially liked, of a pale gray, almost white, shade, called "Morning Bride." She must have some.

In the last week of September he made a three-day excursion to the music festival at Pittsfield. Eva Gauthier had interested him in it during the summer, and he had a pleasant time. "I am glad I could get up here. The concerts are beautiful, and there is an interesting crowd of people up," he wrote his mother. On one evening, at the home of Ulysses Buehler, he, Tuthill, Barrère, Sokoloff, Hugo Kortschak, and several others gathered for music. Griffes played the Franck violin *Sonata* with Barrère, who carried the violin part on the flute.

As October came on he accelerated his rate of activity, utilizing every odd moment and sometimes working into the hours of the night. To Miss Broughton, who had recently returned from abroad and sent him a book, he replied on October 15th: "Pardon for not answering your book sooner. I haven't been feeling well for the last few days and just managed to keep necessary things going. I find the Hymnal very interesting and worth studying — especially the Gregorian things you mentioned. I also enjoyed reading the preface. What a different attitude they have towards church music in England!

"I was quite surprised to hear that you were back, as I rather thought you might stay awhile. But I suppose the conditions do not invite one to stay now.

"I am rushed to death now. Everything comes with me at once. The Boston Symphony is to give the first performance of

my symphonic poem *The Pleasure-Dome of Kubla Khan* on
Nov. 28th, the Philadelphia Orchestra gives the first performance of a set of four pieces for orchestra this fall, and the New
York Symphony gives for the first time on Nov. 16th a new
Poem for solo flute and orchestra. All these things have to be
put in final shape and parts prepared. Also I am finishing up my
music for the Neighborhood Playhouse production in January,
which is a tremendous job. Then in addition I have just signed
a five years' contract with the Duo-Art Reproducing Piano to
make records only for them. I am to make six of my own pieces
the first year and must start in a couple days. They are paying
me very well. I will tell you more about it later. Now I am too
busy. What a nuisance lessons are! "

Nuisance or not, he fulfilled his obligations and continued
with lessons well into October. On Sunday nights he faithfully
conducted his musicales for the boys, playing till he deemed
sufficient for Nevin's *Good Night*. He even satisfied after a
fashion and so far as he was able the broader requirements of
his position. No one who had experienced the recurrent crises
and humiliations of his own adolescence could be entirely in-
sensitive to the disappointments of boyhood. Young Smith on
October 18th entered in his diary: "Lost a football game to
St. Paul's at Garden City, L. I. Coming back to school on the
train, sat with Mr. Griffes. There wasn't much spirit in the
crowd, but he helped to cheer us up."

His trips to the Aeolian Company became mad dashes in
which he could spare only half an hour to record *The White
Peacock* and *The Lake at Evening* and no time at all for correction or revision of these recordings.

From the middle of October the strain of his double profession was almost too much. His resistance was perilously
low, and he was unable to give lessons on some days or even
"keep necessary things going." On the last day of the month

his good friend Rudolph Reuter was playing something of his in a recital at Aeolian Hall, but two days before Griffes wrote him: " I am sick over here at my mother's just now and may not be able to get out to come to the recital on Friday. So if you don't see me then, you will know the reason."

He made occasional visits to the doctor, who recommended good red steaks for the flagging vitality and the drainage on his strength. Nevertheless his exhaustion continued into November. Frederick Smith reported on the 3rd that he " didn't take a music lesson because Mr. Griffes has a bad cold." Other pupils were presently reproducing the same reason in explanation of their own disrupted piano lessons.

The *Poem, Kubla,* the other four pieces, *Salut au Monde,* and the *Sonata* all clamored for his attention. Revision and composition he could only do himself, but the copying of parts he had begun to relegate to a professional copyist. In September and October he had already made some use of this costly service, and now as November drew on, with his three major presentations impossibly close, still more. Though performances brought no financial return, it was necessary for a composer to be heard, even if he must himself pay out money for the privilege. So he had paid out small sums at first — eight dollars, three dollars, five dollars, and ten dollars — then almost a hundred dollars at once at the beginning of November. (Royalties from August 1918 to August 1919 had amounted to $48.70.)

The returned manuscripts must be checked for inaccuracies and incorrectness, and this took almost more time and energy than he could give. He must also copy a great bulk of the music himself. The bandage over his right eye made an occasional reappearance. One of his pupils finding the music instructor tediously copying out reams of music inquired why he did not send out to have it done. Griffes replied that to do so would take more money than he could afford. Once at his mother's he asked that she and his sister mark clefs and bars on manuscript paper for him while he worked. The three busied themselves around the dining-room table.

Rehearsal of the *Poem* took place in due course, and Griffes attended, listening to its "sound," conferring with Barrère, and revising, cutting, and rescoring. On the 16th the piece was performed. *Poem* for flute and orchestra, by Charles T. Griffes, following d'Indy's *Symphony No. 3*, came second in the program. It was received with uproarious approbation. The *New York Tribune* said next day: "Compositions for the flute even when played by such a splendid musician as Georges Barrère do not as a rule give rise to wild enthusiasm, yet yesterday's audience applauded the work and the soloist for several minutes." There was something ironic about its postscript. "If Americans can but continue to produce such works, all talk of the unrequited native composer will be speedily set at rest." It might only too well have been taken in conjunction with the opening sentence of W. J. Henderson's review in the *Sun*: "That Mr. Griffes has real talent was known before yesterday. . . ."

The *New York Herald* said: "Seven recalls were shared by the composer, who must have been pleased by the splendid reception of the work." The *Evening Mail* correctly reported: "Mr. Griffes . . . says that he had no definite program in mind." There was consequently great variety in the description of the piece, ranging from "naïve and elemental as an Irish folk song, but with the difference that it was scored to meet the demands of a modern symphony orchestra," to "rhapsodic and Oriental." Dr. Damrosch, who conducted, had found it Greek in spirit. But on the final estimate there was little difference. Critics vied with one another in praising what has since come to be regarded by many as Griffes's most fulfilled and mature production. At the least they were in agreement with the *New York Herald* that it ranked " among the best works produced by a native composer." Schirmer's devoted a full advertisement to the *Poem*.

Griffes had only a week in which to enjoy his triumph and work on the Philadelphia and Neighborhood Playhouse scores while Monteux was readying *Kubla* in Boston. He was pleased at the commotion over the *Poem* and doubted that the earlier work would meet with a similar success. On November 20th he wrote to Marion Bauer, who had sent him some clippings: " I was really very happy about the kind reception in the press. Such universal favor doesn't happen every day, does it? I doubt if *Kubla Khan* will be so well received. But then, why worry? " Mrs. Elliot noticed this same flippancy in his attitude and inquired whether he were not excited over the acclaim. Griffes smiled confidently in reply, with a curious expression that told her it was unexpected but entirely deserved. It would have been good music whatever had been thought of it.

Dan had been painting a house and so had been unable to share in his friend's glory.

Griffes departed for Boston to attend a rehearsal of *Kubla*. He arrived on Monday morning, the 24th, and was met by Bob, who happened to be in the city. Afterwards he was invited to Harvard for breakfast. The rehearsal went off very smoothly, and, tired as he felt, Griffes kept close track of proceedings. Arthur Shepherd, who was with him, noticed the same detachment that had impressed Mrs. Elliot a week before. " One thing, as indicative of Charles's artistic stature, struck me forcibly: prior to the first rehearsal there was no indication whatever of nervousness or apprehension regarding the effectiveness of his score; one got the impress that ' of course it's *right*, hence it must " come off " satisfactorily.' " In the afternoon he wrote a grateful letter to Adolph Bolm, in Chicago, who had got *Kubla* its chance.

Griffes was feeling ruinously ill. He thought he must have eaten something that disagreed with him at breakfast or lunch. "My Monday's trip was quite successful from every stand-point except that of health," he later wrote Dan, "and there it was very disastrous. . . . I took the 5 P.M. back to New York and thought I would never succeed in getting back to the school." Monteux had been very anxious for him to attend a Wednesday rehearsal, and he made the necessary effort. For he was by now useless at the school. After Monday: "I stayed in bed all the next day and couldn't eat anything (having meanwhile lost everything in my stomach for at least 24 hours). I managed to get up that evening and come down to N. Y. to take the midnight again."

He was busy all Wednesday. Monteux was taking enormous pains with the symphonic poem, and word had spread through-out the Boston musical world that something unusual was about to take place. Excitement ran high. Wherever composers and musicians gathered there was talk of the new composition to be played that week. Charles Martin Loeffler, whose custom it was to bumble in and out of Symphony rehearsals, remarked on the skillful management of the piano: "This was the right way to do it." Griffes had directed that the piano not be played as a solo instrument but be blended in with the other instru-ments by a continual use of both pedals.

A long combination article and interview with Griffes ap-peared in the *Boston Evening Transcript* that evening. "Defi-nitely modern in its technique, yet escaping the imitative emptiness into which so much of this type of American compo-sition has fallen, the music of Mr. Griffes challenges the clos-est study and analysis. It is not easy material to absorb at a single hearing, but invariably there is the feeling that it is worth hearing again." Something was said of the recent suc-cess of the *Poem* in New York, and then followed a preview of the new composition to be played that week. "Mr. Griffes's workmanship is 'ultra Modern' in the common and convenient usage of the words, eventuating in music that is an iridescent web through which occasionally pierce or flash — as it seems in a reading of the score — sharp-set and imaginative harmonies, graphic and imaginative modulations, as keen and felicitous contrasts and combinations of instrumental timbres. . . . Again, so far as the reading eye may gather the quality of the tone poem, Mr. Griffes is not insistently and definitely Oriental in the Russian manner. Rather, such Oriental suggestion as the music may convey is but one thread in a web which would be tapestry, like Coleridge's verse, of fantastic vision. Nor is Mr. Griffes minded to delineative progress through Coleridge's lines after the fashion of pedestrian composers. It is possible to detect in his tone poem 'the mingled measure from the fountain and the caves,' the contrasts of 'sunny pleasure-dome' with 'caves of ice.' No print, no diagram, however, is Mr. Griffes drawing in tones. Instead, he is transmuting into them, in his own voice and manner, a vision and an atmosphere." Mr. Toscanini, the article concluded, had said: "You will be surprised" to an invited audience as they trooped into the dress-rehearsal of a new opera at the Metropolitan. "'You will be surprised,' Mr. Monteux might as reasonably say to his hearers when he opens the score next Friday of *The Pleasure-Dome of Kubla Khan.*"

The next day, Thursday, was Thanksgiving. Griffes sat down and wrote to Dan in the evening. "I think my stomach is beginning to get back in shape again, as I was able to eat a little something solid this noon. But it was a rather pitiful Thanksgiving dinner, alone in a restaurant. I have contracted a pain in my side since last night (I think from cold) which I am trying to nurse with menthol. Between them all I seem to be like the man who fell from one fit into another.

"But there are always some bright spots. A friend of mine [Shepherd] here has put me up at his club [St. Botolph] for my stay here. It is one of the old-time Boston clubs to which a lot of well-known literary people have belonged. So I am awfully comfortable. The rehearsals have gone splendidly, and everybody in the musical and professional world whom I have met has been awfully cordial to me. In fact, I feel like a real celebrity. In the *Boston Transcript* for last evening was a long article about me and my work in general, and the orchestral people seem to expect flattering notices after the concert. In case you show a little more interest in this affair than in the New York Symphony concert last week, I might condescend to show you these things. At any rate let me announce to you now that the orchestra is going to play my work in New York at Carnegie Hall on Thursday night, Dec. 4th, and that this New York performance is the event of which I spoke to you some time ago as the greatest concert honor which can come to a composer in America (at least in my opinion). I cannot offer you any seats, even if you were for once condescending enough to be interested, as there are none to be had now. But don't tell me afterward that you were too busy painting to think of unimportant outside things.

"The concerts here are Friday and Saturday, and I shall take the midnight back to N. Y. I'll be in town Wed., and perhaps if I ask you this long ahead for supper you won't feel it necessary to refuse."

Unhappily the pleasantness of his room at the St. Botolph did not last. The room was poorly heated and drafty, and Griffes suffered considerable discomfort there during the remainder of his stay in Boston.

All his old friends were stricken by the loss of weight and the pallor that had overtaken him in recent months. Even the Hackley boys, who had witnessed the change more gradually throughout the fall, had not been unaware of the physical hardships with which he was contending. His thinness and febrile demeanor, the familiar coughing and colds, had become symptoms almost taken for granted. But to his friends and acquaintances who were first viewing these things — newly aggravated by the tension of the last two or three weeks — it was a truly frightening sight. They plied him with queries and suggestions. Heinrich Gebhard, whom he and Shepherd visited, judged that he was not heavily enough bundled for a sick man in November weather, and urged him to wear heavy overshoes. Carl Engel, who had him out to lunch, also took him to a pharmacist on Winter Street and bought some medicine that he made Griffes swear to take for his cold.

On Friday afternoon, November 28th, the Boston Symphony Orchestra performed *The Pleasure-Dome of Kubla Khan* under the direction of Pierre Monteux. It was a Boston audience but two months removed from the famous police strike that received this new work. Rioting, window-smashing, shooting, robbery, and violence of every sort had reigned openly for two whole nights over the Brahman center. If Boston was the cultural stronghold of the country, events had made uncannily clear that it was one resting on nothing more substantial than the forces of uniformed men that it paid. If Boston was indeed the " Hub " of the universe, there was something organically wrong with the transmutations of the universe. To such an audience, with his deep and burning visions of a beauty that sustains, Griffes might well have come like a missionary from another world. Monteux understood the score and conducted superlatively. He had lavished every care in preparing it, and the men, well rehearsed, played with rare perception. The result was a smash-hit that Griffes could scarcely have looked for even after the anticipatory excitement of the last few days.

The *Boston Evening Transcript* carried a large picture of Griffes next day captioned " Voice of the Orient: Means of the Occident." The long and entirely laudatory write-up reported how in response to the applauding audience he had gone through the corridor and anteroom to the stage, strode across it to shake the conductor's hand, and nodded acknowledgment to all and sundry. " It was good to hear the listeners applauding warmly the music of a youthful and little-known composer because it had manifestly pleased and impressed them. It was good to see him honestly pleasured by such fortune." And the *Boston Traveler* gasped: " An American work by a composer just thirty-five, on a Symphony program! Surely the Boston Symphony Orchestra is progressing. . . . It afforded such pleasure the composer was twice called to the stage to acknowledge the tribute." The critics thoroughly agreed with the audience. " Mr. Griffes's music," said the *Transcript*, " moreover, clearly deserved such reward. His tone poem is a brief piece, since Wagnerian and Straussian lengths are out of the fashion with younger composers the world over. By the same token, it is also laudably concentrated in a mingled economy and astuteness of means. . . .

" Throughout hardly a measure seems to be ' filling'; while not a modulation, a progression, a play of harmony or timbre fails to do its office. There are discernible motives whence the tonal fabric springs; as in the music of Debussy a rhythmic continuity seems to bind the whole together; but there is no ' development' for ' development's ' sake. No more is there any juggling with harmonic and instrumental color as feat of resource and agility which is the newer mode. Mr. Griffes perceives clearly the form in which he would cast his tone poem, the design which he would unfold, the visions he would summon. With surety, with economy, he chooses and applies his means to those ends. Everywhere the outcome is clear, the impression tense, the atmosphere sustained, the illusion compassed. So to compose is to compose with a mind that discerns, sorts, controls. It is a rare, a precious possession for a composer still in relative youth." The review ended: " Music of a mind at every turn of the facture, music of imagery at almost every turn of the illusion, music throughout of a talent and a temperament taking their own visioning and expressing way, music unlike that of any other American composer, yet uncommonly vivid in immediate impression. Mr. Griffes has done well to wait until the mistrustful conductors were ready to accept him." This after Griffes's four years of trying to place the composition. " Neither an audience in New York over the *Poem* for flute nor an audience in Boston over *The Pleasure-Dome of Kubla Khan* has mistrusted at all."

The *Boston Globe* found it to exhibit " genuine originality and power of a sort that entitle its composer to be judged by the same standard as men like Ravel, Rachmaninoff, and Stravinsky, not by that usually applied to orchestral works by unfamiliar Americans.

" It is never imitative, pedantic, bombastic, nor sentimental. Few are the works of American composers which succeed in avoiding all four of these pitfalls, and in calling forth an outburst of genuine applause instead of the routine polite handclapping. Mr. Griffes was obliged by the insistence of the audience and the friendly compulsion of Mr. Monteux to come on the stage and bow his acknowledgments.

" The orchestration of this tone poem is often masterly. The piano becomes what it almost never is, an orchestral instrument instead of a more or less superfluous ' added attraction.' Like Berlioz and Rimsky-Korsakov, Mr. Griffes proves the saying that the highest form of art is to conceal art, by gaining his effects in ways which are not immediately obvious to the listener.

"Best of all, they are never effects for the sake of effects, but always subordinate to his genuine and individual creative impulse. It is to be hoped that this piece will be repeated during the present season, and others by the same composer added to the active repertory of the orchestra."

Perhaps the most impressive notice was that of Philip Hale, respected dean of Boston music critics, in the *Boston Herald*. "Any composer girding up his loins to turn Coleridge's *Kubla Khan* into a vocal work, cantata or what not, would start on a perilous adventure for, to quote Swinburne, this poem is 'the supreme model of music in our language.' 'In reading it,' said the master of rhythm and verbal euphony, 'we seem rapt into that paradise revealed to Swedenborg, where music and color and perfume were one, where you could hear the hues and see the harmonies of heaven.' Any composer meditating a symphonic poem fully 'illustrative' of *Kubla Khan*, a tonal interlinear translation, would undertake a fool's task.

"Mr. Griffes, born in New York State thirty-five years ago, wisely chose extracts from the poem, lines describing the stately pleasure-dome, 'the sunny pleasure-dome with caves of ice,' 'the miracle of rare device,' the gardens and the 'sunny spots of greenery.' By a legitimate stretch of the imagination he hears and reproduces the sounds of revelry that might well take place in this strange palace, mentioned first by travelers, whose description led Coleridge, dreaming, to write the fragment that is enough to make his name illustrious.

"Instrumental music may add wings to even a romantically poetic flight. No one hearing this music of Mr. Griffes will feel that the poem itself has been belittled; that its splendor has been tarnished; for this composer is blessed with what is rare with American musicians, imagination. His gift of expression is pronounced. He might have been extravagant; his music might have been merely bizarre. In either case he would have incurred

Page of the unfinished *Five Pieces*

the reproach of affectation. He has succeeded in being musically, aesthetically, successfully unusual. He studied composition in Berlin; but there are no Germanisms, either orthodox or heterodox, in his style. Nor does it seem that he has worshipped too devoutly in any one of the modern Parisian chapels. If he has been influenced at all, the influence is that of Rimsky-Korsakov, Borodin, and the barbaric gorgeousness of the Russian Ballet; but Mr. Griffes has decided and refreshing individuality; he has found an Oriental expression that is his own, as he has found new harmonic and orchestral colors. His ' Alph, the sacred river' is not the Terek of Balakirev's *Thamar;* his measures of wild revelry are not those that Rimsky-Korsakov heard in Sinbad's palace. The music, from the strange, unearthly opening, which at once arrests the attention, to the exquisitely fanciful ending, is fascinating throughout."

Everywhere there was the same agreement. Another critic, Olin Downes, stacked him up against his American contemporaries. "Mr. Griffes is a man to watch with care. He is not a mere objectivist and a man of ultra-refinement in his music, like John Alden Carpenter, for example. Nor is he a man possessed of the broadly nationalistic ideals in the music of Henry Gilbert.

"But he is a young American, full of spirit and receptivity, astonishingly progressive, as shown by the texture of a score of a man who was musically educated in composition in Germany; he has temperament in great abundance; he loves to write."

There was another triumphant performance of *Kubla* on Saturday evening, and Griffes spent some time with Rudolph Ganz and other of his friends, then bade them farewell. "He spoke of his depleted energies and the exhausting labors that his work entailed," Shepherd later recollected.

And after all the tumult and the glory it was back to lessons at the school. The Boston Symphony, which left on Sunday for a two weeks' trip, would play in New York in a few days, and that was something to look forward to. He must also get on with his other work. During this interval he encountered Leslie Hodgson while in New York and spoke to him of the *Sonata*. He visited the doctor. He showed A. Walter Kramer the spectacular reviews that he had garnered in Boston. In an article Kramer later recalled " Griffes showing me his notices of the Boston performances; he felt he had done something in gaining the approval of those ' doctors of music ' in the Athens of America! "

And presently it came about, "the greatest concert honor which can come to a composer in America." The Boston Symphony played his composition in Carnegie Hall on Thursday evening, December 4th. Once more it was an overpowering success. The audience applauded wildly, as did Monteux from the stage, and again and again Griffes had to rise to bow acknowledgments from the box in the first tier where he was seated. " He seemed more surprised than his hearers," remarked James Gibbons Huneker in the *World* next day.

After the concert he was once more surrounded by admiring friends and flooded with the congratulations of all who knew him.

The New York press reactions paralleled those that he had received in Boston, and one review, with shocking audacity, amazingly and crudely plagiarized Philip Hale's. The *Evening Journal* smugly reflected that Griffes's success proved one thing conclusively: " The American composer, in a word, has no difficulties more than another, provided he be a good composer as well as an American one." Huneker found that " there is no mistaking the authenticity of the mood, or moods, evoked by the interesting combinations of Griffes." He rejected a scintillant catalogue to end all catalogues: " You think of

Rimsky-Korsakov, sometimes of Tchaikovsky, of Liszt, Berlioz, and Richard Strauss. Yet it is, all said and done, Griffes. He has individuality." Huneker commented also on the structure: "Formally speaking, the loop is a wide, loose wire; however, a loop is there, not a mere arabesque, but a narrative tone that carries you on to the mystic close."

In the days that followed Griffes enjoyed the sensation of having experienced perhaps the most phenomenal acclaim ever accorded a serious American composer. He continued at his work and at the school. He attended an uninteresting symphony concert that included, however, *L'Apprenti Sorcier*, which he had never heard before. He visited the doctor. He was interviewed by the *Evening Sun* for an article that would appear some two weeks hence. And though he had never had any luck in obtaining wealthy sponsorship he was not above dropping a hint. "Mr. Griffes said himself to this paper that he had spent the last fourteen years of his life since coming home from Germany at the Hackley School at Tarrytown-on-the-Hudson, and that when he wasn't teaching music or playing the piano he has been composing."

He had been planning to go to Atlantic City during the Christmas vacation in order to regain strength and resistance. That began to seem distant, however, and he resolved to leave at once even before school let out. He began packing his bags, and announced to his pupils that he would be leaving on the 10th. But two days before then the inevitable occurred, and Griffes, taken suddenly ill, collapsed, was brought to the Master's house, put to bed, and a doctor summoned. He had pleurisy, the doctor said, but might be able to leave in a few days.

Soon recovered a little, Griffes was confined to bed, where he worked on his music and sent brief notes to friends about his ill fortune. Walter Kramer had written him admiringly of *Kubla*, and he replied on the 10th. "I have been feeling miserably all fall and decided to give up my work here before our vacation came and go to Atlantic City for a week or two. To-day was the day set for going, and then I had the bad luck to get pleurisy two days ago. The doctor thinks I may be able to go by Saturday." Another note went the same day to Leslie Hodgson, who had asked about the *Sonata*. "Sorry about the *Sonata*, but I'm sick in bed with pleurisy just now — I've had one darned thing after another this fall until there is nothing left of me but a wreck. If I could have gotten away I was to have gone to Atlantic City today, but of course there is nothing doing. My only feeling is one of absolute fury as every old plan I had made up till Jan. 6th is busted up now. Perhaps I can play you the *Sonata* later. Just now I haven't even a copy of it. Bauer has one, Rudolph Reuter another, and the third is in Boston. I may get the last one back soon and perhaps can play it for you sometime before Christmas week. I'll keep you posted."

Two days later he wrote to Rudolph Reuter: "I hope you have not given me up as a bad job. I have been up and down from a sick bed ever since you played in New York. Just now I am in bed again with pleurisy." A young musician in Kentucky had recently communicated with Griffes about private lessons. "I have been unable to write him yet, but shall in a day or two. When I get back to New York in January, I think I can take him. . . . I believe he doesn't come to New York until sometime in January anyway." He spoke again of the *Sonata*. "Shepherd was tremendously interested that you were going to play my new *Sonata*, which he likes very much. He wondered if it would be possible for you to take an evening while you are there and play it at the Boston Composers' Club, which consists of all the composers of prominence in Boston, old and young. There is plenty of time to think it over and arrange matters if you want to do it. In that case I might go up to Boston myself for a day or two." He also told of his latest success: "The Boston Symphony gave four performances of *Kubla Khan;* two in Boston, one in Washington, and one in New York. Wasn't that splendid? It had an enormous success everywhere. . . . At present, Stock has the score and parts, and I believe he intends to produce it sometime this month. Be sure and hear it!

"As soon as I get well enough, I am going down to Atlantic City for a while and see if I can get back enough strength to start in with my work again by the second week in January. It has been a miserable fall. Stokowski is performing the end of this month a new set of four orchestra pieces. I hope to go down if possible."

Miss Broughton had written to inquire about his silence. On the 13th he replied to her in a short note to which he pinned a flower. "Didn't mean to wait so long before writing you, but I couldn't do otherwise. I have been so miserable the whole fall that I could only do the most necessary work. I haven't even given lessons part of the time. Now again I am in bed with pleurisy but hope to be up in a few days at most. I've had two extraordinary successes this year which have sort of brought me fame overnight. Especially in Boston I was the musical lion of the day. I have many long and splendid reviews to send you when I can get energy to collect them and cut them out. As soon as I am well enough I leave the school and go to Atlantic City probably. I am all run down."

The next day Frederick Smith visited him and recorded: "Went to see Mr. Griffes at Mrs. Gage's. He seems discouraged."

Chapter XIX

BECAUSE her son did not wish to alarm her, Mrs. Griffes had not immediately been summoned to his bedside. When the doctor at last rendered a verdict of pneumonia, Griffes, fearstricken, had still insisted that Mrs. Gage not inform his mother. That was what his father had died of. Nighttimes he asked that his door be left ajar so that the light might dispel the imageridden darkness. Finally, on December 13th, he telephoned his mother. Two days later Florence came out to Hackley to see him. She found the invalid propped up in bed assiduously working away at the four orchestral sketches to be played by Stokowski later in the month. "Good gosh, what are you doing here!" he greeted her. His doctor complained of the patient's preoccupation with work, and when that had been straightened out in a day or two, Florence left to fetch her mother.

Mrs. Griffes arrived on the 18th in wintry and difficult weather. She wore a hat with turned-down brim and purple feather, quite modish to her taste, but her son's sense of humor had not been depleted by his exhaustion. "Where did you ever get that hat?" he inquired after the preliminary endearments, and solemnly explained that it must be replaced.

Griffes was comfortably accommodated in the Gages' guest room, Mrs. Gage having waited upon him faithfully till his mother's arrival. He felt grateful for her sympathetic nursing. After consulting doctors had been called in, two nurses were secured, and they also were given quarters. Mrs. Griffes occupied the room belonging to Mr. Gage's young son; a cot was added for her daughter or any other member of the family who might wish to visit.

The days passed by with little show of improvement in the patient's condition. He seemed almost too fatigued and worn out to make a quick recovery any more. His friends began to send messages upon learning the news. Mrs. Elliot made two anxious visits to Hackley. To her beloved friend she reaffirmed more than ever her belief that Christian Science might save him. Weary and disheartened, he must still not abandon the effort to live. He must affirm. She repeated her pleas with insistent and challenging devotion. But Griffes had no faith in Christian Science, and he was tired now beyond the reach of this kind of encouragement. He asked his mother to remain in the room during Mrs. Elliot's second visit so that she would not attempt her ministrations.

Dan came to see him once, and Griffes, happy and expectant, instructed him not to reveal to outsiders that he was a policeman. But it was a sad visit. The idyllic trip to Boston they had planned together was now a thing of breath and words.

Some of the boys had visited him at first. One had brought him a *Science and Health;* and they had gladly run errands to get his prescriptions filled. Then no more visits were allowed. They sent him gifts.

He slept poorly, was restless, feverish, and sometimes short of breath. One day as he tossed in delirium his mother entered the room and, awaking, he asked: "What are all these people doing here?" They were alone. Frightened, Mrs. Griffes assured him that they were there together. Griffes then lapsed back into calm and rest. "I thought I was in a great Oriental chamber hung with tapestries; you don't know how much I've lived in my imagination these last few weeks." Huneker and Hale had been right: imagination. He had once written a friend who was assigned a dull and unvarying routine: ". . . I know you don't mind the terrible monotony of prospect which would be maddening to some people. . . . With some people I might call this a pleasure in thinking of distant and invisible things, but with you I am afraid it is only a greater pleasure in present surroundings." He did not say it, but he was one of "some people," who had had for a long time to rely on "distant and invisible things" for inner support.

A faculty neighbor departing for California vowed that she would like to take him along. That would cure him all right. And Griffes, thinking of his old wish to see the Pacific, sighed assent.

The performance of his four pieces by Stokowski on December 19th had roused little excitement. At first he had been restless and perturbed because he could not be there. They would not do it right without him. But even that he accepted. The reviews came back favorable from Philadelphia. "His score," said one, "has piquancy and pungency, and it is one of the hopeful intimations for the future of American music." Another said: "In their instrumental coloring and in the poetic atmosphere by which they are enveloped they reflect the influence of Debussy, but they are less vague and their tonality is less elusive than is the case with that composer's music, and they evince that gift of melody which only a few possess and which after all is the most precious of any composer's endowment."

Less than a week after the Philadelphia concert, the *Musical Courier* announced that Charles T. Griffes, the composer, "lies seriously ill in Tarrytown, N. Y. This brief statement serves to inform those interested of his enforced absence from

New York." The notice appeared in the Christmas issue. Griffes, lying worn in his sick bed, had scarcely observed the approach of the season. But he had a small Christmas tree in his room. The Gage boy had thoughtfully suggested to his parents that their sick guest share in the festivities, and they had decorated and brought it in to him. There was also a great tree standing in the center of the quadrangle outside, which glittered exquisitely in the sun. Griffes, unable to see it quite from where he lay, made his mother describe it in close detail. The Gages, off to spend the holidays in Philadelphia, considerately left their two maids behind so that the whole Griffes family might celebrate Christmas together.

The Chicago Symphony was going to play *Kubla Khan* in January, and Rudolph Reuter, inviting the composer to be his guest on this occasion, received an answer from Mrs. Griffes. It was dated January 9th, 1920, and explained that her son was down under an attack of pleurisy with pneumonic tendencies. " I am glad to tell you that he is slowly recovering — but very slowly — and we fear it will be a matter of weeks before he can take up his work.

"He is here at Hackley — has been under the care of two nurses for three weeks, and I have also been with him for that time. This forced relinquishing of everything in which he was so much interested is an intense disappointment to him, and he feels rather 'blue' at times — but we are hoping that there will soon be such a decided improvement in his condition that he will be filled with courage."

There was no decided improvement, however, and no resumption of work. On the 16th Stock and the Chicago Symphony played *Kubla*. Reuter had played three of his things the week before, and Chicago, by now somewhat familiar with his works, raved over the new poem. On the 17th, Mrs. Griffes replied to Schirmer's, who had sent a package of proofs. " At my son's request I am returning package sent him by you as he is still severely ill and will be unable to do work of any kind for several weeks." Things indeed had gone further than that. In the second week of January rumors had begun to spread among the Hackley boys that their music instructor was consumptive. Specialists were called in from New York, and plans were made for his removal elsewhere. Griffes dictated a letter to Schirmer's the day after his mother's. "I leave tomorrow for Loomis Sanatorium, Loomis, New York. Any important information you can send me there, but as yet I cannot write myself nor do any work at all so please don't send me any more proofs. I don't know how long I shall be there but probably several weeks. Will have to let the piano version of the flute piece go for a while as it is absolutely impossible to do anything. It will be one of the first things I shall do when I can work at all again." The same day, January 18th, he dictated another letter, to Dan: "I leave tomorrow morning for Loomis Sanatorium, Loomis, New York, supposed to be the highest point in the Catskills. Can't walk yet and am still more or less bedridden.

"Please write me at once. As soon as I can write I'll let you know how things are."

The trip to Loomis was encompassed without mishap in bitter weather next day. Mrs. Griffes, a nurse, and a driver accompanied the patient in the car leaving Hackley, and they were met at the ferry by his sister Marguerite and a brother-in-law, who took them the rest of the way. At Loomis's because of the ice and fierce snows, Griffes had to be placed in a bob-sled and taken up the hill to his destination.

He patiently submitted to the diagnostic questionnaire put to him upon arrival. Occupation? "Musical Composer." Religious denomination? "None." And Charles T. Griffes, composer, was assigned his room in a tuberculosis sanatorium.

Loomis Sanatorium, founded in 1896, was situated in the heart of the Catskill Mountains, more than two thousand feet above sea level. There was a neighboring town, Liberty, and New York itself was only about a hundred miles away, but as far as the eye could see there were only spans of trees and a horizon of misty mountain ridges. The porches and cabins that lined the institution were all designed to take advantage of the high atmosphere. Though it was doubtful that Griffes had tuberculosis, there was little doubt that he would benefit from the sanatorium's fundamental program. "The cure is— *Rest*," according to their circular. "It must be *complete* rest." That was why Griffes's doctor, writing to Loomis of his decision on January 12th, had remarked: ". . . I believe that whether tuberculous or not he will make a much more rapid and satisfactory convalescence under your care than elsewhere. There are no complications, and the case I think is a suitable one for Loomis and interesting as a study. He would require infirmary care and want privacy."

Griffes was by now indeed "interesting as a study." His consignment to a sanatorium had depressed him beyond words. The nurse who accompanied him and of whom he had grown rather fond soon departed for New York, and he was left with his mother at Loomis to wait out what might be.

Mrs. Elliot redoubled her efforts to inspirit new life in her friend. She had acquired a Christian Science healer to work *in absentia* for him, and she now began an impassioned stream of letters, vehemently in earnest, hortatory in tone, and with all crucial passages many times underscored. They were letters beautiful in the purity of their love.

Apart from Mrs. Elliot's faith in Science it should be taken into account that there was on foot a widespread revival of religious inspiration along similar lines at that time. As compensation to the physically and psychologically mutilated left strewn in the trail of the war, the same doctrines were springing up everywhere. Mrs. Elliot herself mentioned these conditions in one letter: "These letters may be entirely too heavy for you, and may fatigue you instead of bringing inspiration. . . . But you see New York is inundated with this kind of thought this year.

"Sir Oliver Lodge with his 'Spiritual Serum of Life,' his 'What Is Life,' his theory of etheric energy, is lecturing all over the place. Maeterlinck with his theory that the soul of man has power to build its own body — and that psychic and spiritual power can move external matter without contact — is also talking, talking, talking. A man from England is speaking from the altar of several Episcopal churches, in the city, and healing people in the church at the altar. In France simply unbelievable experiments in psychology and therapeutics are being carried on."

After Griffes's removal from Tarrytown, Mrs. Elliot wrote him encouragingly at once that he had now "been released from those first surroundings of sickness and bondage." She entreated him to live. "I cannot believe that a man who has had so much the touch of genius" could go through these hours, days, and weeks, without discovering the healing revelation.

Yet it made little impression one way or the other on Griffes. "Prostration was very marked," his sanatorium doctor later wrote, "even after the patient had had some opportunity to recover from his fatiguing trip to Loomis."

It was to his mother that he turned for strength during these hard weeks. "I will tell your mother," said Mr. Hare to John Norton, the character in Moore's *Celibates* with whom Griffes identified himself in certain respects, "I will tell your mother what you say. . . . I agree with you that no one but ourselves can determine what duties we should accept."

"Ah! if you would only explain that to my mother. You have expressed my feelings exactly. . . ."

But Griffes had been confused. He had thought that his personal life must remain an unrevealed and invisible barrier between him and his mother, precluding any intimate mutual understanding between them; and that the necessity of playing Mr. Hyde among ever-widening circles of American musical society constituted a further estrangement. For her part Mrs. Griffes may have felt that she and her family problems acted as a hindrance to her son in the carrying out of his mission in life. Also that she had never known how, adequately, to express the very real admiration that she felt for the things he was achieving in a music outside her ken.

They had both been wrong. For he had followed the course necessary to the individuation of his personal and creative beings, and she had required only that which is any mother's right in age. Impediments were trivial beside the true strength of their devotion. Griffes felt the bond between them now more keenly than ever before. He had few intimates among his many friends. In almost grimly literal fulfillment of his boyhood wish, there were very few who, like Dan or Mrs. Elliot or the Bolms, even addressed him by his first name.

He could not get enough of his mother now. She had borrowed a pink sweater from his sister on first coming out to Hackley, and he greatly admired it on her. She must wear pink often henceforth. She had discarded her atrocious hat for something more becoming. He complimented her on the change at once. She had begun knitting a black and white sweater, and he watched its progress with interest, praising it boundlessly when she had done.

She was his constant companion during the long days and nights. His bed was on casters, and he spent most of each day on the porch adjoining his sleeping room. Hands warmly mit-

tened, knitted toboggan cap drawn down and the coverlets
up, so that only his face showed, he was content thus to be
wheeled each day to the invigorating air of his porch, whence
he could view the neighboring hills and other patients on
their chairs and couches. His mother would sit quietly by
him knitting; or if the weather proved exceptionally inclement
the two would remain indoors conversing and reading. Once
in a while some acquaintance among the hardier patients would
visit him.

Mrs. Griffes was lodged at the Administration Building,
which was a distance from his quarters. Sometimes she would
come to him twice a day, but usually only once, for she had to
plow through banks of snow and ice. The ground was not
level, and once when the snow came up above her knees she
floundered and did not know whether she would get to the
hospital division or not.

One night Griffes feverishly imagined that his sister Marguerite had been in to see him. She had not, but she soon came
to relieve her mother, who was ill for a week.

On the 23rd of January, after an exploratory puncture in his
lower right axillary region, thoracentesis was performed on
Griffes, and over a liter of pus withdrawn. His fever lingered,
his pulse continued extremely rapid, and his condition remained so grave, indeed so nearly moribund, that the doctor
decided to attempt such immediate relief as was possible, and
applied apparatus designed to maintain suction and evacuation
of the chest. It had been purchased for the purpose and was
used for the first time on Griffes. Nevertheless the procedure
proved entirely unsatisfactory and was finally abandoned. The
empyema cavity was emptied and irrigated, at first daily, then
every other day, by means of two needles. In early February,
Griffes rallied a little. He had at any rate emerged from the
stage in which death seemed imminent.

He was in pain much of the time now, and his mother would sit by his side holding his hand. Sometimes worn out with her vigil she fell asleep thus, his hand in hers. So great did his dependence on her become that the nurse at Loomis vowed he was a spoiled child. Once he drowsed off while awaiting her arrival, leaving a note: " If asleep, please wait as I want to see you."

Mrs. Elliot did not relax her implorations despite the horrified protests of attendants at Loomis when they learned that their patient was receiving letters from a Christian Scientist. Indeed it was their opinion that this correspondence should be intercepted. But whatever the merit of her religious theories, Mrs. Elliot realistically appreciated what her friend had been through during the last few years and the last few months. On the 30th of January she wrote him: " I hear through your mother that you have been having a hard time. It is hard to ask you to have more patience after you have suffered so long. But, Charles, just keep your grip, your patience, a little longer. Relief will certainly come soon now. You have had a terrible time, and I know you feel worn out. But surely it can't go on being so bad. Relief will certainly come soon now. It is hard to go through with what you have had to endure — and to have any patience or strength left. But if you can get and keep your grip it will help to hasten your recovery. Life is very strong and omnipotent, Charles. God be with you." She followed it immediately with another agitated note the same day.

Through February her letters became more and more urgent all the time. " I know that you are having to endure a very great deal of suffering — and I know that its being so prolonged wears you out and takes the heart out of you. I do not say to you as others say to you: 'You must help yourself by your courage and mental condition.' I say this: 'I believe that there is a Principle in the Being of every man born on this earth that

makes for Life and Fulfillment.'" She besought him to practice these meditations for her sake.

At the end of January, Schirmer's had sent him a contract for
the *Poem* for flute and orchestra. On reading it he felt himself
unprotected once more and asked his brother-in-law to return
it to Schirmer's and explain. (Griffes had been forced to have
the orchestral parts of the three Macleod songs multigraphed
at his own expense.) But an old question brought an old response. The assistant manager of Schirmer's replied on February 11th in a letter that minced no words. "Your brother-in-
law returned the contracts for your *Poem* to us with your
query, but we really do not see that any added clauses are necessary. In the event of your making any reductions or arrangements of the composition and our publishing them, your royalty percentage holds good for them just as for the original
work. The contract definitely states this, and whether we publish them or no, you are privileged to make as many arrangements as you choose, such arrangements being your own property and affair, so I see no reason for any changes in the contract
and if you will sign them and return one copy to us, we shall
be obliged."

February stretched on in pain and tedium. There were occasional notes from his pupils and friends. The doctor considered
that surgical interference would be advisable but feared that
a trip to New York might prove difficult and hazardous. There
had been no findings whatsoever of tuberculosis. The empyema was the outstanding feature and the one requiring immediate and serious attention.

Griffes could not help becoming disconsolate and even mor-
bidly imaginative. One day when some workmen were digging
a frozen water main about a quarter of a mile away from his
porch he became obsessed with the idea that there was a funeral in progress. He was certain that he saw everything from

beginning to end, although it was, he conceded, a strange location for a funeral. A workman's black coat hanging on a door, the black paint at the end of the building he could barely see, every stray bit contributed to his mournful impression. Nor could he see why his mother should wish to deceive him with a more cheering interpretation.

On the afternoon of February 24th, Nikolai Sokoloff and the Cleveland Orchestra played the revised version of *Sho-Jo* in Cleveland, but if Griffes any longer knew or cared he no longer said. Indeed, had he cared he might have discovered his name sprinkled as liberally as always on concert programs during the period of his illness. His things were played, sung, and danced, all the while he lay abed.

The day after the Cleveland concert Mrs. Elliot wrote: "You are really 'missed,' Charles — and more now than when you were first taken ill." Many had called her to inquire of him. She had just heard from Leslie Hodgson. "The Lewisohns come home today — Wednesday. They will learn definitely for the first time about how severe your illness has been."

The Lewisohns, who had been traveling and thus missed the news, were eager to proceed with their plans for *Salut au Monde*. They got in touch with their musical collaborator, suggesting if he were unable to continue the work himself that he name a successor to finish it. But Griffes raged to his mother: "I've got it all planned out in my mind, and I don't want anyone else to do it!"

It was a noticeable and peculiar circumstance that he never spoke of music any more, except when the necessity of answering communications forced it upon his attention. And from this time he never once referred to the subject again.

Rudolph Reuter, having learned of Griffes's continued sickness and recalling his erstwhile hopes for the *Sonata*, thought to cheer him by a performance of the work. Accordingly, in a

Wednesday morning recital on March 10th at the Ziegfeld Theater in Chicago he played the *Sonata* from manuscript, with Leo Sowerby, an American composer, turning pages for him. It claimed much the same reaction that it had at Griffes's own performances. One critic, W. L. Hubbard, in a review headed "This New Sonata Has One Virtue, Anyway — It's Brief," said: "Themes of sufficient distinction to be grasped were sought in vain, and meaning, purpose, mood, or suggestion to say nothing of tonal euphony and beauty, failed wholly to be discovered. It may be music, but it seemed notes and then more notes." Another, Edward C. Moore, summed up: "One could perceive that the work was continuous, varying ever and anon in mood, and that was about all."

But whatever the thrill at ultimate performance or disappointment at reception, neither was any more known to Griffes. He was too far gone, too lapsed into coma, when his sister tried to inform him, and he never learned that his *Sonata* had been performed. In the second week of March it was decided that his metabolism had attained a degree of equilibrium where the trip to New York might prove a safe risk. It was the time of prohibition, and Ann Parke was requisitioned for some brandy, which she kindly furnished as stimulant for the invalid before his journey. Griffes's old friend Dr. Bancroft was called in on the case. On March 19th the doctor at Loomis wrote a long letter to Dr. Bancroft, and the next day Griffes, his thin wasted body having been hoisted through a train window, was transferred to the New York Hospital. "Do get well and get back within reach of us — where we can see you. You do not know how we all miss you," wrote Mrs. Elliot. Helen Marot sent Joyce's *Portrait of the Artist as a Young Man*.

Dr. Bancroft provided him with a friendly, quiet, and understanding nurse, for whom he was grateful. Then the agonizing ceremonies resumed: rubber tubes inserted into the wound and removed from the wound, constant irrigations, changes of dressing, and medication. He coughed continually, slept restlessly and seldom, and felt pain in his wound. Once he sat up for ten minutes. Otherwise he lay on his back alternately coughing and dozing at intervals. Sometimes the pain was almost unbearable. He would think of simple near things, the happiness and strength that he might take in his mother and family. As with her, so with them, and for similar reasons, he had felt himself slightly alienated. But that was over now. Katharine had written that they were all counting on him to get well. She had set aside a room in her home, and her children were all thinking of ways to wait on him, serve him, and make him comfortable. He was deeply touched — it was so kind of the children. Katharine sent a pillow that she had made for him, and he was again grateful. The whole family had shown him so much kindness. When Marguerite said: "But Charles, that's what big families are for," he could only reply: "Yes, but I never knew that before."

He elaborated the things that he would do upon his recovery. They would have dinner together, his mother and Marguerite and he, at Bloomfield; and he tentatively sketched the items of the menu, which would surely include apple pie.

His good nurse had been replaced by a noisy, garrulous one, and he asked his mother to do for him now. He asked her to stroke his head. There was a difference between stroking and rubbing, he said, that nurses did not understand. Once when, pale and trembling, he was seized by a final palsy and his very being seemed at an end, she hugged him close to her and, as she felt, by dint of sheer blandishment and love kept him alive.

A friend who was permitted to see him at this time was stunned by Griffes's emaciated appearance. "I can only remember kneeling and kissing his hand and saying: 'God bless you.' . . . I was profoundly moved, and the emotional reaction remains with me to this day." Griffes was too weak to say anything.

He no longer smiled with fresh ironic humor at things that were said as he had been able to while yet at Loomis. There he had cheerily looked off to the distant hills and said that if he were still confined the next spring his mother must take a mountain cabin.

From day to day he languished on a final rack of pain as the tubes were inserted, removed, inserted, removed, the irrigations continued, and the dressings endlessly changed. There were bloody discharges on his dressing now. Once in suffering he told his mother: "I don't know why I want to live." And when she replied: "Don't talk like that," he persisted: "But what have I to live for?" Mrs. Griffes wisely forbore mention of the music and beauty that had led him to this point and answered simply: "For me."

On the 1st of April he had a hemorrhage. His nurse wrote on her chart: "Patient expectorating bright red blood," and hours later: "Patient extremely nervous." It had been almost the worst experience of all. When the position of his head and neck became unbearably tiring and he wished his mother to place her arm beneath his neck he remembered the hemorrhage and was afraid to let her try. There might be another terrible choking-up sensation.

April 4th was Easter Sunday. Griffes's room was filled and banked with flowers. He asked Marguerite, whose birthday he had been unable to honor a few days before, to take the best of them. Mrs. Elliot had left a note for him. "Please give this to Mr. Griffes on Easter morning." It was brief, and began: "The truest Easter greeting which I can send you is for me to know the truth of the gospel of Christ and the Power of God. . . ." It ended with the Biblical inspiration: "For lo, I am with you always."

On the 5th he was wheeled to the operating room. He was declining rapidly, and Dr. Bancroft wished to leave no stone unturned on his behalf. With the aid of local anesthesia, about six inches of the eighth and ninth ribs were resected, the cavity opened wide, and good drainage established. A foreign body was also removed. This was a small metal portion of the vacuum apparatus that had been used earlier at Loomis. The doctor there had written: ". . . The small metal portion which is devised for freeing the cannula of obstruction must have become detached and is probably somewhere in the patient's chest. At least we have missed it and have been unable to find it. Perhaps you are familiar with the instrument. If not, I may say that a small piece of metal of rather cylindrical form, about the size of the eraser on the end of a pencil, is used for this purpose." And unknown to Griffes and the others this had been lodged in his chest all the while until the operation.

The operation made little difference in his condition. He coughed still and complained of pain when coughing. The pain also grew more severe, though most often now it was mitigated by opiates. The next day he was uncomfortable all day, coughing frequently and eager for air. He was nervous and irritable. His pulse was changeable and thready at times, and he seemed to have difficulty in breathing. Dr. Bancroft, who had been in and out all the time, scarcely leaving this case for others, began to prepare Mrs. Griffes with the news that her son would not be able to resume his work should he recover. And he would be a little bent over on one side. Perhaps it would be better if . . . At about eight o'clock Griffes's nurse recorded: "Seems excited this evening."

Mrs. Griffes sat up with him. Dr. Bancroft had promised that he should have his old nurse back the next day, and they spoke of that. The evening wore on, and it grew late. He was feeling tired and weak. Together they recited the words of *Sweet and*

Low. How he longed to rest his head upon her breast, he told her. Then suddenly he noticed an absolute stillness in the air, not the faintest sound of unrest or stirring anywhere. How strangely quiet it was, he murmured. His nurse bustled into the room, gaily proclaiming that his old nurse was coming back in the morning and that it was late and that Mrs. Griffes must go away now and get some rest. In fact she would absolutely insist upon it. Griffes agreed.

He died at 6:25 A.M.

Conclusion

ALTHOUGH Griffes had died on April 8th, 1920, obituary notices did not begin to appear in the newspapers till the 10th. His demise was incorrectly attributed to tuberculosis in the earlier reports. Nevertheless it was of empyema, abscesses of the lungs, resultant upon influenza, that he had died. The autopsy revealed no tuberculous processes and indicated, in the words of his doctor, "that neither operative nor medical treatment would have offered him any eventual hope." Indeed, it appears to have been the consensus of medical opinion that Griffes was already lost from the date of his first trip to Boston, and that the subsequent episodes of his confinement are medically irrelevant. In this there is a certain resemblance to Mozart's death, of which a French doctor has written: "Two factors hastened Mozart's death. The first was a chronic cause, dating from his earliest years and increasing every day. This was simply excessive work, continual fatigue, and profound misery. One should be able to say of a man as of a machine: 'This machine is used up, it has been worked too much.' The word *used* applies perfectly to Mozart. Mozart arrived at the age of thirty-five worn out, having expended all his vital power.

"It was at that moment that the disease which carried him off laid hold of him. . . ."

Funeral services were held in the Community Chapel of the Church of the Messiah, 34th Street and Park Avenue, at two o'clock on Saturday afternoon, April 10th. It had been decided to have no music, but the Bach Trombone Choir from the parapet of the 71st Regiment Armory across the street (where a music festival was in progress) provided unexpected accompaniment as the services began. Miss Broughton, recalling her student's long devotion to Bach, later commemorated the incident in a poem:

> 'Twas fitting, Bach, that in that last sad hour,
> . . . 'twas thy music, flung upon the air
> Should be his Requiem.

The Reverend John Haynes Holmes officiated, reading as eulogy Robert Browning's *Abt Vogler,* with its felicitous concluding reference to "the C major of this life." Musicians, composers, writers, and artists attended the services, and all the important musical organizations of New York and Boston sent representatives. The body was then interred at Bloomfield, New Jersey (not Elmira, New York, as erroneously reported).

The ending, pitilessly slow in its ravages upon the composer, came as a sudden blow to the musical world. Many had not even known of his illness. Condolences came thick and fast, but because Griffes had lived his own life away from the associates on whom he depended, none knew precisely whom to condole. His mother came first. On so much there was agreement, and Mrs. Griffes was deluged with wires and letters from every part of the country. Perhaps the most impressive of these tributes was that drawn up in the form of a public statement and affixed with forty-four prominent signatures: ". . . The music of America suffers a great loss. We who keenly feel this loss wish to express our sorrow while offering to the memory of the man and the composer this tribute of admiration and respect." The list included names like Serge Prokofiev, Leopold Stokowski, Pierre Monteux, Frederick Stock, the Flonzaley Quartet, and Marcia van Dresser.

After his mother there was some doubt as to who came next. Many a female musician received cards expressing sympathy for the stark particular loss that must be hers. Miss Broughton, to whom he had repaid in full the money borrowed long ago, and whose own death was to follow his by two years, consoled Schirmer's: "He spoke to me many times of the interest in his work shown by M. Schirmer. He never could have achieved what he did, and his short-lived success was due in large part to M. Schirmer." Schirmer's themselves took publicity in which to shed tears for "the loss American music had suffered by the death of this composer who, true to his artistic ideals, preferred to struggle through years of assimilation and experimentation until he would emerge triumphantly with a message distinctly his own, instead of reaping an easy harvest from his unusual gifts by following the lines of least resistance." They felt privileged in publishing the work of one "to whom, during his lifetime, musicians, critics, and public denied the appreciation so necessary and precious to a composer of lofty ideals — a neglect for which they are now seeking to make just amends." Others comforted a recent performer of Griffes's songs for the loss of a "discovery." Marion Clark wrote Dan: "I know that you filled a place in his life, and brought him happiness that no one else could . . ." At Hackley, where administrative tyranny reached such a pitch that there was a faculty walk-out the following year, the Hackley Alumni Association authorized a resolution on their bereavement. Eva Gauthier, perhaps most appropriately of all, consoled audiences for their loss.

A few of his as yet unpublished works were brought out, including *An Old Song Re-sung* and *Sorrow of Mydath*, of the songs, and the *Sonata*, of the piano music. Adolfo Betti, consulted on the string music, examined one of the two Indian movements that Griffes had written to go with the " Lento e mesto," and, correctly divining the composer's intention, substituted it for the old "Scherzo." The resulting combination was published as *Two Indian Sketches.*

The Pleasure-Dome of Kubla Khan was not engraved until 1929 when it appeared in an edition revised by Dr. Frederick Stock. "I performed this work in Chicago in January 1920," Dr. Stock explained in an introductory note. "In the autumn of that year, I had an opportunity of meeting Mr. Griffes during a festival of chamber music at Pittsfield in Massachusetts, when I suggested to him that the scoring of his work, in some places, could be improved upon. This he readily admitted, and we arranged to meet again in order to go over the score together. The results of this very careful scrutiny are faithfully embodied in this revised version. Nothing has been added that would not have been sanctioned by the composer." Mr. Sonneck, who handled the revised edition of *Kubla*, did not live to approve or reject this final statement in print. Nevertheless Griffes was dead " in the autumn of that year," and Dr. Stock could not have conferred with him then. The autumn of 1919 was meant, but the situation is still incomprehensible. For Griffes not only refers to *Kubla* as remaining " to be put in final shape " seventeen days after the last possible date of collaboration between him and Dr. Stock at Pittsfield, but also, as is well known, revised and altered the work almost up to the time of delivery to Monteux. It is not clear why he should not have incorporated any fruits of his discussion with Dr. Stock in the score that was performed in Boston on November 28th. A faculty colleague at Hackley, moreover, testifies to Griffes's general satisfaction with the sound of *Kubla* at Boston: ". . . He told me that during the rehearsals he had never had to change *one* note. It was produced exactly as he had written it." Mr. Sonneck's earliest communication had merely put forth: ". . . Mr. Frederick Stock told me that Mr. Griffes and he had agreed on certain matters of interpretation. He said he would be glad after his return from Europe to furnish a brief prefatory note to that effect which could be inserted in the score."

In correspondence with the present writer, and after receiving a complete record of the facts, Dr. Stock makes the following contributions to the subject. (1) Anton Bruckner's symphonies as doctored by Schalk and Löwe must have been acceptable to Bruckner, who recognized that these men knew their métier; so the new edition of Bruckner's symphonies replaces the original in almost every detail, and presentations of these symphonies are now publicized as being performed in the original version. (2) *Kubla* suffers from the same defects that are to be found in Hugo Wolf's *Penthesilia*, in much of Moussorgsky's music, and the symphonies of Robert Schumann, all music of exceptional value, but also music that could be greatly enhanced by more expert instrumentation. (3) He is not satisfied with his revision of *Kubla*. (4) He can add nothing to the original introductory note. (5) "It might almost be best to ignore all reference to the revised *Kubla*."

Let it be emphasized here—as it was emphasized to Dr. Stock before his reply—that the comparative merits of the two scores are not under discussion. The references to Bruckner and Moussorgsky are irrelevant to the plain historical problem of whether Dr. Stock erred in regarding himself Griffes's amanuensis and his revised *Kubla* the posthumous handiwork of the composer. It is true that Griffes had not yet mastered the full resources of the symphony orchestra sufficiently to realize his individual effects. Unquestionably he would have made further revisions. To the composer's sister Mr. Sonneck wrote: "It is a pity that your brother did not live to make certain changes in the instrumentation of *Kubla Khan* which he had in mind. We discussed the matter when I last saw him. . . ." Even Dr. Stock's revision can stand revision. One conductor offers as professional counsel: ". . . It is evident what Griffes wanted and that the means he took to achieve it were inadequate. Even in the newer score [Stock's] there are still spots where passages in a woodwind or two would add to the effect if they could be heard through the texture, but, as a conductor, let me say that with the required dynamic effects at these points, these passages cannot be made audible. For example see the parts for second and bass clarinets in the third and fourth measures after R; the first flute part in the same fourth measure; both again a few bars later; the bassoon parts in the first measure of page 31, and the previous measure will not sound; the bass clarinet again in the first measure of page 5, and the next will need to be blown FF to be heard." It is certainly arguable that the effects obtained by Dr. Stock in the last eight measures of the revision are quite different from the original score. Nevertheless the problem is historical, not aesthetic, and in view of the inconsistencies related above, and pending the introduction of fresh evidence, it might be safest to treat Dr. Stock's text simply as his own revision, to be estimated on its own merits as a revision.

In addition to the works previously mentioned, other of Griffes's manuscripts were collated. The piano *Notturno*, the orchestral *Notturno*, and the orchestral *Nocturne* were compared and seen to be three distinct creations and not three versions of the same work. An *Intermezzo* for piano had been composed at Leslie Hodgson's request merely to serve as a breather on Hodgson's programs. There were no traces of a modern children's opera for the Metropolitan — inspired by Humperdinck's *Königskinder* — that Griffes had contemplated during his last year. On November 16th, 1920, the New York Cham-

ber Music Society performed for the first time the three compositions that Griffes had arranged for them. The scoring was
for piano, two violins, viola, violoncello, double bass, flute,
oboe, clarinet, bassoon, and French horn. On the 24th of the
same month there was held a memorial concert of his compositions at the MacDowell Club. "I hate such things, for they
always seem so sort of constrained and empty," Griffes had
written in 1904 of the memorial concert to Ernst Jedliczka.
Duo-Art released his roll of *The White Peacock* as revised and
corrected by some pianist friends. *Salut au Monde*, filled in and
completed by Edmond Rickett,[1] was presented at the Neighborhood Playhouse on April 22nd, 1922. The orchestration
was for no strings, one flute, one clarinet, one trumpet, one
horn, two trombones, two harps, tympani, and piano. "Musically, it is astonishing to realize the effect he obtained with such
a small group of players and singers," commented Georges
Barrère, who directed the production. "There is nothing of the
so-called ultra-modern in the music. Griffes is always modern,
from inner conviction and with sincerity, not as a fad."

It is worth noting that even after Griffes's canonization the
music critics exhibited their customary deftness in approaching
his work. Deems Taylor, who was later to write of Griffes's
death as "the greatest musical loss this country has sustained,"
reviewed *Salut au Monde* for the *World*. "The most interesting part of the performance, musically," wrote Mr. Taylor,
"was the second, with its five symbolic religious scenes, which
embodied not only Griffes's music but authentic chants and
dances. . . ." Over the second part, however, Mr. Rickett had
inscribed: "There is no Griffes in this Act." Simple inquiry, if
not a personal inspection of the deciphered score, would have
ascertained the same information.

Beyond a certain point and despite the posthumous clamor

---

[1] See Appendix III.

over his name, there was a sense in which Griffes could not gain a hearing. When some of his friends sought to interest Walter Damrosch in a lesser known work, one of Dr. Damrosch's closest associates handled the matter. "I didn't talk to Mr. Damrosch about your proposition as I was sure to get an unfavorable answer.

"Mr. Damrosch has never shown so very great interest in our friend's composition up to the time [Barrère] played the *Poem* for flute and orchestra — this was really the first time some Griffes music was played by him, and it was not his choice but [Barrère's].

"He will be quite reluctant now, I am sure, to emphasize the reputation of a composer whom he scarcely recognized during his life. The only way to get at it would be to make an official statement from a Committee to which he would answer *officially*.

"Personally he would just have let it drop without any hope of reconsidering."

The code of the American musical world is immutable and sacred after its own fashion.

Soon after Griffes's death the incontrovertible facts of his life began to be known and penetrated even into the strongholds that had upheld him as a model of the American composer rewarded. Commentaries and articles on the appalling social implications of his end began to appear. The *New York Times* devoted an editorial to him. "Mr. Griffes underwent for a good many years the drudgery of teaching in a boys' school, which necessarily left him little leisure for composition and for the meditation and reflection that in some form or other are a condition precedent to composition. . . . We speak with pity or scorn of a public that could let a Mozart or a Schubert die and think that those bad old days are gone, but from time to time something uncomfortably like them and of the same sort is revealed in the present." *Musical America* carried a long elegy by A. Walter Kramer entitled "Charles T. Griffes: Cut Down in His Prime, a Victim of Our Barbarous Neglect of Genius" and subcaptioned "American Composer Whose Art Was Blossoming into Glorious Fruition Died as the Result of Overwork." The conclusion forced by the circumstances of Griffes's death was substantially correct. "American music needs no patting on the back today. Of that I am certain." There were several other attempts on the part of critics and musicians honestly to apprise themselves of the real significance of the catastrophe that had occurred within their sight.

What next followed, however, was one of those grisly jests of fame that perhaps only Griffes himself, with his ironic sense of humor, could have appreciated. Before long the musical world, with its knack for converting sentiment to sentimentality, expanded the story. Griffes became a poor artist literally starving for his music. One pianist with true mnemonic virtuosity even recalled the time that he had come hungry to her studio, begging a meal. Each retelling wrought new embellishments on the Griffes legend. He had been utterly unheard of till the performance of *Kubla* (despite the fact that the musical press had often referred to him as a well-known American composer). He had died of poverty and want. The tuberculosis rumors outlived their correction, and the handicap of consumption was assigned him as yet another melodramatic touch. Those who favored a happy ending had him flooded with redeeming missionary orders just before his death. American musicians, unwilling and often unable to rely on the musical value of their programs, seized on the Griffes legend with joyous alacrity. It was a dull program that yielded no hushed introduction to some Griffes number, the sad story of the composer's life newly adorned with the latest legendary details. They moaned, they grieved, they ranted, they prattled, but always without sensibility or direction. Even the little scheme for a "Griffes Fellowship" to the MacDowell Colony, originated at his memorial concert in November, came to nothing in the end. They indulged in the sublime hypocrisy of lamenting the things he might have lived to compose while remembering him chiefly for *The Pleasure-Dome of Kubla Khan* (composed in 1912, revised in 1916) and *The White Peacock* (composed in 1915, orchestrated in 1919). A trio of musicians took the name "Griffes Group" and toured the country, including one composition by their patron saint on every program. In short Griffes had become, as one critic remarked, "the object of an almost religious veneration."

What is perhaps most regrettable in all this misrepresentation is that there is a core of truth in each romanticism, a factual basis to every exaggeration, and that the significance of his story is warped by sentimentalizing. He was not overlooked. His talent was well appreciated in his time. He was not a garret-ridden bohemian. He was a practical manager who saved his money and who budgeted every penny towards the establishment of his freedom to compose. He was not hopelessly austere or removed from the current of his day. He made every concession to clique and to popularity that a real artist might legitimately make without injury to his art. Lawrence Gilman, critic for the *New York Herald Tribune*, commented: "Had he been endowed with the priceless instinct for publicity — that knack of tempting the shy radiance of the limelight which is God's most precious gift to the American genius — he might perhaps have won an encouragement and a leisure that would have resulted in an extensive contribution to his country's art. But he lacked that excellent and indispensable trait, and so he was obliged to divert the greater part of his time and his energy to activities that were merely utilitarian and sustaining. He must needs instruct youthful mediocrity to afflict the world, while those subtle fantasies of beauty that haunted his imagination were set aside for a more propitious hour, or became, it might be, fugitive and irrecoverable. . . . Griffes was dead, worn out by drudgery and a stupid world's misuse." If Gilman meant that Griffes did not try by every means at his command to tempt that " shy radiance," he was wrong. Griffes left no stone unturned. It was an integral part of the drudgery. But if he meant that Griffes simply had not the stomach for such things and suffered by the lack, he was correct, and the admission is most damaging to the musical setup, coming from Mr. Gilman, who was in a position to know.

In the end, when all considerations are added together, one thing stands out. Charles T. Griffes, despite critical recognition and popular approval, despite his most untiring and single-minded perseverance, found it impossible to function in American life as a composer.

Yet his life was a triumph. Fighting tiredness and discouragement, he had preserved the shape of an inner vision and refused to compromise with his own intuition of the highest. He had persisted with a sensitive and critical intelligence that enabled him to resolve each new challenge with wholeness and surety as though he were the first to meet it. He had persisted with a veracity of expression and a depth of feeling that make him the true musical conscience of his country at the beginning of the century.

One does not require the testimony of his biography for these things. There is his music. Probably never again in America will there arise his equal as a composer of art songs. *The White Peacock* and *The Pleasure-Dome of Kubla Khan* seem destined to hold their wide popularity with concert audiences. And his more advanced work — *The Kairn of Koridwen; Sho-*

Jo; the *Notturno,* 1918; the piano *Sonata;* the *Poem* for flute and orchestra; the *Nocturne,* 1919; the best of the songs and the piano pieces — will also, one may hope, gain their proper audience with time and understanding. For Charles T. Griffes, lost in the moment of fulfillment, nevertheless made his small but imperishable contribution to the music of the world.

Appendix I

A *Synopsis of* The Kairn of Koridwen *as Set Forth in the Original Program*

IT IS NIGHT and the druidesses of Sène are assembling about the kairn or sanctuary, to perform their rites to Koridwen, the Goddess of the Moon. They build the sacred fire (their symbol of the mystic force in life) and prepare in the caldron a potion from the herbs and berries of the woods. The ceremony, accompanied by rhythmic movements, describes the circle of the universe and unfolds to them the three planes of existence. One by one they respond to the spell, and interpret in esoteric language the principles of their faith — individuality and universality, liberty and light.

In the midst of these rites they are interrupted by Mordred, a Gallic warrior, who has come from the mainland to seek adventure and to demand a prophecy which he knows can be revealed to him only by winning the love of a druidess.

Enraged at his daring sacrilege, the Sène rush upon him and prepare to sacrifice him according to their custom, but Awena, the high priestess, confers the privilege of sacrifice upon Carmelis. Just as Carmelis is prepared to strike with upraised sword, she sees for the first time the eyes of her victim appealing to her for mercy. The sword falls to the ground. Mordred realizes that he has conquered. The druidesses, filled with horror at her defiance of her vows, hurl curses upon their sister, rush wildly over the cliffs, and sail away.

According to their austere law, after three days of grace, they will come back to demand in exchange for the life of the warrior the life of her who has broken her vow. Meanwhile Carmelis and Mordred forget themselves in the happiness of their love, and it is only when Mordred unconsciously gathers and offers to her the berries of the sacred belladonna that Carmelis is reminded of the doom awaiting her.

Overcome by the futility of her efforts to conquer her fate, Carmelis becomes the visionary and seer; she foretells Mordred's future, first his victory, then his bondage, and reveals to him the secrets of the druid faith — the three planes of existence beginning with darkness and ending in universal light. Then handing him her torch, the symbol of her soul, which will forever lead him onward, she sends him forth to his destiny.

The legend tells us that the boat disappears and that she sees its light dimly in the darkness, her voice is carried far across the sea in soft and savage intensity: "I was yours in life; in death, I will possess and never leave you. You shall feel me in the moonlight. I shall be with you in the shadows."

For her, there remains the sacred belladonna. Will she not find in death a greater promise of life?

When the Sène return, they find Carmelis lying beside the sanctuary, the empty horn by her side. They solemnly encircle her, repeating to themselves the austere law of their faith: "What is to be, will be."

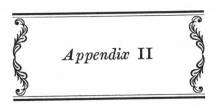

Appendix II

Paul Rosenfeld's Review of The Kairn of Koridwen *in the* Seven Arts

MR. GRIFFES EN ROUTE

IT IS DOUBTFUL whether the Neighborhood Playhouse on Grand Street has mounted anything more interesting than *The Kairn of Koridwen*, the little dance drama presented for the first time on February 10th. Not that the mimic elements of the production showed a salutary revolution on the part of the artistic direction. Quite the contrary. Never before had the resources of the Playhouse seemed so inadequate. The *mise en scène*, devised by the Misses Lewisohn, seemed unusually monotonous and ineffective. The poses and gestures of the Neighborhood's Festival Dancers, led by Miss Blanche Talmud, betrayed none of the far-famed Talmudic subtlety. The want of a single dynamic controlling intelligence was again painfully evident throughout the entire production. And yet, it was gratifying to have assisted at a performance of *The Kairn of Koridwen*. One could at least return home with the sense of having undergone an experience. That was made possible by the musical setting, the work of Mr. Charles T. Griffes. It alone lifted the little dance drama from mediocrity into importance.

For Mr. Griffes's score is something more than an able setting. It is a felicitous and often brilliant piece of work. In the light of the difficulties, inherent in the action he was asked to clothe, that beset him, it is an amazing one. It abounds in passages of rare loveliness. It is skillful and imaginative. There is no question of its incidentalness. For in this case, it was the miming that was incidental, the music that was the primary and important matter. Better than anything that occurred on the stage, it expressed the essential idea that underlay the drama.

Mr. Griffes's score is significant for another reason. For in it, his talent for the first time has made a satisfactory manifestation. An idiom a little undecided, a little derivative, a personal expression a little hesitant, has become formed and individual and respectable. The music for *The Kairn of Koridwen* should bring Mr. Griffes reputation more surely than his piano music, more surely, indeed, than anything that he has hitherto composed. Taken alone as a *tour de force*, quite apart from its musical value, it is frankly astonishing. The resources of the little orchestra of piano, celesta, flute, clarinets, horns, and harp, placed at the composer's disposal, have been exploited with a deftness that calls to mind the feats of Strauss in *Ariadne auf Naxos*. Mr. Griffes has drawn effects from his curious assemblage of instruments quite as the prestidigitator draws objects from a silk hat, and quite as amazingly. The unusual conjunction of timbres, split horn and piano, chromatic harp, chromatic flute and celesta, the happy superposition of conflicting tonalities, the knitting of strongly contrary rhythms that abound throughout the work, should make a musicians' holiday. Today, there can be no more question of Mr. Griffes's rare ability.

The real beauty of the music, however, lies in the completeness with which it makes plastic the Misses Lewisohn's conception. The authors had drawn their stuff from a Celtic legend. And their drama, quite apart from any modern valuation of the story of the druidess who will not leave the shrine to which she is dedicated, and goes rather to death in the sanctuary than into the world with her lover, was, in intention, at least, of the coloration that we recognize as Celtic. The action itself was laid in the kairn sacred to Koridwen, the Gallic moon goddess. A good deal of the stage business represented the rites of the goddess in her shrine by the oceanside. There were dances signifying the circle of the universe and the three planes of existence, potions brewed in seething caldrons out of herbs and berries of the wood, visions and ecstasies, all in a pattern of oak branches, torches, bronze altars, mistletoe, and, in the first scene at least, moonlight. It was just that druidic, sublunary coloring that Mr. Griffes captured in his music. Whatever Celtic glamour there was in the production mounted from it. From the initial measure of the short prelude, from the moment the clarinet uttered its half mournful, half glowing phrase, there expanded a music unified by a single quality, a quality that better than anything else evoked the druid rite there in the moonlight. It was the music that urged the imagination continuously, that expressed the ardors and the ecstasies of the celebrant druidesses, that laved the stage with actual moonfire. There were the gestures, the poses, the abandon that the authors of *The Kairn of Koridwen* had dreamed, more fully, more beautifully than their stage could realize them. Indeed, only once, in all that first scene, were the miming and the music in accord. That moment occurred after the first frenzy of the rite had passed. The druidesses were prostrate before the altar. From the muted piano and the celesta, shrouded by the other instruments, there emerged, tenderly, painfully, phrases that flowered out, piercingly sweet, in the stillness. And on the stage, in a sort of ecstasy, shadowy torso after torso raised itself toward the moon in an aspiration of every nerve, every tendon, and then sank back prostrate. It was the one compelling moment of the presentation, and as such, unforgettable.

No doubt, Mr. Griffes's score is uneven. The music for the second scene, for instance, is not quite as eloquent as that of the first. Not even Carmelis's dance with the branches, nor the episode where she and Mordred, the intrusive Gallic warrior, lie on the promontory and gaze out over the sea, could make it so. But perhaps the chief weakness of Mr. Griffes's score lies in the comparative weightlessness of the dramatic moments. Besides the snap, the life of the descriptive passages, and the dance movements, they are a trifle insipid. The fault does not lie with Mr. Griffes but with his librettists. In some matters the Misses Lewisohn were very generous with their composer. They engaged Mr. Nikolai Sokoloff to rehearse and conduct the music, the Barrère Ensemble to perform it. In others, they were unduly withholding. For instance, they deprived the composer of all opportunity to do anything with the dramatic and passionate moments by eliding them as often as they could, and when they could not, by passing them over as quickly as possible. The ending of the first scene is a good example of the want of symmetry in the construction caused by this somewhat undue aversion to passionate love scenes, and other passionate scenes. Mordred had intruded into the kairn. Carmelis had been commanded to kill him, and had disobeyed. Like another in a like situation, she might have said

> *Er sah mir in die Augen.*
> *Das Schwert, ich liess es fallen.*

The rest of the druidesses had rushed off, leaving her alone with him. At this point, the curtain chastely fell. One needs to be neither salacious nor Wagnerian to wish it had remained up. For a very beautiful scene might have been enacted and Mr. Griffes might have had an opportunity to write some directly dramatic music, and not have had to end the scene so abruptly.

Nor was he vouchsafed greater opportunity for variety and action in the second scene. Here there was more drama, but an unfortunate conjunction of episodes of similar character forced a certain monotony on the music again. The finale was most ineffectual, though this time the fault was Mr. Griffes's. "Finding Carmelis dead," the libretto prescribed, "the Sène solemnly encircle her, repeating to themselves the austere law of their faith: 'What is to be, will be.'" It is obvious that by the time he reached that part, Mr. Griffes was a trifle bored with the whole business. And so he wrote a little conventional death music, just reminiscent enough of the *Götterdämmerung* funeral music to give the audience its cue, and let the "austere law of their faith" go at that. Perhaps his very boredom at that point is further proof of his artistic sensibility.

One would like to see him try his hand at a more grateful subject. If he could be kindled to such production by the rather meager action of *The Kairn of Koridwen*, what could we not expect if he occupied himself with, say, *The Shadowy Waters* of Yeats, or some other dream-stuff of Celtic inspiration? But, whatever he undertakes, it is impossible any longer to entertain only slight expectations in regard to him. The music he wrote for the Neighborhood Playhouse precludes that. For it seems to offer positive assurance that Mr. Griffes is indeed *en route* for actual achievement.

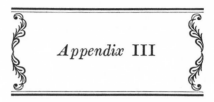

Appendix III

Letter from Edmond Rickett Explaining His Work on Salut au Monde

AT THE TIME of his death, Griffes was engaged upon the composition of this work, which was to be produced at the Neighborhood Theater as a sort of pageant, with the poem recited by a chorus of male voices, and illustrated on the stage in pantomime and dance. None of the work was scored, but he had filled several notebooks with pencil drafts of the various scenes. Many were, harmonically, quite complete, and there were fortunately sufficient indications as to their relative position in the play. I understand that the Misses Lewisohn had had this MS. draft inspected by several musicians, but without result. Finally they asked me to look it over, and see whether I could do anything with it. At first sight it was a formidable job, the different sections being set down in no order at all, jumping here and there in the action with no indication as to their connection. However, a month or two of patient study, and I began to appreciate the way the composer's mind had been working, and at last managed to connect the sequences of the various scenes. When I had finally prepared a pianoforte score, I found I had only to supply a few quite short connecting links, using Griffes's own tunes and harmonies, to have a complete picture of the first act, which was the only portion he had worked on. I played this to the Misses Lewisohn and to . . . Mrs. Laura Elliot. . . .

So there it is! The whole of this first act is Griffes's own work. Even the orchestral arrangement is his, as, while he did no actual scoring, the indications as to this detail were very clear in the notes. It was scored (as I remember) for an orchestra of wind instruments, harps, and percussion — no strings, except a string bass — and at the production was very ably played by Mr. Barrère's ensemble. . . .

This first act, then, is entirely Griffes. As I have said, where connecting sections were necessary, I used his own themes and harmonies for the purpose. The third act is wholly mine; I may have used some of the Griffes material where possible, but this I could not say without reference to the score. As for the second act, this consisted of a sequence of pictures of the religious worship of all nations, and the music used was from various sources as indicated — I believe I arranged some Gregorian music for the Christian picture; a Hindu friend provided the Buddhist ritual; a Jewish authority the Hebrew melodies, and so on.

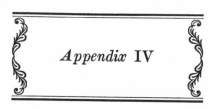

Appendix IV

Recordings of Griffes's Works

1. *By a Lonely Forest Pathway*
   Alexander Kisselburgh   Columbia 189–M
   Glenn Darwin   Victor 36224

2. *The Fountain of the Acqua Paola*, Op. 7, No. 1
   Rudolph Gruen   Roycroft 171

3. *The Lament of Ian the Proud*, Op. 11, No. 1
   William Hain, tenor, and Jerome T. Bohm, piano
              Friends of Recorded Music 5–B

4. *The Pleasure-Dome of Kubla Khan*
   Eugene Ormandy and the Minneapolis Symphony
                                Victor 7957

5. *Sonata*
   Harrison Potter   Friends of Recorded Music 10 and 11
   Jeanne Behrend   Victor Album (forthcoming)

6. *The White Peacock*, Op. 7, No. 1
   Myra Hess   Columbia 9072–M
   Olga Samaroff   Victor 7384

7. *The White Peacock*
  Howard Barlow and Columbia Broadcasting Symphony
  Columbia 17140–D

  Howard Hanson and Eastman-Rochester Symphony Orchestra   Victor 15659

8. *Two Sketches Based on Indian Themes*
  Coolidge Quartet   Victor Album 558
  Kreiner Quartet   (the "Lento")
  Friends of Recorded Music 5–A

(*A complete bibliography of Griffes's works is now in progress; meanwhile, the list of his published compositions, including arrangements by others, may be found in G. Schirmer's catalogue.*)

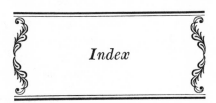

Index

72004